Christy Mathewson

Christy Mathewson
A Biography

MICHAEL HARTLEY

McFarland & Company, Inc., Publishers
Jefferson, North Carolina, and London

LIBRARY OF CONGRESS CATALOGUING-IN-PUBLICATION DATA

Hartley, Michael.
    Christy Mathewson : a biography / Michael Hartley.
       p.   cm.
    Includes bibliographical references and index.

    ISBN 0-7864-1653-X (softcover : 50# alkaline paper)

    1. Mathewson, Christy, 1880–1925. 2. Baseball players—
United States—Biography. 3. New York Giants (Baseball
team) I. Title.
GV865.M327H37   2004
796.357'092—dc22   2003021300

British Library cataloguing data are available

©2004 Michael Hartley. All rights reserved

*No part of this book may be reproduced or transmitted in any form
or by any means, electronic or mechanical, including photocopying
or recording, or by any information storage and retrieval system,
without permission in writing from the publisher.*

On the cover: Christy Mathewson at West Side Grounds, 1905
(*Chicago Daily News* negative collection, Chicago Historical Society)

Manufactured in the United States of America

McFarland & Company, Inc., Publishers
   Box 611, Jefferson, North Carolina 28640
     www.mcfarlandpub.com

To my parents,
George and Sni

ACKNOWLEDGMENTS

I wish to thank the following persons for their assistance as I endeavored to complete this work. I may have imposed on their lives for only a day or an hour, but their helpfulness and graciousness is appreciated: Dorothy Cavalier, the Rev. Garford F. Williams, Grace Mathewson Van Lengen, Mary Lee Caterson, Harold and Carolyn Reynolds, Betty Cook, Mary Hotaling, Edna Finn, Diane Bowerman, and Mary Reely.

I am also grateful to Betty Phillips, Keith Wrigley, Mike Sparrow, Darren Maria, Robert E. Mooney, Jr., Nancy McGuire, Narda Tafuri, Bruce Freed, Doris Dysinger, Paul Spaeth, Al Kermisch, Marian G. Gibbs, Bill Chambers, Robert F. Bluthardt, Timothy J. Wiles, William C. Burdick, and Daniel J.J. Ross.

Robert Loveland carefully read the manuscript and generously contributed appropriate volumes from his own library of hard-to-find and interesting baseball books.

I also wish to express my appreciation of the following libraries and historical societies for the courtesy and care with which they house their collections: James Prendergast Library, Jamestown, New York; Ellen Bertrand Library, Bucknell University, Lewisburg, Pennsylvania; Miller Library, Keystone College, La Plume, Pennsylvania; Cleveland Public Library; and the microfilm lending library of the Society for American Baseball Research (SABR), Cleveland, Ohio, and the society itself.

Other libraries deserving my thanks include the Corry Public Library, Corry, Pennsylvania; Erie County Library, Erie, Pennsylvania; Warren County Library, Warren, Pennsylvania; Friedsam Library, St. Bonaventure University, St. Bonaventure, New York; Saranac Lake Free Library, Saranac Lake, New York; Lawrence Lee Pelletier Library, Allegheny College, Meadville, Pennsylvania; and the Romeo District Library, Romeo, Michigan.

I found the following historical societies of particular help: The

Wyoming County Historical Society, Tunkhannock, Pennsylvania; Ohio Historical Society, Columbus, Ohio; Mahoning Valley Historical Society, Youngstown, Ohio; Union County Historical Society, Lewisburg, Pennsylvania; and Historic Saranac Lake, Saranac Lake, New York.

TABLE OF CONTENTS

Acknowledgments   vii
Preface   1

1. EARLY INNINGS   3
2. NEW YORK, NEW YORK   19
3. DISPUTED CHAMPIONS   32
4. WORLD CHAMPIONS   41
5. TO THE BONE   50
6. CHAMPIONS AGAIN   73
7. BUT NOT WORLD CHAMPIONS   94
8. SOMEONE ELSE'S TURN   107
9. CINCINNATI   119
10. WAR, THEN THE BLACK SOX   136
11. PATH TO GLORY   151

Epilogue   170
Notes   173
Bibliography   185
Index   189

PREFACE

At one point during this project, I encountered a prominent baseball writer's opinion that Christy Mathewson does not seem interesting enough to merit a serious biography. The clear implication was that Mathewson was just not flawed enough as a man to attract, or hold, the interest of modern readers raised to venerate the antihero.

It is true that Mathewson was not driven by furies as was Ty Cobb, nor was he larger-than-life like Babe Ruth, nor even a man of immense contradictions like Mathewson's own friend and mentor, John McGraw. Compared with these compelling figures, Mathewson was merely a man of high accomplishments, who had a keen sense of what he regarded as private and public obligations.

But if Aristotle were alive today, besides the beyond-a-reasonable-doubt assumption that he would be a baseball fan, he would find Mathewson a far more intriguing figure than Cobb, Ruth, McGraw, and a host of other baseball heroes, anti- or otherwise. As Aristotle knew, the opportunities for missing the mark in life are infinite. Hitting the mark is difficult. Mathewson's pinpoint accuracy as a pitcher can be regarded as a metaphor for his accuracy, moral accuracy, as a man throughout his life—both on and off the playing field.

Mathewson was a child of his times. He would have won a lot of games for whichever team he pitched, but probably not 373 in his career without the good fortune to play for John McGraw and John Brush on the New York Giants. He became a great pitcher by honing his craft against skilled competitors like Mordecai "Three Finger" Brown and batsmen like Honus Wagner, Sherry Magee, and Joe Tinker. His pitching greatness became such that, in moments of professional failure and no matter by how tight a margin, when he failed he failed notably—witness the most famous at-bats of "Home Run" Baker and Tris Speaker.

Yet it is the crucible beyond the playing field which enables us to glimpse the true man. The loyalty and nature of his personal relationships, both as giver and receiver, do not disappoint; but this, gratefully, is not uncommon among humankind. The strength of his personality was inherited from, and instilled into him by, an equally well-endowed personality, his mother; in many ways his essential being is an extension of hers. Minerva Mathewson steeped herself in Christian faith, and her son benefited from her faith. In marriage he was blessed with a loving, strong partner who both complemented and sustained his desire to keep, and acquire more, middle-class respectability in its higher manifestations and without hypocrisy.

After his playing career ended, we can see, in his direct reactions to corruption, war, and sickness, that the sterling quality of his character become evident in more than one dimension. More than a few Hall of Famers, more than a few major leaguers, and more than a few men, are made of like stuff as Mathewson. But only a relative handful are given, or confronted with, these kinds of dramatic circumstances to test them so publicly as well as privately. To my mind, respecting the tempered grace with which they rose to each occasion, Eddie Collins and Jackie Robinson are among the very few Hall of Famers who can be regarded in a similar manner.

Uncomplimentary things can be fairly said about Christy Mathewson. Teammates sometimes found him stand-offish, even conceited. Autograph seekers, especially during his playing career, approached him at their peril. When his son was born, he should have been home with his wife and not hunting in Michigan with Frank Bowerman. He liked money. He was a capable writer, but if he had written a clearer, more forceful, affidavit when Hal Chase was accused of throwing baseball games in 1918, the major leagues' severest scandal might have been nipped in the bud and the Black Sox World Series of 1919 would never have occurred. But none of the flaws suggested by these examples proved personally fatal to him, and on the whole Mathewson was a remarkably integrated personality. If myth is derived from truth, the legend persists that Mathewson's integrity was so highly regarded by those who knew him that umpires would look for his reaction to affirm whether they had made a close call correctly.

Mathewson was, at heart, a reticent man not inclined to speak of his feelings. He much preferred to let actions speak for him. Having therefore slight choice in the matter, I have endeavored to portray Mathewson's life in that same way—to let his life speak for itself. So, for those modern readers who do not pride themselves as being too jaded, I recommend these pages to look upon a man whom Aristotle would have described as virtuous and perhaps, because of the equanimity in which he took all things, even happy.

Corry, Pennsylvania

1
Early Innings

In the year 1880 James Garfield defeated Winfield Hancock for the presidency of the United States. The last president born in a log cabin, Garfield, before assassinated, briefly presided over 50 million persons living in the 38 states, eight territories, and the District of Columbia. According to the nation's tenth census, blacksmiths outnumbered lawyers in the population by nearly three to one.

Among those born in 1880 was a son, Christopher, on August 12, to Gilbert and Minerva Mathewson, who lived in a house with Minerva's mother and stepfather on the main street of a village called Factoryville, nestled along a branch of the Tunkhannock Creek in northeastern Pennsylvania. The factory, a cotton mill, for which Factoryville was named, had long since ceased operation. Built during the War of 1812, the mill went bankrupt shortly thereafter. With no factories since, the village endured as the hub of a farming community. Thirty-three-year-old Gilbert worked as a barkeeper in the hotel near the train depot. The newborn was given the same name as Gilbert's Uncle Christopher, who operated the hotel. Having no sons of his own, the uncle had offered $1,000 to thus perpetuate his name.

"Christy" was descended, both paternally and maternally, from among the first settlers in the valley, Baptists who came in the early part of the century from Rhode Island. Minerva Mathewson was a daughter of her father's second marriage. A patriarch in the valley, George Capwell had died at age 77 when she was but four. Several of Capwell's grandchildren by his first wife were well into adulthood by the time Minerva was born, and her half-brothers—more like granduncles—were themselves well-established in the community.

When George Capwell died in 1860, he left a large estate. In a will prepared that same year he bequeathed his town dwelling to his wife Christiana and his "old farm" to the surviving children of his first marriage. He entrusted Christiana with his gristmill, sawmill, and a large

Matty, winner of 373 big-league games, pictured here circa 1915. (National Baseball Hall of Fame Library, Cooperstown, N.Y.)

tract of land until the youngest of their three minor children, Minerva, turned 18. At that time the mills went to their son, and the land and remaining personal property was divided, share and share alike, among Christiana, son, and two daughters. Some of the grandchildren of the patriarch's first marriage, perhaps knowing the intent of an earlier will and certainly feeling excluded by the later one, took their complaint to court. A jury of 12 men found in favor of Christiana and her children. Christiana, a widow at age 41, later married Nelson Doolittle, a clergyman.[1]

In the valley the descendants of the "Rhode Island" Baptists tended to worship at the General Six Principle Church, the smaller of the community's two Baptist congregations. There an Arminian view of the availability of God's grace to all was preached. At the larger Factoryville Baptist Church the elect heard a Calvinistic view. Questions of theology aside, Factoryville First Baptist has endured as a living entity into the 21st century, while the physical structure of the Six Principle church yet stands as the town hall.[2]

Gilbert's father Henry had a house and barn, also on the main street and not far from the Union School where his new wife, Frances, had been a teacher. Henry Mathewson, who turned 58 in 1880, owned the tannery at the edge of town. Four years previously he divorced his first wife Janette for reasons not mentioned in the docket of court records.[3] Henry and Frances now had a girl child, Jessie, just two years old. Frances herself was only a few years older than Minerva.

In their youth Gilbert and Minerva were educated at the Keystone Academy, a Baptist preparatory school founded on 20 acres purchased from the estate of Minerva's father. Funded with local money and built by local hands, the school was a treasure in the eyes of the community and considered one of the finest such institutions of learning in this part of the state. Here sons and daughters were taught in a strictly moral and religious atmosphere.

Minerva, it was said, had been engaged to Gilbert's younger brother Wellington, but Wellington had gone on a western journey and was killed. If so, it is an early example of the tragedy and grief that followed this intelligent, strong, resourceful woman all her days. "Gib" is an interesting second choice. Surviving photographs indicate that he was handsome enough, and Minerva does not seem the type, even in her early 20s, to suffer a man whose wits and sensibilities were not as keen as her own. Still, for a Baptist preacher's stepdaughter who would become a longstanding leader in the local chapter of the Woman's Christian Temperance Union, Minerva's acceptance of Gilbert hints of a sentimentality over the lost brother or a bit of rebel in the young woman, or perhaps both. That she settled on a barkeeper is neither in keeping with her upbringing nor her later years. Of course, Gilbert did not remain a barkeeper. Throughout his life he seems to have been a jack-of-all-trades and master-of-none, and preferred to regard and describe himself as a gentleman-farmer. For a few years, when the Republican politics were right, he went to Washington to work in the senate post office. A family tradition lingers that he resorted to many clever hiding places in and around his home to keep his liquor from his wife, reserving for himself the right to imbibe now and then.

More children were born. Cyril did not survive a year; the infant was buried in the Capwell family plot in the cemetery above Factoryville's main street. Edith Christine was born in 1884 and Henry in 1886; in between Minerva's mother died and was buried alongside her first husband. In 1888 Jane was born, and in the next year came Gilbert and Minerva's last child, another son, Nicholas.

Because Nelson and Christiana Doolittle had two teenaged sons, Albert and Benjamin, of their own, the household in which Gilbert and Minerva began their married life was crowded—and the trains of the Delaware, Lackawanna, and Western Railroad passed not far from the back door.[4] Even so, it was not until 1886, the year after her mother's death, that Minerva agreed to purchase a modest home on a hill overlooking the Keystone Academy.

The house contained cozy rooms with high ceilings and pleasing woodwork, more pine than hardwood. The entrance led to a six-sided parlor, which featured a melodeon—a small keyboard organ with pedals to operate tone-producing bellows. Minerva insisted that her children learn to play music. French doors separated the parlor from the dining room, and the stairway to the bedrooms upstairs was adorned with a stained-glass window. A one-story section attached to the rear of the dwelling served for cooking and washing. A side door opened to a well-tended garden, and in the yard chickens pecked. Adjoining the yard was an orchard of apple and cherry trees; much of the surrounding land either came with the house or already belonged to Minerva. Also behind the house stood a small barn for the family's dairy cows.[5]

When Gilbert and Minerva married, he borrowed from her $500 which he never repaid. During the early years of their marriage, they invested together in real estate, a portion of which they sold to his mother, Janette, who seems to have returned to Factoryville after several years of post-divorce exile in Scranton. But when it came time to purchase the home in which they would raise their family, Minerva evidently decided that the deed should be recorded in her name alone. At the time, she probably could have afforded a more lavish house, but Baptists of this era were not generally at ease with displays of wealth. And this was Factoryville, after all—there just were not big fancy houses. Whether Baptist or Methodist (the community's two main denominations), the better sorts of people worried as much or more about their heavenly home as about their earthly one.[6]

All the while, Christy grew into an intelligent, athletic boy, liking all sorts of outdoors activity, and going to Union School for his elementary education. With Jessie Mathewson, when she was about 10 and he was about eight, he snuck away at a wedding party and began eating the icing from the cake well before the bride and groom were ready to cut it.[7]

For a magazine article written in 1912, Christy Mathewson reminisced about how, when he was eight or nine, an older cousin instructed him in the art of throwing stones: how to make a flat stone tumble end-over-end through the air, or, by holding its flat surface at an acute angle, to make a stone curve horizontally. Christy practiced throwing stones a great deal, attaining the proficiency, according to his own recollection, of going into the woods and being able to bring down squirrels and birds with the round stones he chose for the best accuracy. His mother enjoyed remembering an occasion when an even younger Christy and some pals used the backside of his uncle's horse as a target. When the horse, "old Charley," got to moving pretty fast in the barn lot, the uncle caught Christy and gave him a good talking-to and a spanking. It was, said Minerva's eldest son as the tale improved with age, the one occasion of his life when pitching control was neither a virtue nor an advantage.[8]

About the time he was ten, Christy became mascot, or bat boy, for the local baseball team of grown, sometimes bewhiskered, men. He would recall how he swelled with pride at being connected with this club. Besides tending the bats and carrying water, he performed the function of "second catcher"; that is, he was allowed to chase all the foul balls the regular players could not reach.

A pitcher on the team showed young Mathewson how to grip the ball and snap his wrist to throw an "out-curve," the venerable pitch that, when thrown by a right-hander, curves away from a right-handed batter. Sometimes with an old mattress propped against the barn, sometimes with another boy who had a glove, Christy practiced the pitch and, for a youngster, got fair control of it. He also threw what he considered, at the age of 12, to be an "in-curve," but what he later learned was more aptly a right-handed fastball which by its nature tended to tail in on a right-handed batter—in modern parlance a "two-seamer."

"Husk," as Christy was known because of his size, played baseball mostly with older boys, but, because they did not like being shown up by the kid's pitching, he was usually sent to right field. As is yet generally the case with a boy sent by other boys to right field, he was better at chasing balls than catching them on the fly. He left something to be desired as a hitter too, for he held the bat "cross-handed"; in other words, he held the bat with his left hand over his right.

Part of the genius of Ted Williams is ascribed to the fact that, as a natural right-hander, he had the disposition at an early age to bat left-handed. Since most pitching is right-handed, the advantages to a left-handed hitter, besides a nearer distance to first base, are a partial negation of the curveball and perhaps an extra fraction of a second to see the ball as it is delivered. That extra moment is precious in the almost instinctual determination to swing. As Williams practiced his craft and then taught what he learned to others, the key to a successful at-bat is for the batter to recognize "his pitch"—just as the pitcher is doing all he can to deceive the batter into visualizing something else.

Whatever his youthful insights into the science of pitching, Christy did not have them to a similar degree as a hitter. Though he threw right-handed, he may actually have been more naturally a left-hander when it came to hitting; but no one in Factoryville had enough baseball acumen to suggest that. In later years he wondered if his early awkwardness with a bat stemmed from his childhood chores of hoeing in the garden or chopping wood; in the performance of these chores he held his left hand over his right for his own comfort and with no ill-effect. But, he said, "I batted as if I was hoeing potatoes and seldom obtained a hit."[9] He flailed at the ball too—for, as big as he was and in spite of his awkward swing, when he connected the ball went a long way.

One Saturday the Factoryville team was preparing to play in a neighboring town. However, the Factoryville pitcher took ill and the second pitcher was away. "That Mathewson kid can pitch pretty well," someone said. The excited 14 year old climbed into the carriage with the men for the ride to the rival ballplaying community. Christy pitched gamely and remembered the outcome all the days of his life: Factoryville won, 19–17. "The thrill that lasted me twenty years," he described it.[10]

Soon after this triumph Christy began his course of study at Keystone Academy. A bell atop the main building called the students to rise, to meals, to classes, and to chapel. Christy was a day student. His mother hoped he would become a minister, though her son never seriously considered the notion. The Mathewsons donated $1,000 to the academy, and Gilbert was elected a trustee for life. Christy, like all students, was required to gain competency in English, algebra, geometry, chemistry, physiology, botany, natural philosophy (as physics was called then), astronomy, rhetoric, composition, and Latin. Musical training was an elective, but not for Minerva Mathewson's offspring. United States, Roman, and Greek history, bible study, mental philosophy (psychology), commercial law, French, and German were some of the other classes available, and Christy's graceful handwriting as an adult was no doubt developed by the strong emphasis placed on penmanship. Graduation required written and oral examinations, as well as an original paper on a subject selected by the student and approved by the faculty. All students were required to attend church on Sunday, to be punctual in attending class and chapel, and to observe study hours faithfully. How faithfully Christy observed study hours is a matter for conjecture, but by now it had to have been apparent that he possessed a fine retentive memory; and, if his later collegiate record is indicative, he did well as a student.

At Keystone Christy found a small band of kindred spirits, including Ernest Sterling who came from a farm near the hamlet of Brooklyn, Pennsylvania, and who boarded with the Mathewsons. These intimates consisted of five boys, plus one girl who was accepted "as a pal and equal." Among these friends Christy found a niche. They, and they alone, called him "Taffy"—the nickname was not used outside the group. He felt comfortable with them, his reserved, almost taciturn, personality notwithstanding, for they accepted that he largely kept his thoughts and motives to himself. He dealt with the myriad of confusing situations and emotions encountered by all youth by disciplining himself to show a calm exterior and to keep a cool mind in order to grasp "the lay of the land" before deciding how to act.[11]

His mother welcomed his friends at the Mathewson home. On Sunday mornings a special event was her breakfasts of buckwheat pancakes drenched with honey from the beehives Christy kept behind the barn. Christy never revealed how he got to know so much about bees or bragged about his ability with them; he somehow acquired the knowledge and could undeniably get honey.

That his mother took a boarder, even one as pleasant as Ernest Sterling, is illustrative of the family's tightened financial circumstances. Minerva's inheritance evidently was by now quite a bit used up. The $1,000 donation to the academy had been more a gesture of former wealth than of continued affluence. To make ends meet, Minerva and her children milked the dairy cows and maintained a milk route. Frugal, hard-working Minerva would keep the route even after her eldest, and generous, son became a big-league pitching star.

Christy's control of his "out-curve" improved, and as he grew his fastball got faster. During the summer he again pitched for the Factoryville team. When they disbanded late in the August during which he turned 15, Christy was approached by the team captain from nearby Mill City and offered a dollar a game to pitch for them on Saturday afternoons. To a boy who would rather play ball than eat, and the growing boy liked to eat, the offer was just icing on the cake. He usually had to walk the five miles or so to and from the playing field, but the dollar in his pocket made it worthwhile. That he was being paid money to play baseball with grown men was a considerable tonic and made other boys seem inferior—at least in terms of ballplaying ability. But, for boys that age, what other criteria are there?

During his first year at the academy, Christy had played second base for Keystone, since the older boys did not want to relinquish the pitcher's position. In his second year, with the aura of the Mill City dollars, he was elected team captain. As captain, with the approval of faculty member Bromley Smith who assumed the additional duties as coach and trainer of the academy's athletic teams, Christy chose to pitch, but only against the stronger competition. A couple of the boys could pitch fairly well but were not so good at fielding or hitting, and Christy would insert one of them as pitcher against a weaker team while putting himself back at second base.

As his time at Keystone continued, so remembered Ernest Sterling, Christy was not considered a "boy wonder" destined for greatness. His chief distinguishing characteristics were his size, strength, and ability to "wallop the tar" out of the other boys should that necessity arise. He showed an early indication of his coolness under pressure one day at an entertainment in the school auditorium. Christy was slated to recite "The Raven" by Edgar Allan Poe. He took the stage ably enough and got so far as one of the points of "Quoth the Raven 'Nevermore'"—then the remainder of the poem suddenly eluded him. Instead of fumbling through a bad ending of forgotten verses, he nimbly concluded with "and of this tale I know no more," and exited the stage with dignity.

Once, while returning home on a horse-drawn sleigh with his friends from an ice-fishing trip to a nearby pond, Christy, struggling to keep warm in an old buffalo robe, became so fed up with trying to keep his bucket of water, bait, and fish from slopping on him as they traveled over the bumps that, without a word of warning, he finally threw the bucket and its contents over a stone wall. As far as he was concerned that was all there was to it, and there was no point in going back or worrying about whether he should have simply poured out the contents and saved the bucket.

Another time, near graduation, in a height of recklessness and possible disgrace, Christy and his male comrades slipped off to Scranton, some 15 miles away, to see the naughty French musical comedienne Anna Held perform "Won't You Come and Play Wiz Me."[12]

What reputation Christy did have at Keystone was more as a football player than as a baseball player. The football and baseball teams consisted mostly of the same boys, including his mainstay friends. They "were almost sure to be licked" by Wyoming Seminary, but had a fighting chance against the high schools of Scranton and Binghamton, New York. (The St. Thomas School of Scranton, whose players were the sons of coal miners, was considered a particularly tough opponent.) Perhaps due to an increasing awareness of his family's financial difficulties, Christy practiced drop-kicking a football and throwing a baseball with renewed diligence during his last year at the academy. Given the frenzied interest in collegiate athletics at the time (has it ever ended?), once he got to college, he may have reasoned, athletic ability could keep him there. Again, as with beehives, his determination for drop-kicking or pitching excellence was not something he talked about or of which his friends were much aware. He just went out and did it.

Friends of the University of Pennsylvania and of Lafayette College urged him to apply his football skills at one of those institutions. Instead he decided on Bucknell, the Baptist university in Lewisburg, Pennsylvania. It was probably an easy decision to make. His best friend, Ernest Sterling, was also going there, as were two other close friends. Affordability had something to do with it as well. On the day Christy graduated from the academy, his mother had to scrape together enough money to pay his remaining tuition balance in order for her son to receive his diploma.

Keystone served as a "feeder" academy to Bucknell, and close relations existed between them. In fact, the former principal of the Keystone Academy and pastor of the First Baptist Church in Factoryville, Dr. John Howard Harris, had, in 1889, been called to the presidency of Bucknell. Therefore young Christy would not be going entirely among strangers.

During the summer that Christy turned 18, Admiral Dewey was already in Manila and Theodore Roosevelt led the Rough Riders at the battle of San Juan Hill. Whatever youthful thoughts about war he may have pondered, Christy struck out 15 in a game for the Scranton YMCA and was offered $20 a month plus board to pitch for the Honesdale Reds, in a town about 30 miles east of Factoryville. He accepted the offer. It seemed a lot of money to Christy, and he spoke of "J.P. Morgan and me."[13]

On his first Sunday at Bucknell, Christy was invited to dinner at the residence of Dr. Harris; along with Christy came Frank Stanton, a fellow freshman. It must have been a full household for, according to Stanton's recollection, the 51-year-old university president had seven sons and a daughter Mary. With an enrollment of less than 500, Dr. Harris was able to, and did, take a *loco parentis* interest in the lives of his students—and, from his days in Factoryville, at the dinner remembered Christy as a boy who sat up straight during sermons.[14]

Founded by subscriptions from Baptist communities throughout Pennsylvania and originally called the University of Lewisburg, Bucknell strived to provide Baptist sons, and at the Female Institute to daughters as well, an academic excellence in the Susquehanna Valley similar to that offered by Brown University to Baptists in New England. It had been an unceasing struggle for the university to afford its high standards until a generous benefactor from Philadelphia, William Bucknell, was elected chairman of trustees.

Christy respected the general quality of his fellow Bucknellians, and he quickly made his own presence known among them. The freshman kicked the extra point after Bucknell's solitary touchdown in a 6–0 victory over Wyoming Seminary. In those days a touchdown was five points; so was a field goal—and it must have given the young man, as a college student, a special satisfaction to play a hand in beating the same seminarians who had so enjoyed roughing up the Keystone football team. By the third contest of the season, in which Navy beat Bucknell 11–0, Christy was the regular punter. In the fifth game, Bucknell 34, Swarthmore 18, Christy scored two touchdowns and returned kick-offs. When Penn State shut out Bucknell 16–0, he had a busy day punting—averaging 38 yards in 11 attempts. And, in an 11–11 tie with Franklin and Marshall, Christy drop-kicked his first collegiate field goal from a distance of 15 yards. His gridiron performances could not have done otherwise than elicit from his classmates the freshman yell:

> Who Ra! Who Ra! Who Ra! Who!
>
> Boomerang! Boomerang! Boomerang! Boo!
>
> Bucknell! Bucknell! Nineteen-oh-two![15]

A drop kick, as opposed to a place kick, is a lost art of the gridiron. The ball carrier, instead of running the ball across the line of scrimmage, "dropped" the football to the ground and kicked it. If the ball traveled through the goal posts and over the crossbar, his team was awarded a field goal. If the ball merely traveled downfield, the opposing team could return it. The trick was to kick the ball with the toe or instep just as the point of the ball rebounded from the ground. A football was bulkier and less oblong than nowadays, but even so the drop kick had few reliable practitioners. As Christy's collegiate football career developed, his only rival in drop-kicking ability was Frank Hudson, a Pueblo Indian from the Carlisle School.

Football as played between colleges in the 1890s is described as the "red meat era." There was no forward pass, only laterals. There were no temporary substitutions; once a player left the field, he could not return. The team with the ball had three downs to advance it five yards. The dominant strategy was mass movement, the flying wedge as the most famous example. Actually the flying wedge was anything but fleet afoot.

Christy Mathewson (front, center) with college friends ca. 1898. (National Baseball Hall of Fame Library, Cooperstown, N.Y.)

Mass movement plays were ponderous and slow-moving, and required an immense amount of shoving, tackling, pushing, and wrestling by the defense against the offense in order to get to the ball carrier and bring him down.

"What matters a few broken bones to the glories of intercollegiate sport?" declaimed Theodore Roosevelt at a Harvard Club dinner, even as, not far away, a very recent football player lay paralyzed for life in a hospital bed.[16] Eye gouging, bone fractures, and on-field brawls were accepted by most as part of the game. Players did not have much protective equipment, mainly just thick, padded knickers and heavy woolen sweaters.

Collegiate Christy was proud of his football accomplishments. He came, he played, he conquered. Returning to Factoryville with Ernest Sterling and two other friends, he went with them to a local photographer to have a portrait taken. As his life unfolded, Christy Mathewson became accustomed to posing, whether he sought it or not, as the centerpiece in photographs with both friends and teammates. This Factoryville photograph is an early example. The other young gentlemen, attired in suits and ties, are situated around the seated football hero. Lest there be any question of Christy's status, his neck is entirely swallowed by the bulky turtleneck of his Bucknell sweater, which he somehow managed to contain within his suit jacket.

At Bucknell Christy's course of study is recorded as "Latin Philosophical," and his grade report indicates that he was an "A" student. During his freshman year he studied geometry and trigonometry, French and German, and Tacitus and Livy. Perhaps influenced by fellow Pennsylvanian Gifford Pinchot, Christy contemplated a career in forestry. He talked about it and made plans with Ernest Sterling, with whom he shared a dormitory room. (Sterling later transferred to the school of forestry at Cornell and went on to a distinguished career in that field.) He joined the Euepia Literary Society, one of two such societies on campus organized for the purpose of debating and presenting papers on issues of the day, although, by the time Christy came to Bucknell, the literary societies, both formed in 1850, were considered not as vigorous as they once had been. He also joined the Phi Gamma Delta fraternity and played the bass horn, known more familiarly as the tuba, in the university band.

Football was the only sport Christy played during his freshman year. The following summer he returned to Honesdale and the ball field near the silk-mill flats along the Lackawaxen River. This season the team called itself the Eagles, and Christy's sojourn among the Eagles improved his raw baseball talent. First, he resolved to stop batting cross-handed. He still could look awkward at the plate as he struggled to adjust, but, with his right hand now over his left, in the long run he became a fair hitter—"for a pitcher," that is.

Second, Honesdale had a left-handed pitcher named Dave Williams who would eventually appear in three games in the American League. Williams had what was considered a freak pitch. He could throw an "out-curve" to a right-handed batter. Though Williams did not have reliable control over his unconventional pitch, Christy wondered why a right-handed pitcher such as he could not learn to throw an "out-curve" to a left-handed batter. Provided he could avoid a telltale sign in the delivery, the oddball pitch might one day prove a valuable piece in his repertoire.[17]

Williams showed Christy, known now increasingly as Matty among his peers, how he held the ball and threw his unusual offering. Matty applied the logic to the long fingers of his own right-handed delivery and practiced. When throwing a conventional curveball, as the ball leaves the hand, the inward snap of the wrist turns the palm skyward and the ball's spinning motion is imparted to it by the pressure of the middle finger upon the seam. (It is the spinning motion and the resultant high and low air pressure areas acting upon the ball that cause the curving trajectory.)

When developing his unconventional curveball, Matty held the ball lightly between his forefingers and thumb, and that is where the similarity between the two types of curves pretty much ended. The index finger, rather than the middle finger, rested upon or along the seam, and, rather than skyward, the wrist movement snapped the palm toward the ground. Because of the awkwardness of the wrist motion, the pitch was difficult to control. It would be a while before Matty felt confident enough to use it in a game situation.[18]

Meanwhile his fastball, fisting in on the hands of right-handed batters, was formidable, the more so as he learned to incorporate the strength of his football-player legs into the delivery. But what was really distinguishing him among pitchers was his ability to complement his "roundhouse" curve and his fastball with his "drop ball," which would suddenly break low over the outside edge of the plate against a right-handed batter. The "drop" was Matty's best pitch, and he saved it for situations in which things were "serious," for, at the Honesdale level of competition, the drop was "a surprise for all the batters." In July he was offered $90 a month to finish the season with Taunton of the New England League, and he gladly accepted. On the way to join his new team, he stopped in Boston to watch Kid Nichols pitch against Cy Young. It was the first major-league game Matty ever saw.[19]

Taunton was mired in last place, and it was not due to a whim of fate. On July 22 against Manchester in his debut, Matty kept his team in the game and lost, 6–5. A few days later he lost 13–4 against Brockton. It went on like that for the rest of the season. To make matters worse the $90 per month was illusory; Matty was hard pressed at times just to get $5 to pay his landlady. Eventually the club declared itself bankrupt, but the players, in order to salvage something, elected to stay together, finish the season, and divide among themselves whatever gate receipts became available.

Near the end of the season, Matty pitched against Portland and lost 19–11, but he had enough movement on the ball to attract the attention of Portland's manager, "Phenomenal John" Smith. Smith, a former big-league pitcher, decided to speak after the game with young Mathewson. During the conversation Smith stated that the New England League would fold at the season's conclusion, but, because he expected to manage another club elsewhere next year, he wanted to secure Matty's services as a pitcher. Smith's home was in Bristol, Pennsylvania, near Philadelphia. Matty's faith in minor-league contracts at this point could have been no more than problematic. However, he politely agreed to meet Smith in October when Bucknell came to play football at Penn, should Phenomenal John still have an interest at that time.

Glad to get back to Bucknell, Matty may not have been wealthier but he was at least wiser in the ways of the world. Few eyebrows seem to have raised when the erstwhile professional athlete returned to the amateur football field; rules opposite to that sort of dualism were a few years yet in coming. Matty had a momentous season as kicker and fullback, and Bucknell had a winning record.

One exception to the win column was the game against the University of Pennsylvania. Penn, coached by George Woodruff, implemented a "guards back" offense, which left only five men on the line of scrimmage and placed two guards alongside the quarterback. This offense was primarily mass movement; but, with a lateral or two, wide-open enough to keep the defense off-balance. In the preceding five years Penn had a remarkable streak of 65 wins, 2 losses. Bucknell, in previous outings with Penn, had failed even to score. As they checked into their hotel, the team did not expect to win: They just hoped to avoid another "whitewashing." The Bucknell coaches even offered a prize, a handsome new raincoat, to the first of their players to score. Another prize, a new pair of shoes, was offered in the event of a second score.

True to his word, Phenomenal John Smith came to meet Matty at the hotel. Smith had signed as manager and outfielder for the Norfolk club of the Virginia League. He offered Matty a contract for $80 a month to pitch for Norfolk during the next baseball season.

"Why, Mr. Smith," Matty replied coyly, "I had a contract with Manager Kellogg for ninety dollars per month."

"But how much did you receive?" Smith answered. "We will pay you $80 per month, and you'll be paid every dollar of it." Smith added that the Norfolk club had a $1,200 limit on its combined monthly salaries and he was committed not to exceed it.[30]

Matty eyed the veteran baseball man. Phenomenal John seemed genuine enough. He signed the contract.

Smith said he was planning to attend the football game that afternoon and left the hotel feeling he had landed a fine prospect. As Phenomenal John took his seat at Franklin Field, he saw Connie Mack nearby. He went to shake hands with Mack and pointed out the Bucknell fullback.

"I've signed him to pitch for the Norfolk Club of the Virginia League and I won't be surprised if you sign him next season," Smith said confidently.

Matty did not disappoint that afternoon. Bucknell drove into Penn's territory, and he drop-kicked a field goal. Soon he kicked another and also had a long run. At the half Penn led by a single point, 11 to 10. Pleased and proud that his prospect showed himself to such good effect against heavy odds, and before Connie Mack, Smith resolved then and there to revise the contract to $90 a month, limit or no limit.

Bucknell's moment of glory ended in the second half. Penn went on to win 47 to 10. Matty, along with the rest of the team, was physically battered by the end of the contest. He felt that he had rightfully earned the raincoat and shoes. After the game Phenomenal John approached him again, complimented his effort, and presented a new contract for $90 a month.

At 6 feet 1½ inches, Matty played center on the basketball team during his sophomore year. Basketball was a much different game then as well—a typical score for an entire game was State College 11, Bucknell 8. And in the spring he played on the college baseball team for the first and only time. The catcher, O'Brien, did not like to go behind the plate for Matty because of his dropball. O'Brien would not call for the pitch because he had such a hard time digging it out. Frank Stanton, the same Frank Stanton who went with Matty to Dr. Harris's home for dinner that first Sunday at Bucknell, could handle the dropball as well as Matty's fastballs (almost always right on the mark), and thus became Matty's battery mate.

Nearly 50 years after catching Matty's dropball, Stanton reminisced that, as with everybody and without being specific, Matty left a few uncomplimentary memories; nonetheless he described Matty as "way above average" as a student and Christian gentleman. At the training table Matty liked oatmeal and fruit had had a healthy appetite. "Milk should be taken with a spoon," he would say humorously, and that is how he took it.[21] One day Matty unveiled a new stunt of spinning a plate on the tip of his finger—without dropping it. Even Ernest Sterling had no idea when or where his friend learned this skill.

Matty's contract commenced with Norfolk on May 1. In the first inning of his first start he promptly yielded three straight bases on balls and an untimely triple; followed by an out, a single, another out, then another triple. Phenomenal John ran in from right field and asked the problem.

"I don't know. Everything I serve, they blast it."

"Take it easy," Smith answered. "You're going to finish this game if they score a hundred runs."[22]

Smith ran back to right field, and Matty—his mind perhaps turning to what the manager's confidence in him might do to his ERA—thereafter found his form. The opposition did not score again as Matty completed the game, and Norfolk came back to win, 6–5.

He would go on to win 20 games for Norfolk, including a no-hitter, all by mid-season.[23] He lost twice, in the second defeat going 12 innings before giving up the solitary run scored in the contest. Phenomenal John gave his young ace the benefit of his own big-league pitching experience, but, in the financially-strapped Virginia League, Smith did not coddle him either. When not pitching Matty played the outfield, and in 46 games he attained a batting average of .289. The Norfolk management touted their pitching star to the New York Giants and Philadelphia Athletics—hoping to turn a nice profit on their $90 per month investment. One day Phenomenal John came to Matty and said that both New York and Philadelphia had expressed an interest in him and made more or less equal offers. Therefore Matty could choose which big-league club he preferred.

Matty said he would like a day or two to think about it. He compared what he knew about the Philadelphia and New York pitching staffs. The Athletics appeared stronger in that department. The Giants were a last-place club. It seemed to the calculating young man, still not quite 20, that he would have a better chance of working on a regular basis with New York.

2

NEW YORK, NEW YORK

George Davis, playing manager of the Giants, summoned Matty during a morning practice. Davis, who hit .337 in over 400 at-bats the previous year and, seven years before, had connected for base hits in 33 consecutive games, took a bat and went to the plate. Matty, his arm warmed, stood ready on the mound.

"I want you to throw everything you've got," Davis instructed Matty.

Matty threw a hard one.

"That's a pretty good fast ball you've got there. Now let's have a look at your curve."

Matty delivered his "roundhouse," of which he was proud and with which he had great success in the Virginia League. Davis sent it deep into center field.

"The 'old roundhouse' ain't so good in this company!" Davis declared. "You can see that start to break all the way from the pitcher's box. A man with paralysis in both arms could get himself set in time to hit that one. Haven't you got a drop ball?"

Matty answered affirmatively and threw it.

"Now that's what we call a curve ball in the big league," Davis pronounced. "As for that other big one you just threw me—forget it! Got anything else?"

"I've a sort of a freak ball that I never use in a game," Matty replied.

"Well, let's see it."

Matty threw the pitch that he had picked up in Honesdale. Fortunately he got it to move in a way he wanted it to go.

"What's that ball? Can you control it?" Davis asked.

"Not very well."

"Try it again."

Davis swung and missed.

"That's a good one. That's all right!" the manager chirped. "It's a slow in-curve to a right-handed batter. A change of pace with a curve. A regular fadeaway. That's a good ball."

Thus, by Matty's own recollection, the "fadeaway" was christened by George Davis on a summer morning in the Polo Grounds. The pitch had been seen before. Charles "Old Hoss" Radbourn had a "reverse curve" or "inshoot" with the Providence Grays when Matty was a toddler. Mickey Welch, a star with the Giants a decade prior to Matty's arrival, in later years claimed to have had a "fadeaway" too, though he did not call it by that or any other special name.

The pitch was afterward rechristened the "screwball" by Carl Hubbell, perhaps its greatest practitioner and who at first did not know the pitch had earlier manifestations. Not only difficult to master, the pitch exacts a physical price. Retired from baseball, when Hubbell relaxed his throwing arm along his side, his palm turned to the outside—a living reminder of all the times his forefinger and thumb, and the force of his arm, imparted an "unnatural" movement on the seam of the ball. Matty himself, as his career progressed, used the delivery selectively. "Pitching it ten or twelve times in a game kills my arm," he said.

"I want you to practice on that fadeaway ball of yours, and get so that you can control it," Davis told Matty. "It's going to be a valuable curve."

What Davis told others was not necessarily the same thing. Sportswriter Bozeman Bulger remembered some reporters asking the manager about the newcomer. "Some kid who is supposed to be a pitcher," Davis remarked. "I don't think much of his motion, though. It's too hard on his arm, and if he shows anything, his arm won't stand the big league racket long."[1]

On July 17, 1900, New York City coped with the third day of intense heat. People succumbed in the streets as the temperature hung in the mid-90s throughout the afternoon. The city listed six adult deaths due to heat. Small children were more vulnerable. The Bellevue morgue reported 33 heat-related deaths of children to five years of age.

That same afternoon, at Washington Park in Brooklyn, the home team scored three runs in the fifth inning to tie. With no outs and two men on base, Davis pulled pitcher Ed Doheny from the mound and brought in the big kid from Norfolk. Brooklyn promptly scored another two runs; in the next inning they scored five more times and went on to win, in what seems the only thing breezy about the whole day, 13–7. New York fielded poorly; while Matty, relying on speed, hit three batsmen, walked two, and struck out one. The following day he could read in one of the great newspapers of the land his name incorrectly spelled with two "t's."[2]

A couple days later, from the bench, Matty saw John McGraw for probably the first time as St. Louis came to town for a three-game series. He did not see McGraw long—the Cardinals' third baseman was ejected in the second inning for arguing with an umpire. On July 25, after a rain delay and before an attendance of just 500 persons, Matty would no longer have to wonder what it was like pitching to Honus Wagner. "What's his 'groove'?" Matty asked his catcher, the veteran Jack Warner. "A base on balls," was the unsmiling reply. It was not Wagner, however, but Fred Clarke who smacked a home run, and Pittsburgh's hurler Happy Jack Chesbro welcomed Matty to the big league with a fast one behind the ears as the college man stood in the batter's box. The Pirates won handily, 11–3.[3]

Matty appeared infrequently the rest of the season. On September 13, his first start, he pitched well enough against Chicago that on several occasions the Giants could have won the game had they made a timely base hit. Two weeks later he came in against Boston in the fifth inning with a large lead and his wildness cost his team the game. On Saturday, October 13, at the Polo Grounds, first-place Brooklyn defeated the cellar-dwelling Giants in the last contest of the season, 1–0. That same day the football team of Lehigh University beat Bucknell, 12–6. Matty left for Lewisburg, a few weeks late for the beginning of the fall term.

However ignominiously the Giants ended, Matty returned to campus a conquering hero. He resumed his football exploits, earning an All-American accolade from Walter Camp. He was elected junior-class president; he sang in the glee club; he grappled with classes in psychology, embryology, and ethics; he participated in planning the junior ball—and he soon if not already had more than a passing interest for a willowy 20 year old with gray-blue eyes and chestnut hair. Jeanette Stoughton, whom family and friends called Jane, took courses in music and French at the Female Institute affiliated with Bucknell and lived with her parents and two sisters in a town house on Market Street, not far from the Presbyterian church where she taught Sunday school. Her father was Lewisburg's stationmaster.[4]

Matty was unsure which, if any, big-league team he would play for the next season. Andrew Freedman, the Giants' owner, made known his displeasure at shelling out $1,500 for the contract of a kid who had won no games and lost three. Freedman refused, allegedly, to complete the transaction with Norfolk and persuaded Cincinnati to pick up the rights to Matty at a fire-sale price.

In Lewisburg, Matty knew only that Freedman had not honored the obligation to Norfolk—and not that Cincinnati had claimed him. Connie Mack was still interested in the college man and sent an advance of $50. Matty needed money for books and other expenses so he accepted. Meanwhile, the mercurial Freedman traded Amos Rusie, who had not

Matty, young pitching phenomenon of the New York Giants, circa 1903. (National Baseball Hall of Fame Library, Cooperstown, N.Y.)

pitched for two years, to Cincinnati in order to get Matty back. When Freedman heard of the Athletics' advance, Matty received a "red hot" communication to report to Freedman's office in New York as soon as possible. Since Freedman's demand included an offer to pick up his traveling costs, Matty complied—only to be summarily upbraided during the meeting as a deserter to the American League and an unwise one at that since, in Freedman's opinion, the new league was doomed to fail. Freedman said that he would send the Athletics an amount equal to the advance already received and threatened a lawsuit if Matty did not show for spring training. Matty wrote to Mack asking if he would stand by him if it came to a court case. He received no reply.[5]

The second term of the academic year ended in late March, and Matty left for spring training, not for somewhere in the sunny South but for the brisk winds of Manhattan Field in New York City. Matty said goodbye, for a time, to Jane. Whether he realized it or not, he was also saying goodbye, for good, to his formal education. He would come back to Lewisburg often and fondly, and would be remembered as a Bucknell man. But he would take no more courses there, or anywhere, and leave his degree uncompleted.[6]

Manager Davis trained his club as best he could in April in New York. This inclement situation was due to the penuriousness of Freedman, who, owning the National League's potentially most lucrative franchise, was determined to minimize investment and maximize return. Since pre-season crowds flocked to exhibition games in New York in numbers equal to or surpassing those of crowds attending exhibitions in every town between Hot Springs and Harlem, Freedman saw little reason to take the team south and incur all that expense.

Soggy and cold weather prevented the Giants from limbering up regularly on the ball field. Instead they practiced signals or went to the handball court. When Matty, after receiving some salary, learned that Freedman had not sent Connie Mack any money as promised, he returned the $50 advance himself. Mack sent back the check and announced publicly that he intended to hold the young man to his contract with the Athletics, but, even though the contract would soon become a very valuable property, Mack evidently relented and instead allowed Matty to hold a place on a big-league roster untroubled by legal wrangling.[7]

A shellacking of Luther "Dummy" Taylor, the deaf mute pitcher, in Boston contributed to the decision by George Davis to assign Matty the start when the Giants opened at home in late April. Nearly 10,000 persons paid to witness the event. Above the horseshoe-shaped grandstand hundreds more watched for free from Coogan's Bluff or, with the old Polo Grounds—now called Manhattan Field—intervening, from the vantage of the 155th Street Viaduct. Beyond the outfield, along Eighth

Avenue, elevated trains clacked to and from the bridge over the Harlem River or to the routing yard northeast of the ballpark. Other than a soggy right field, the grounds were in good shape, and a Catholic preparatory school band played as the home team in white and the visiting Brooklyn club in gray marched festively around the field in the pre-game ceremony.[8]

Matty pitched splendidly. In shutting out the opposition, he yielded four hits, two walks, and struck out eight. He also hit a single and scored a run as the Giants won their first home opener in six years.

On the road he beat Philadelphia with a three-hitter and Boston with a five-hitter. On May 6, in his second appearance of the year at the Polo Grounds, he struck out the Phillies' lead-off batter with just three pitches and went on to record his second shutout. On May 11 Brooklyn's largest crowd of the season to date came to see Matty hold the home team, then known as the Superbas, hitless through five innings and allow only two hits thereafter. Some of the veteran Superbas tried hard to rattle the young man with chatter, but to no avail. Four days later the featured hero of Mathewson Day at the Polo Grounds shut out Chicago 4–0. By May 24 and the conclusion of his eighth consecutive complete game, another shutout, he had surrendered during that eight-game span a grand total of 34 hits and seven runs scored. The combined record of the other pitchers on the club was six wins, seven losses. Because of Matty's eight victories the Giants had an overall winning percentage of .650 and a perch atop the standings.

Moreover, the young lion of the Giants had religious principles, too. Honoring his mother's devout wishes, Matty refused to appear in a professional baseball uniform on Sunday, and held to this practice throughout his playing career. As he skyrocketed into the public's imagination during this unapologetically religious time, this well-publicized stand enhanced the fervor in which he was held. The only fans who may have disliked him for it were those who could not see him pitch because they had to work the other six days of the week. The issue might seem quaint and archaic now; then Sunday baseball sparked lively debate. In the National League it was the eastern cities, New York, Brooklyn, Boston, Philadelphia, and Pittsburgh, with blue laws that forbade Sunday baseball. Andrew Freedman tolerated Matty's stand and no doubt welcomed the good publicity, but none of the eastern owners could afford a clubhouse of similarly scrupulous men since, on the road in Chicago, Cincinnati, and St. Louis, their organizations were expected to honor Sunday dates, and it was not lost on the owners that Sunday crowds in those cities tended to be large.

When St. Louis scored a single run at the Polo Grounds on May 28, it proved enough to give Matty his first loss. John McGraw was no longer with the Cardinals. During the off-season he became manager and part-owner of the Baltimore Orioles in the American League. Largely due to the efforts of its president, Ban Johnson, and to the uncapped salaries which lured—diluting Matty's achievements somewhat—more than a hundred former National Leaguers into its ranks, the American League was engaged in its first bona fide major-league season.

McGraw brought marquee value to Ban Johnson's league. But these two domineering and ambitious personalities were destined to clash. Johnson sought a reputation of probity for his domain and had little patience for McGraw's vituperative and manipulative treatment of umpires. With the season less than a month old, the Orioles' manager already had felt the sting of a five-day suspension for repeated outbursts in a series with the Athletics. Antagonism between the two men increased on another count as McGraw fretted and fumed about Johnson's intentions toward the Oriole franchise. Johnson aimed to have his league enter the New York market and, to make room in the league for that metropolis, the Baltimore club seemed the most likely to fall by the wayside.

The size of the crowds at the Polo Grounds in late May and early June underscored the value of the New York market. On Memorial Day the grandstand and bleachers were filled to capacity and additional spectators stood two and three deep along the rope stretching around the outfield. They clamored to see Matty. With the score tied in the seventh, he relieved Roger "Peaceful Valley" Denzer and thwarted St. Louis until the tenth. In that inning a passed ball by catcher Frank Bowerman allowed a runner to reach third and then to score on a long fly ball. In the bottom of the inning, an unassisted double play by Cardinals' second baseman Tom Padden ruined the Giants' hopes.

Matty proved a drawing card on the road, too. Something about the tall, handsome, well-mannered, and well-publicized college man from Bucknell struck a responsive chord with people. The turnstiles at League Park in St. Louis recorded one of the largest crowds of the season as Matty yielded six hits in a one-run loss; recognizing that the kid's delivery tended to be lumbering, Tom Padden, leading from third base and relishing the opportunity to dash the young hero's hopes again, obtained the win for the Cardinals by stealing home.[9] Matty was cheered on by many of the 11,000 in attendance in Cincinnati as he came to bat in the third inning, and rapped New York's first hit of the afternoon, a single. He would lose the game 6–4. The very next day, though, the fleetingness of all this glory became intimated as the once great Amos Rusie, the man for whom Matty was traded, was sent to relieve in the fifth inning of a laugher. Having already scored 15 runs, the Giants against Rusie hit safely another 15 times and scored ten more runs.

On July 15 Matty threw a no-hitter in St. Louis. Jack Warner caught the 5–0 victory. Kip Selbach made two base hits and in the ninth preserved the no-hitter by coming up with Jesse Burkett's low fly ball to left. The pitching feat was the only such gem thrown in the league that season. (The game lasted just one hour, 35 minutes!) The team, however, was otherwise faltering. After the no-hitter, the fourth-place Giants journeyed to Chicago only to be swept in a five-game series. Matty lost five of his next six starts, and the Giants dropped further in the standings.

On September 6, 1901, the whole nation felt shock as news spread that President McKinley, attending the Pan-American Exposition in Buffalo, New York, had been shot by a young anarchist. McKinley lingered eight days; then Theodore Roosevelt, the bespectacled apostle of American manhood, fulfilled Senator Mark Hanna's fear that there had been only "one life between this madman and the Presidency."[10] Five days after McKinley's burial, Matty, suffering from a cold, pitched poorly against the team about to clinch the pennant, Pittsburgh.

Matty's first full season in the big leagues was an eye-opener. He began with an arm that could do no wrong and ended with an arm that did not feel right. No man could have been unaffected by the idolization he met throughout the country. But too intelligent to miss the object lesson offered by Amos Rusie, who in later years became a watchman at the Polo Grounds, or to fail to notice that people were more interested in the successes of his right arm than its aches and pains, Matty stayed loyal to family and friends. Fame and people eager just to see and touch him, let alone know him, did not change his inherent shyness and taciturnity. Consequently he seemed to many standoffish and even conceited. Once he visited an office in Philadelphia where his friend Ernest Sterling worked. By the time he was ready to leave, word had spread. Employees clamored around him, patted his shoulders, and called him "Christy" and "Big Six." Becoming tight-lipped, he exited the office in as straight a line as possible.

He was, according to sportswriter Fred Lieb, "Matty" to his wife, the New York fans, and invariably to his teammates. "Big Six" was a popular nickname for him, thought by some to have been derived from his height—a *Scientific American* article in 1915 cited the average height of major-league ballplayers as 5 feet 9½ inches. Others thought the nickname was derived from the numerical designation of the supposedly most reliable fire station in New York. It was not derived from any number on his jersey; that did not become a baseball convention until well after Matty's on-field career was over.[11]

A photograph of Matty at this age reveals striking handsomeness. His looks, fame, education, and ballplayer's salary could not have failed to attract feminine notice. Social opportunities of which his mother would have approved, however, were likely relatively rare. Ballplayers tended to fall in with fast company, and showgirls and ballplayers seemed to find each other. Besides to the places of bright lights, whether Matty accompanied players on nocturnal visits to the red-lighted tenderloins of the great cities to which they came is left to conjecture, other than to say two things: It is a temptation many virile young men have to confront at some point in their unmarried lives, but no such scandal has ever been attached to Mathewson's name from either his married or unmarried days.

During the off-season Matty returned to Lewisburg from time to time. He visited his college friends and could bask in their admiration. Yet they were preparing for graduation, something he was not doing, and Matty's personality was too proud to overstay a welcome. Mostly, though, he came to Lewisburg to see the stationmaster's daughter. He must have delighted, on a winter's day, bounding up the steps to the large door of the narrow town house, to receive admittance from one of the sisters, to remove his coat in the foyer, and to await Jane Stoughton's appearance. No showgirl had anything on her, and she did it with no more artifice than a Presbyterian upbringing allowed. More than that, her character was steady and intelligent, somewhat like Mathewson's mother's, though not as austere. She was someone beautiful upon whom to lean.

They made plans. From a family of Democrats, she told him she would become, like him, a Republican. He told her he would become, like her, a Presbyterian. If another season proved his right arm was no fluke and he could expect a career in the big leagues, they would marry. Meanwhile he would save a nest egg, and they would keep their engagement quiet. Matty now had plenty of incentive to keep himself in shape, which he did as a winter outdoorsman and in the gymnasiums of Keystone and Bucknell. For leisure, in addition to card playing—the college yearbook identified him with "three decks and a box of chips"—he played checkers.[12] Like beekeeping and spinning a plate on his finger, checkers was an avocation he pursued purposefully.

In 1902 the Giants again did their spring training in Manhattan. The popular George Davis had enough of Andrew Freedman and left to play for the Chicago White Stockings. The new manager, Horace Fogel, a sportswriter by profession, found his best-laid training plans plagued by rain and cold weather. By mid–April another sportswriter, being generous, described the team as physically fit and "drilled in a course of signs and signals to a degree which borders on perfection."[13]

Hope springs eternal. Never more so than on opening day—the day when, so goes the saying, there is no past, only future. Among the thousands who came to the Polo Grounds on this inaugural day was the famous fan with the powerful larynx known as "Well, well, well!"[14] They cheered as the Giants and Phillies marched around the field to the tune "There'll Be a Hot Time in the Old Town Tonight." They stood when the players came to a halt in front of the grandstand and a regimental band struck up "The Star-Spangled Banner." Matty took his place on the mound and, shortly after 3:30, umpire Hank O'Day called the first pitch a strike. An ovation shook the edifice. Matty threw a four-hit "whitewash," with six strikeouts, while the New York bats connected for seven runs.

The Giants jumped to a good start in the standings, and Horace Fogel had his headiest days as a manager. But the team faded. When Matty's arm hurt, Fogel sent him to see a doctor. Despite pain, on Memorial Day in the morning game, Matty had a 3–1 lead in the eighth inning against the visiting Phillies. Two walks, a wild pitch, and two singles later, the game was tied. A relief pitcher was summoned, but Philadelphia went on to win, 5–4. When the Giants lost the afternoon game, they dropped to fifth place. Soon thereafter Freedman intervened. Second baseman George Smith received appointment as playing manager; Fogel was now designated an agent for securing players.

A pall literally hung over the Polo Grounds—over the entire city for that matter. A bitter strike in the anthracite coal region made soft coal all that was available to burn. In June a game tied after 11 innings was called on account of the smoky darkness. Matty could read in the papers that he was a "fading idol," and, in a relief appearance for Tully Sparks, "no great improvement." The same articles did not mention that his arm continued to pain him and that he still won as many games as he lost for a team that, by June 27, had sole possession of last place with a 20 and 33 record. Nor did these articles mention that some teammates, jealous of his youth, talent, and publicity, occasionally made less than an honest effort when he was on the mound. Finally Matty griped: "I cannot win with them behind me!"

The organizational leadership grasped at straws. Matty could hit singles fairly consistently, and an experiment sent him to play first base. There he committed five errors in three games. Some infielders, teammate Jack Hendricks remarked, threw wide deliberately.[15]

Meanwhile, John McGraw's second season as a playing manager in the American League was even less congenial than the first. He and Ban Johnson seemed to go out of their way to battle over umpires. McGraw baited them, and Johnson suspended him for his conduct. About the kindest thing McGraw had to say about umpires was that the good ones "are born, not made, and the born variety is remarkably scarce." His on-field tirades, when quoted euphemistically in the press, contained remarks like "You're a piece of cheese!" or "You're the hole in a piece of cheese!"[16] His invective spewed against opposing players too, and how some of them regarded him found expression when Detroit baserunner Dick Harley, refusing to submit to a sure tag at third base by McGraw, savaged McGraw's left knee instead with a spikes-first slide.

Popular opinion correctly predicted that Baltimore would be the city sacrificed by Johnson to enter the New York market and incorrectly predicted that McGraw would be the manager of the new club. At this time, the extent to which each man detested the other for real or for show was blurred to observers. As much as Johnson wanted the apple of New York, he privately no longer wanted the thorn in his side represented by McGraw. Andrew Freedman wanted to discourage Johnson from making a competitive inroad upon the New York market and thought one way to do so was by taking what he perceived as the anointed manager of his potential rival. Besides, McGraw, whether fans loved him or loved to hate him, was good box office, and, as the big leagues' most dauntless competitor, he could restore credibility to Freedman's last-place club. Freedman, however, sought to wreak more havoc upon the American League than merely secure the services of one of its famous managers.

McGraw, nursing his knee injury and with the Orioles playing in the West under the guidance of his friend Wilbert Robinson, slipped into Manhattan for a talk with Freedman. There, with some discreet advice from former star player and now attorney John Ward, he held his own with the wily Tammany and real estate operative, and, together with John T. Brush, owner of the Cincinnati Reds, the three of them formed a plan to dismember the Baltimore franchise. First, McGraw orchestrated his release from Baltimore and sold his stock in the club to its president, John Mahon; then, back in New York, he publicly signed a contract to manage the Giants, to go along with the secret one with which he had protected himself by signing some days before. To complete the tight-knit scheme, Freedman and Brush purchased a controlling interest in the Baltimore franchise from Mahon and Oriole stockholder, and Oriole outfielder, Joe Kelley.[17]

As the Orioles' new principal owner, Freedman ordered the release of six players, not by mere coincidence the team's best. Joe McGinnity, Dan McGann, Roger Bresnahan, and Jack Cronin would go to New York; Joe Kelley and Cy Seymour went to Cincinnati. Ban Johnson, to preserve the American League from its enemies, summarily declared the Baltimore franchise vacant. Freedman and Brush did not put up much argument; in their raid they had gotten what they wanted, which did not include having their methods scrutinized in a court of law. Johnson borrowed enough players from other clubs to reconstitute an Oriole team, with Wilbert Robinson as manager. The American League president would remain in office a quarter century more. The new Giants manager would finally relinquish the reins of the team after three decades. The enmity between these two men never ceased.

Meanwhile, in Cincinnati, Matty and the other Giants learned that, on instructions from McGraw, four players were receiving ten-days' notice prior to release. When the team returned to New York, two more received the same news.

A large crowd came to see McGraw's debut. The Giants loaded the bases in the bottom of the ninth, but newcomer Bresnahan popped out and Philadelphia won, 4–3. A few days later in Brooklyn, Matty made his first start for the new manager, who, his knee better, watched him closely from the shortstop position and was not disappointed in Matty's performance as he struck out 11 and walked just one. McGraw liked to brag that, from this point, Matty's days as first baseman were over. McGraw had brought Dan McGann with him anyway. However, in the weeks to follow and somewhat contrary to the recollection of McGraw's autobiography that, from the moment he took the job as manager, the development of his young star pitcher was a special concern, Matty was occasionally sent to play right field, probably because base runners were reluctant to challenge his throwing arm and his bat was capable of registering as many hits as those of the other outfielders available. Nonetheless, without question the days of lackluster support for Matty's pitching were at an end.

McGraw marveled at how he never had to tell Matty anything a second time. From Joe McGinnity Matty learned how better to use a change-of-pace pitch; also from the "Iron Man" he learned the importance of pacing himself in the course of a game in order to have that little extra to call upon in the critical moments—"pitching in a pinch," Matty called it. He acquired the duality of performing both as a control artist and as a fireball hurler; in large measure it was a matter of self-preservation, for sometimes he was being started with just three days' rest. Most of all, in regard to both his current promise and future success, the pinpoint control which he developed complemented his ability to remember the strengths and weaknesses of every opposing batter. The presence of Matty brightened the Giants' horizon, but for the time being the team continued to lose twice as many games as it won. McGraw adroitly sidestepped immediate responsibility, saying, "Of course, the pennant is out of our reach as this season's playing goes, but look out for us next year."[18]

Matty lost the Polo Grounds' season closer to Brooklyn. The same day Andrew Freedman announced the sale of the Giants to John Brush. Freedman had decided to concentrate his energies and resources on the financing of New York's first subway, the Interborough Rapid Transit system. McGraw suspected there was more to it than just that. He believed Freedman regretted the autonomy guaranteed in his four-year contract and especially the salaries McGraw intended to lavish on the veteran ballplayers whom he, McGraw, would seek to recruit from the

American League. Consequently, according to McGraw, Freedman chose to get out of the business.

The gaunt, 57-year-old Brush required two canes with which to walk; a disease of the lower spine caused him difficulty in coordinating the muscle movements of his legs, though it did not cause him to lose his shrewd eyes and hard nose for business. Orphaned at age four, he had, like McGraw, a damaged childhood in rural upstate New York. He served in the Civil War and became a clerk after it. Brush thrived in merchandising and became rich from his big Indianapolis department store. Sportswriter Joe Vila liked to remark in his columns for *The Sporting News* that the "T" in John T. Brush stood for "Tooth." Prior to buying the Giants, he sold his Cincinnati club to political boss George Cox and the brothers Julius and Max Fleischmann of the yeast and gin fortune. Brush said he expected to make New York his home and, perhaps thinking of the four-year guaranteed contract, added that "Manager McGraw will be a fixture."[19] Guaranteed contract or not, in the years to come the association between the club owner and club manager proved eminently successful.

The Giants concluded the season 53½ games behind pennant-winning Pittsburgh. Having lost his last five decisions, Matty's record was 14 and 17. He pitched 277 innings with an earned run average of 2.11. His big-league credentials thus seemed established, and therefore it was pleasant to return to Lewisburg and make plans with Jane.

3

DISPUTED CHAMPIONS

In December 1902, John Brush cast a dissenting vote in the election of Harry Pulliam, 33-year-old secretary of the Pittsburgh Pirates, as the new president of the National League. Brush also opposed the peace talks with Ban Johnson that commenced early in the new year. The resulting National Agreement between the two leagues ended costly player raiding, deliberately conflicting schedules, and, except for the bitterness of Brush and McGraw, opposition to an American League entry in New York City. Business among the two major leagues and soon most of the minors as well was to be overseen by a three-man National Commission, composed of Johnson, Pulliam, and, from the Cincinnati organization, August "Garry" Herrmann, president of the Reds, political lieutenant of George Cox, and, from Johnson's days as a newspaperman in Cincinnati, a friend of the American League president.

In February Matty signed a $4,000 contract with the Giants, accompanied by a $1,000 bonus. The following day he and Jane announced their engagement.[1]

At high noon on Thursday, March 5, 1903, the marriage took place at the Stoughton residence with the Reverend Welling Thomas of Lewisburg's First Presbyterian Church officiating. The bride wore crepe de Chine trimmed with pearls. Ernest Sterling stood as best man and Jane's younger sister Margaret was maid of honor. Jane's relations were in attendance along with many of the couple's friends from Bucknell. Matty's parents, with his sister Christine and cousin Harry Sisk, came from Factoryville. After the ceremony the newlyweds were escorted to the train station in nearby Milton and boarded the Buffalo Flyer for Washington. On the train prior to its departure, some 20 Phi Gamma Delta fraternity brothers distributed handbills announcing: "Christy Mathewson, New York's great baseball pitcher, and newly wedded wife are on this train. Make them feel at home as there may be 'Something Doing.' Note: He will be easily recognized by his boyish countenance and Apollo-like form."[2]

From the Chesapeake the newlyweds took a coastal voyage—during which Matty suffered seasickness—to Savannah, where the Giants congregated for spring training. With McGraw as manager, the team would no longer have to endure training in Manhattan. Now they just had to endure McGraw. The short and combative manager took the tall and aloof Mathewson, seven years his junior, under his wing. When their wives first warily eyed each other in a hotel lobby, Blanche McGraw thought Jane was dressed rather nicely in a Sunday-school-teacher-way. Appraising Blanche's dazzling engagement ring, Jane thought "only a hussy would wear a ring like that." Soon, however, they were exchanging these and other confidences as they whiled the time during which their husbands practiced on the ball field. The two couples agreed to share an apartment once they returned to New York.[3]

The National Agreement foiled McGraw's attempt to make an immediate pennant winner by means of John Brush's checkbook. From the American League McGraw sought to sign Detroit's Kid Elberfeld, Washington's Ed Delahanty, and from Chicago, Fielder Jones and George Davis. But Harry Pulliam, in the spirit of the National Agreement, ruled that none of these players should put on a Giants uniform unless their American League clubs granted their release, which, understandably, none of these clubs were willing to do.

On April 8 the team arrived in New York. The McGraws and Mathewsons made their residence in a ground-floor apartment at 85th Street and Columbus Avenue, near Central Park and the elevated train to the Polo Grounds. They shared seven rooms and $50-a-month rent. Blanche and Jane were close in age, but, as the manager's wife and with more experience in the big city, it seems plausible that Blanche assumed at least a slight ascendancy in the household. As a Presbyterian, Jane may have had qualms about living with Catholics, yet, if Jane had any difficulties in the living arrangement, she possessed the good grace not to let them go further than her husband, if they went that far. Fortunately, especially for her own husband, Blanche had intelligence and even-tempered grace of her own. The McGraws had been married only a year themselves. Five feet tall with dark eyes and luxuriant black hair, Blanche was the daughter of a successful Baltimore building contractor. Like Jane she did not begin her marriage particularly baseball-minded, but in the years to come she would enjoy not only the game but also the respectful veneration among the fans at the Polo Grounds who came to regard her as an icon, seated in her accustomed place in box 19, just to the left of the home-team dugout. Her husband's life and therefore Blanche's own were seldom untroubled by controversy, the effects of which were ameliorated by the hearty affection her husband and she received on countless occasions from the baseball-loving people of New York—such as the cheers this springtime when her husband, hobbling on a reinjured leg, appeared as a coach in an exhibition game against the collegians of Fordham.[4]

Matty won eight of his first ten starts plus another win in relief. Giants rooters had something to cheer about as the team flitted between second and third place; no matter how well they played they could not keep up with the formidable Pirates. McGraw wanted a smart team, full of fight: Bill Gilbert, another former Oriole, now played second base; from the Phillies for cash came George Browne to patrol right field; Roger Bresnahan played center and muscular Sam Mertes, left field. Bresnahan, as the lead-off hitter, came within six points of capturing the batting crown from Honus Wagner. Mertes led the league with 104 RBI and stole 45 bases. Dan McGann hit clean-up and anchored the infield at first base. Warner and Bowerman shared the catching duties.

Joe McGinnity's nickname, "The Iron Man," originated in his off-season work at his father-in-law's foundry in Oklahoma but is remembered for such feats such as he performed on successive weekends in early August, when he pitched both ends of two Saturday double-headers, completing all 36 innings and winning all four games. Employing "Old Sal," his underhand curve, he worked so quickly that batters had little time to think about adjustments. The round-faced McGinnity stood 5 feet 11 inches and weighed over 200 pounds. His submarine delivery did not propel the ball very fast and thus tantalized batters all the more; with his control, however, the ball had so much movement that batters could seldom connect other than too high or too low resulting in ground outs and pop-ups. McGinnity this season would pitch 434 innings and win 31 games.

Pittsburgh, nonetheless, paraded to the National League championship, and Barney Dreyfuss, the club owner, challenged the American League pennant winners, Boston, to a post-season series. For non-pennant winners, post-season contests between National and American crosstown rivals were already being arranged in Philadelphia, Chicago, and St. Louis. But the whole situation did not sit well with Brush and McGraw; both already had bad blood for Dreyfuss and the man whom they regarded as his lackey, Harry Pulliam. That Dreyfuss and Pulliam wanted to give the American League, and Ban Johnson, the chance to prove their status as equals, or even superiors, on the playing fields of a "World Series" only confirmed their opinions. As for a post-season contest so popularly clamored for between the American League entry in New York, the Highlanders, and the Giants, Brush said: "I do not care to recognize the American League in New York. I do not know who these people are."[5]

The Giants clinched second place. Within a year McGraw had turned them from also-rans into contenders. Matty, for his part, had an excellent campaign. He started 42 games, completed 37, won 30, lost 13, with an earned run average of 2.26. Three relief appearances netted for him one win and two (of what later would be known as) saves. He struck out 267 batters in 366⅓ innings. He would have, in terms of wins and losses and earned run average, even more excellent campaigns, but this does represent the high mark of his strikeouts per season.

The Mathewsons spent the winter in Lewisburg. In early March they once again journeyed to Savannah. During the winter McGraw had already been south, to Hot Springs, Arkansas, where he and another man were arrested for unlicensed gambling—pitching silver dollars at a hotel.[6]

Matty engaged in games with ordinary people too. Not normally garrulous, he could go on about the "Old Fourteenth" or some other checker strategy for as long as someone cared to listen. He occasionally visited firehouses for challenges with local checker champions; McGraw affirmed that this was one of Matty's favorite "stunts" on the road, playing as many as eight "checker experts" at one time and beating them all. So comfortably did Matty have the numbered positions of a checkerboard in his memory that he would even play blindfolded and win consistently. Less publicly Matty continued to play poker, and on at least one occasion McGraw did not like it. In the midst of a pennant race, the manager fined Matty $500, not for playing at cards but for having the poor judgment to win, at high stakes, from his own teammates. McGraw scolded that Matty knew better and that for anyone else the fine would have been less—and the fine apparently was not rescinded.[7]

In 1904 the major leagues increased their season from 140 to 154 games. McGraw, of course, had been concerned with more during the off-season than fleecing locals for silver dollars. To Brooklyn he traded Charley Babb and Jack Cronin for shortstop "Bad Bill" Dahlen, a 13-year veteran. To some Dahlen appeared lazy and indifferent; to others he was the second best shortstop in the league, not necessarily faint praise, since the indisputable best was Honus Wagner. To McGraw, Dahlen was an icy cool competitor, who, because he insisted on knowing the pitch to be delivered, ably positioned himself and the other infielders. Dahlen's presence made easier the decision to go with rookie Art Devlin at third base. A smart, dauntless player from Georgetown University, Devlin also had two years' experience in the Eastern League. McGraw liked having college men on his roster, believing that, given the right temperament and physical ability, an educated man had a better chance at succeeding in baseball than an unlettered one.

In Brooklyn, soon after the season began, for the first time and in the face of the blue law, a Sunday contest was offered at Washington Park. Nearly 12,000 people came to see Ned Hanlon's no-longer-quite-so-Superbas play Boston. Charles Ebbets, Brooklyn's president, sought to skirt the law by, rather than directly charging admission, encouraging patrons instead to buy programs for 25, 50, or 75 cents, not the usual nickel. Ebbets reported that there were only two to three hundred "deadheads"—those who took advantage of the situation to pay nothing.[8]

The Giant organization, also uncontent to let their coffers remain unplenished one-seventh of the week, that same Sunday sent, as had been their wont for quite some time, most of their players across the river to Newark, where Sunday ball was legal, to engage a minor-league club there. The star pitchers, of course, were exempted from these exhibitions; on this particular Sunday young Leon "Red" Ames did the chore, and later in the season Claude Elliott was purchased from Cincinnati for essentially this purpose.

Police Commissioner William McAdoo waffled on Sunday baseball. He refused to countenance it in Manhattan because the Polo Grounds was too near populated neighborhoods, but he felt the sanctity of the day might be less disturbed in the less inhabited environs of Brooklyn's Washington Park. McAdoo wanted the matter resolved in the courts, and Ebbets scheduled another Sunday contest to facilitate just that. In an apparent prearrangement, after the first two pitches, the police arrested the pitcher, catcher, and lead-off hitter—the catcher and batter were reserve players and the starting pitcher was coming off an 8 and 13 season. After this bit of farce, the game was allowed to go on.

Matty's refusal to play Sunday ball was not without precedent, though being a pitcher made adhering to the decision easier. After all, it was, concerning him, a factor only in the Giants' road appearances west of the Alleghenies, in Cincinnati, Chicago, and St. Louis. Boston's Fred Tenney, from Brown University, an everyday player and an established star in the league for ten years, for much of his career also chose not to play on Sundays. Talent and stature did have something to do with having the privilege to make this choice. When Branch Rickey—then an obscure catcher assigned to the Sabbath-violating Reds, and whose respect for his mother's devout wishes was just as profound as Matty's and whose religious fervor probably more so—told his manager, Joe Kelley, that he would not play on Sunday, Kelley, McGraw's teammate on the old Orioles, berated the young man badly, and Rickey never did see big-league duty in a Cincinnati uniform.[9]

In May the Giants returned to New York from a long road trip in third place, just two games out of first. They took five straight from Brooklyn, including McGinnity's 11th and 12th victories in a row, the latter due largely to Jack Warner's dramatic tenth-inning home run into the bleachers behind the Polo Grounds' short right field. The Giants now shared first place.

Fans thronged to the Polo Grounds to share the excitement. John

Brush came to realize that with McGraw and team he had a figurative gold mine on his hands, and the sooner he could increase seating capacity at his stadium the better for his financial account. When Brush took over the franchise, the grandstand could accommodate 5,500 patrons and the bleachers another 5,000. That many and more squeezed in on Saturday, June 11, to see McGinnity go for his 15th in a row. Chicago trailed New York by one-and-a-half games. Bob Wicker, whose own competitive fire peaked this day, took the mound for the Cubs. McGinnity pitched a shutout through 11 innings. So did Wicker; in fact Wicker did not allow a hit until the tenth. In the top of the 12th, a combination of slap hits and heady base-running enabled Frank Chance to score against the Iron Man. Wicker held in the bottom of the inning to win.

Chicago, managed by Frank Selee, had come to play a three-game series. Wicker threw his no-hitter in the second meeting. Matty had pitched the opener. From the vantage of the visitors' bench, Mordecai Peter Centennial Brown could have watched Matty make what Brown later described as one of his typically lordly entrances: "He'd wait until about ten minutes before game time, then he'd come from the clubhouse across the field in a long linen duster like auto drivers wore in those days, and at every step the crowd would yell louder and louder." As Dizzy Dean would remark, "It ain't bragging if you can do it." Matty, in the opener, shut out the Cubs 5–0.[10]

The third game took place the following Monday. McGraw chose to start Matty a turn early, in place of Luther Taylor. Matty's opponent would be the colorfully-named Brown. Four years older than Matty but only in his second year in the big leagues, "Three Finger" Brown had grown up in Indiana, where, as a boy on a farm, he put his right hand into a corn grinder and lost nearly all of the index finger and severely disfigured the middle one. He turned the accident to advantage, however, by using his peculiar grip on the seams of a baseball to develop a tremendous curve. After a lackluster season in St. Louis, Brown was dealt to the Cubs for Jack Taylor, an established 20-game winner who had offended Cubs' president Jim Hart. Though the trade may have seemed a fire sale at the time, within a few years it had all the marks of a shrewd investment to Chicago fans. One of its earliest dividends occurred this day when Brown outdueled Matty, 3–2. Chicago left town one-half game ahead.

The Giants went on a tear, due largely to the ineffectiveness of Brooklyn and Boston. Chicago could not keep pace. When Matty took the mound at the Polo Grounds for the afternoon game on July 4, he sought his fifth victory since his one-run loss to Three Finger Brown; for that matter the team sought its 18th win in a row. Matty yielded just four hits to the Phillies through seven innings when Red Ames relieved to wrap things up. When the scene shifted to Huntington Park in Philadelphia, the Phillies, against the combined efforts of McGinnity and Taylor, managed to halt the Giants' win streak with a bloop hit in extra innings (the Giants had almost won it in the ninth when McGraw substituted himself as a baserunner and was nipped at the plate on a close call). The following day the Giants resumed winning ways as Matty threw another one-sided victory, again with Ames going in to mop up after seven innings. McGraw's men now had a record of 49 and 17 in the standings, their lead swelling to ten games.

Judge William Gaynor of Brooklyn ruled against the playing of Sunday ball in that borough. He found the inflated price of scorecards, in lieu of direct admission, a sham that could not remedy the fact that an undeniably professional sporting event had occurred. Commissioner McAdoo now instructed his officers to arrest all, not just token, offenders. Charles Ebbets canceled Sunday contests for the rest of the year.

John Brush and Jim Hart announced plans for a "world tour" of their respective clubs to take place at the end of the season. The tour did not take place, but clearly the intent was to cut short the public's natural assumption that another "World Series" would occur. Brush and McGraw continued to delight in their antagonism for Ban Johnson and his territory-infringing league. Johnson and McGraw traded insults in the newspapers, and Brush contemptuously dismissed all discussion of a post-season series with the champions of a "minor league."[11] Though entrepreneurial to his fingertips, this particular issue, at least in the short term, meant more to Brush than dollars. The Giants were already attracting a new club record at the gate, but a World Series, especially since it appeared the Highlanders might well dethrone Boston for the American League crown, was a sure promise of even greater receipts.

The Giants maintained a ten-game lead in early August, but McGraw was not comfortable. He wanted to be sure he was in a position to snub Ban Johnson come October. In Cincinnati manager Joe Kelley was known to be anxious to be rid of his star hitter and number one discipline problem, Mike Donlin. McGraw had managed Donlin before, in Baltimore; since then "Turkey Mike," so nicknamed because of his strutting walk, had done time in jail for assaulting a woman, caught on with the Reds, and was currently suspended by Kelley for drunken behavior. McGraw believed that he could handle any ballplayer. The Reds were so willing to part with the man who had hit .351 for them the year before, that it cost the Giants just reserve outfielder Harry "Moose" McCormick to make the deal. That Donlin was already banned from the American League and no other National League club wanted him also had something to do with it.

McGraw rather liked seeing or hearing references to himself as the

"Little Napoleon" of baseball. He did not take the coach's box often in 1904; instead he ran things with a tight rein from the bench. He rode players hard for physical and mental errors and reserved all responsibility for strategy to himself. "Do what I tell you," he said time and time again, "and I'll take the blame for mistakes."[12]

Luther Taylor's presence on the club induced McGraw to order his team to learn sign language. Not only did this improve conversations with Taylor, it gave the Giants a backup to their ball-field signs. If someone missed, say, the manager's cloth-on-cloth for a pitch-out or the third base coach's legs straddling the chalk line for a steal, McGraw could bark for the player's attention and spell out the instruction, or some sort of reminder, with his hands. But smart competitors were always looking to steal signs, and Johnny Evers and Tommy Leach took up the study of sign language in order to "listen in" as the Giants communicated to Taylor and to one another. McGraw realized this particular method of relaying tactics would have to go when one day from across the diamond he and Evers were trading barbs by signing their fingers.

On September 22 the Giants clinched both their one hundredth victory and the pennant. To spice things up for the hometown faithful, and anticipating Bill Veeck and Minnie Minoso by more than a half-century, McGraw placed "Orator Jim" O'Rourke on the roster. In 1876, playing with the Boston Red Stockings, O'Rourke recorded the first official National League hit; in 1888 and '89 he was the starting left fielder as the Giants won pennants in those years. Leaving the Giants in 1892, O'Rourke farmed, practiced law, and was a guiding figure, as well as player, in the Connecticut League. At 54 he was obviously still in good shape. Not only did O'Rourke appear in the September 22 game against the Reds, he caught all nine innings for Joe McGinnity. Orator Jim went one-for-four at the plate, as the Iron Man notched his 34th win of the year.

Brush and McGraw remained adamant that there would be no World Series. Talk of a world tour was replaced by talk of a tour of Cuba, but that also aroused little or no enthusiasm. Nothing allayed the disappointment, among both the players and fans, at Brush and McGraw's stubbornness.

Without anything more to aspire to, namely post-season money, the Giants became, putting it mildly, uninspired. Matty succumbed as well; on September 29 Tinker to Evers to Chance turned as easy a double play as they ever did by nabbing Frank Bowerman at second and throwing out Matty as he loped to first with his bat yet in hand. Crowds dwindled at the Polo Grounds as the team dropped six in a row. But many celebrities and others did show up enthusiastically at a gala staged at Klaw and Erlanger's Theatre on Broadway for the pennant winners, the proceeds going as a bonus to the ballplayers' salaries. Tod Sloan, the jockey said to have been the inspiration for George M. Cohan's *Little Johnny Jones*, acted as master of ceremonies. Prominent Broadway performers and vaudevillians, including Dave Montgomery and Fred Stone, famous for their roles in *The Wizard of Oz*, made stage appearances. Capping the evening for the packed house, Joe Humphreys, the Giants' megaphone announcer, introduced the team, dressed in tuxedos and basking in the wild applause. A loving cup was presented, and Harry Stevens, the scorecard and concession impresario, gave gold cuff buttons to McGraw. Most pleasing of all to the players, the event netted as much as $10,000 to be divided among them.[13]

The next day McGraw did not appear for the game against St. Louis. Another esteemed relic, Dan Brouthers, filled in as manager and at first base. Matty, however, roused himself from the general lethargy and struck out 16 Cardinals in his 33rd victory against 12 defeats. Only 300 patrons witnessed his effort.

The Giants ended with a record of 106 and 47. Two thousand persons came to a Giants' "field day" held just after the season ended; it featured an exhibition game and other assorted athletic contests, including matches between professional boxers, mostly Irish. Real baseball excitement in New York, though, had already gravitated to the Giants' crosstown rivals. Jack Chesbro's spitball had kept the Highlanders neck-and-neck with the Boston Americans. When Chesbro faltered in the next-to-last game of the season, and inasmuch as John Brush continued to ignore their pleas for a World Series, the Royal Rooters of Boston—who, as events would prove, with some reason considered themselves a force to be reckoned with—claimed the title of "World Baseball Champions" for their Red Sox and their city. Convinced the Giants had the best pitching anywhere, Joe McGinnity left New York angry at the fact of no post-season play. Mike Donlin left "sore" too, saying that McGraw had conned Brush into preventing everyone, including Brush, from making more money.[14]

4

WORLD CHAMPIONS

McGraw dealt Jack Warner to St. Louis. Warner was not happy about it. The catcher felt that McGraw had reneged on an understanding that he, Warner, should have instead received extra compensation for having done so much in the development of the Giants' pitching staff.[1] McGraw evinced little sympathy as his team's bitterness about the previous season's lack of post-season play gave way to the joyousness of a new beginning and high expectations. The Giants once again trained in Savannah. During their circuitous route north, they played an exhibition in Indianapolis, where, when "Sandow" Mertes hit a triple, "Happy," the Giants' canine mascot, chased him around the bases. For pennant winners, this sort of thing delighted crowds and did not irk the manager.

On opening day at the Polo Grounds, the grandstand, colored in a fresh coat of yellow paint with red trim and festooned with bunting, looked especially bright beneath a blue sky. Flags, taut in the April breeze, flew from every eminence. A cordon of city police kept the throng of fans from flowing onto the field, and at two o'clock the band struck its first air. Mayor George McClellan, son of the Civil War general, arrived in the company of Commissioner McAdoo and other public dignitaries. Harry Pulliam took his seat, as did baseball venerables John Ward and Cap Anson and heavyweight boxing champion Jim Jeffries.

Shortly after 3 P.M. the Giant players, to a rousing ovation marched onto the field: McGraw first, then Matty, Browne, Dahlen, Devlin, and so on until Iron Man McGinnity appeared. They hoisted on a staff a large pennant, dark blue with gold lettering; it proclaimed:

Giants
Champion Baseball Club of National League
1904

The mayor tossed the ceremonial first ball, and the Boston Beaneaters, led by playing manager Fred Tenney, lost to McGinnity 10–1.

For his pennant winners John Brush lavished a remodeled clubhouse, acknowledged as the finest in the major leagues. On a game day McGraw expected his players to report by ten o'clock in the morning, usually not much of a problem as long as they observed the manager's rule of being in bed by 11 every night except Saturday. They were greeted by Enos Joseph, the clubhouse keeper, and Happy the dog. Harry Tuthill served as trainer; he also developed prize fighters. Each player had a large, open-wire locker with his name painted over it. A whirlpool adjoined the showers. A wide balcony, overlooking right field, was attached to the upper floor of the clubhouse; sometimes players rested there in the shade after practice. Matty, Bill Gilbert, and Roger Bresnahan maintained sartorial reputations as the most "dudish" dressers on the team. Red Ames's tenor voice often began a popular song and others joined in unison. Luther Taylor exhibited his jiu-jitsu exercises and let out a cacophonous laugh whenever Bowerman's fingers repeated a good clubhouse jest. By 10:30 the team was on the field for a two-hour session; afterward they could go eat—often they went to a nearby luncheonette or had worshipful youngsters fetch sandwiches for them—but they had to be back two hours before the four o'clock game time.[2]

In June the Giants, off to a stellar 36 and 12 start, journeyed to Chicago. The Cubs took the first two games of the series, the Giants scoring but once in the 18 innings. For the third game, on June 13, Mordecai Brown pitched against Matty. Brown was a year away from establishing himself as one of the league's premier pitchers and in the process acquiring the reputation as Matty's particular nemesis. Their match-ups, on the whole, brought out the best in both competitors. Before 9,000 fans and beneath weather that threatened rain, Brown did not yield a solitary run until the ninth inning. Against Matty no Cub even made a hit, although two reached base as the result of errors; one of these runners was doubled-up off first base after a fine catch by George Browne in right field. The only other near-base-hit the Cubs made in their 28 at-bats came in the fifth when center fielder Donlin snagged a line drive by Johnny Evers. Matty and Brown combined for just five strikeouts between them, as if they challenged each other to see who could fool the more batters into pop-ups and ground-outs.

The brief loss of their batting strokes in Chicago notwithstanding, the Giants continued to dominate the league; so much so that in early August they arrived in Pittsburgh with nearly a ten-game lead over the second-place Pirates. McGraw planned to pitch Matty twice in the four-game series, and Matty won the opener 3–1. On their way from and to the Monongahela Hotel where they stayed, the Giants often delighted in agitating the local citizenry. One day their carriage passed a marketplace and, in response to their cockiness, the team was pelted with vegetables and fruit. A cantaloupe struck Sammy Strang in the head, and tomatoes found the seat of Joe McGinnity's pants. At the ballpark, when Matty took the coach's box and began to chatter, Pirate fans and players liked to heckle him because of the high-pitched tenor of his voice; they collectively felt that he was most fond of being called "Big Sis."³

A large attendance came to Exposition Park to see the final game of the series. Matty pitched into the last half of the ninth inning as the Pirates came to bat with the score tied at five. Claude Ritchey hit a double; George Gibson then bunted toward Matty who threw the ball to Art Devlin at third; Ritchey seemed to slide around Devlin and, from his vantage point near home plate, umpire George Bausewine called the runner safe. The Giants immediately appealed to the other umpire in the contest, Bob Emslie, who refused to intervene. When Devlin continued to badger him, Emslie, his temper flaring, threw a punch at the player. McGraw, in the heat of the situation, decided not to risk giving the Pirates the satisfaction of scoring a late-inning victory against Matty, so he simply refused to depart the playing field when the umpires repeatedly ordered him to do so. Bausewine called the game a forfeit to Pittsburgh.

Later in August the Pirates went to New York. McGraw had, as Matty related it, the ability to incite even a Monday crowd just by the way he picked up a pebble and tossed it. The manager took the third-base coaching box with Matty pitching the opener. With a five-run lead already in the sixth inning and with a baserunner leading from third base, McGraw rattled the Pirates' veteran battery of Deacon Phillippe and Heinie Peitz by sending the runner to steal home. And in the eighth McGraw agitated umpire James Johnstone into ejecting him, as the Giants and Matty finished the 10–2 romp without him, although it was McGraw's practice, after being ejected, to hide in the groundskeeper's shed at the Polo Grounds where he still had a clear view of the field and could make his instructions heard on the bench.

Outside the Polo Grounds young Alexander Schacht hawked newspapers which headlined Theodore Roosevelt's diplomatic triumph in successfully sponsoring a negotiated end to the war between Russia and Japan. The youngster sold more papers than other boys by shouting the news in the sports pages. "Matty wins another!" he cried. "Read all about it inside the paper! Matty headin' for thirty victories again! Read about Matty!"⁴

In the American League the Athletics stumbled to the pennant. It had seemed a cakewalk for them until their star pitcher Rube Waddell took a walk of his own. He disappeared for several days and when he returned his arm hurt. Some thought gamblers got to him, others were certain the injury resulted from a scuffle with teammate Andy Coakley. Still others believed Rube could only be Rube, and he simply defied rational explanation. This was, after all, a man who chased fire engines and who, hearing what he thought was a cry for help, once dove from a fog-shrouded steamboat to save a log—and a man who, in behavior not so benign, allegedly in an argument threw a pair of flatirons at his wife's parents. To the same degree that Rube's large hands could grip a baseball, he could not handle a bottle. Connie Mack, it was said, was the only manager, perhaps other than McGraw, who had a chance to keep him in line. But his teammates, with World Series money at stake, were fed up, and Mack, World Series or no World Series, resolved to do without him. The club had other pitchers, and good ones too, though none of them besides Rube, as yet anyway, compared in reputation or proven ability with Matty or the Iron Man.

McGinnity and other Giants made evident their dissatisfaction as another pennant-winning season loomed with no commitment to post-season play. Brush and McGraw, however, had no taste for denying their players or the paying public a World Series a second time. To save face in making this abrupt policy turnaround, McGraw expressed the opinion that he was willing to engage the American League champions in a best-of-seven contest provided the players received 60 percent, not the heretofore offered 40 percent, of the gross receipts from the first four games.[5]

As September began, Frank Bowerman, Matty's main catcher, received word of a family illness and left for his home in rural Michigan. With Roger Bresnahan, who now generally caught the other pitchers, behind the plate, Matty extended a winning streak another four games. When Bowerman returned in mid-month, McGraw was not eager to reinsert his less potent bat into the lineup, but did so at Matty's preference. Matty won two more games, taking his record to 29 and 7. On Saturday, September 23, Matty and Carl Lundgren engaged in a brilliant pitchers' duel in Chicago. With the pennant still on the line, McGraw put Bresnahan behind the plate instead of Bowerman. It represented his first loss since the forfeited game in early August and his first real loss since the Pirates beat him 2–1 on July 18.

The Giants had clinched by now the season series from every club except the Pirates, who led thus far in the head-to-head competition ten games to nine. The Giants went to Pittsburgh for three more games. The Pirates also had won their season series from every other club, though not so decisively, and needed to sweep the Giants to keep alive their pennant hopes. Instead the Pirates fell apart. In the opening inning of the first game, Deacon Phillippe, ordinarily one of the best control pitchers in the league, hit three batters; then with the bases loaded Honus Wagner, of all people, made a wild throw that let in three runs. As the dust cleared and Matty returned to the mound for the second inning, his team had a five-run lead with only one base hit, a single, to its credit. Both clubs sensed the inevitable. Ten runs to four, Matty breezed to his 30th victory.

A few days later the pennant belonged to the Giants, and afterward, with a World Series now promised, there was no ignominious letup as last year. Matty won the team's hundredth victory, and his 31st, in St. Louis on September 29. The Giants spent the last week of the regular season on the road and ended with a 105 and 48 record.

At ten o'clock on the morning of October 9, the Giants arrived in Philadelphia to take on Connie Mack's Athletics. They came in a special car attached to the regular train. Five hundred Giants fans, led by former heavyweight champion James J. Corbett, accompanied them. Stepping onto the platform McGraw walked arm in arm with actor Louis Mann. A band led the way to Columbia Park, and Philadelphians received the visitors with polite applause along the route.

The ballpark filled to capacity, and hundreds stood along the edge of the playing field. With both players and management interested in the total receipts, an exact count of 17,945 was registered. Many more had to be turned away. The Giants' devoted 500 were parceled into one section of the wooden grandstand, and they made up in enthusiasm what they lacked in numbers. About 2:15, the Giants burst onto the field, McGraw leading the way. The players wore dramatic new uniforms obtained for the occasion by their manager: black trousers and blouses with white belts, stockings, and insignia. The New York fans cheered:

> Johnny, get your gun, my son, we've won!
> Johnny, get your gun, it's ten to one!

McGraw doffed his cap and waved. "The odds are too big, boys!" he called. "Take even money!"[6]

The Philadelphians shouted for "Connie Mack, the crack-a-jack!" and brought whistles and bells to make noise for their team. McGraw and Mack agreed that whenever a fair ball went into the crowd surrounding the outfield it would count as a double. At the Giants' bench and scanning the short distance of left field, McGraw demanded of his clean-up batter, McGann, the chances of putting the ball into the outfield crowd. "On this postage stamp!" McGann replied, "You bet!" But pitcher Eddie Plank retired the Giants without a score in the first inning. Plank, five years older than Matty, also a college man, and who after Waddell's abnegation went on to pace the American League with 26 victories, did not have overwhelming speed but his left-handed delivery baffled hitters.

When Matty took the mound, six photographers surrounded him

and he delayed his warm-up to pose. Roger Bresnahan crouched behind the plate, as perhaps the only Giant not in an upbeat mood, Frank Bowerman, looked on. Topsy Hartsel grounded the first pitch to Billy Gilbert for an easy out. Bris Lord flied the next delivery to Mike Donlin in center. Harry Davis hit a come-backer to the mound and Matty snagged it. It had taken Matty four pitches to end the first inning.

He took six pitches to end the second. In contrast, throughout the game, the Giants worked Plank for twice as many pitches as Matty threw. The Giants were lightning on the basepaths as well. In the top of the second, taking advantage of Plank's long delivery, Devlin and Gilbert executed a double-steal, though the batters who followed were unable to get them home. In the fifth inning, with two outs and Bresnahan at second base, Donlin swung at a pitch and missed. A New York fan raised a sign, charcoal on a large sheet of manila paper. "What! A strike on our Mike? It cannot be," it said. Then Donlin drove the ball between Monte Cross at short and Lave Cross at third, and Bresnahan scored as Donlin raced to second. (Although Lafayette Napoleon "Lave" Cross had two brothers who played big-league ball, Montford Montgomery "Monte" Cross was not one of them.) The Athletics then set up a force play by walking the switch-hitting McGann to get at right-handed Sam Mertes, who, in a statistic to render the wisdom of the percentage ploy uneasy, had finished second in the National League in runs-batted-in. Mertes sent the ball into the crowd edging center field for a ground-rule double. McGann and Mertes were stranded when Bill Dahlen flied out, but the Giants led, 2–0.

In the sixth Ossee Schreckengost led the Athletics' half of the inning with a double and was advanced to third base. Hartsel then bunted on a squeeze play but Matty got the ball to Bresnahan in time for the out at the plate. In the eighth Danny Murphy led with a double, and the local rooters attempted to rattle Matty with their whistles, bells, and horns. He responded by striking out Monte Cross; then Schreckengost flied to George Browne in shallow right. Connie Mack chose not to pinch-hit for Plank, who struck out also. Matty had five strikeouts on the entire day, two of them coming in this situation of a man in scoring position and none out.

The Giants scored one more run in the ninth. For the Athletics, Harry Davis knocked a two-out double in the bottom of the inning, but the game ended with Lave Cross's grounder one hour and 47 minutes after it began. Matty and McGraw warmly shook hands near the first-base line, as the Giants rooters climbed out of the stands to hail the victors and as the players themselves hurriedly repaired for the carriages to the train which would take them back to New York.

Thirty thousand raucous fans packed the Polo Grounds the next day to see the Iron Man versus Charles Albert "Chief" Bender. The Athletics took the field in their somewhat tattered maroon-and-gray uniforms which they had worn on the road all season. The Giants again were resplendent in black. Bender, of German-American and Chippewa ancestry, struck out nine batters, including McGann three times and Mertes twice, as the Athletics won, 3–0. The series, in seesaw fashion, was to resume in Philadelphia on Wednesday, October 11, but a dark sky and drizzle augured so ill throughout the morning and early afternoon that only 4,000 patrons, paying on average 75 cents admission, came to the ballpark. The drizzle stopped before game time. The players looked to the sky and to the grandstand and thought of their pocketbooks. Sammy Strang outstretched his arms and implored the rain to fall. McGraw and Mack had a decision to make. The choice they made left a bad taste in the mouths of the 4,000 faithful who braved the weather to see baseball played, and also among the larger baseball public as it became generally known the field condition had been tolerable and the rain did not come.

One choice made easy, however, by the extra day of rest was McGraw's decision to go with Matty in game three. Andy Coakley took the mound for the Athletics. Coakley had a career season in 1905 with a 20 and 7 record, due largely to a superb first half. New York scored two runs in the first inning and five in the fifth. Matty and Bresnahan, in a sophisticated game of catch, mixed pitches marvelously as their overall strategy relied on their fielders. Matty fed the opposition deliveries designed for pop-ups and ground outs until the Athletics got a man on base; then he went for a strikeout. If an Athletic did connect soundly on a certain pitch, he did not see that pitch again. Matty was particularly effective against Socks Seybold, mixing both fast and slow ones, until Seybold just jabbed at the ball with a short-arm motion. The wind departed from the Athletics' sails, and some of their batsmen scarcely tried to beat the throw to first base. And if they got to first base, they hung closely to the bag out of respect for Bresnahan's arm, and because in these circumstances Matty was more likely to challenge the batter with his fastball rather than an easier-to-steal-on breaking pitch. In fact, the Athletics did not steal a base at all until Topsy Hartsel took one in the first inning of the third game. The Giants stole six in the first two contests, and five more against Coakley. Victimized by errors, Coakley allowed nine runs in nine innings, only two of them earned. Matty allowed five hits, struck out nine, and yielded a solitary base on balls. Not only had he pitched a shutout, but no Athletic base runner had even touched third base.[7]

In game four, despite letting Athletics on base in every inning except two, McGinnity beat Plank, 1–0. All four games of the series thus far had ended in shutouts. That night the final receipts from these games, from which the players would receive their money, were counted: The winners' shares were worth over $1,100 each; the losers' shares under $400. McGraw, perhaps to allay suspicions of seeking to prolong the series to enhance the management's portion of the gate, decided to go with Matty for the fifth game, even on just two days' rest, and went over one more time with his pitcher the strengths and weaknesses of the opposing lineup.

In the morning Matty ate his usual late breakfast of eggs, bacon, and fruit. "Lunch makes me feel heavy," he would say; consequently he avoided it on game days. Still he felt logy as he prepared to go to the Polo Grounds.[8] The stands swelled to capacity for the Saturday game; in the excitement to see Matty pitch for the championship the bad feelings engendered by the postponed game quickly wore off. Fans, in contrast to the previous day's attendance of 13,598, stood ten deep behind the ropes extending between the left- and right-field bleachers. A band played Broadway tunes as Chief Bender warmed up in a temperature approaching 70 degrees.

"Back to the teepee for you!" someone hooted, and others imitated Indian yells. Bender was remarked by the press as only smiling in reply; but, in the years ahead as he became at home in the big leagues, Bender would occasionally lash back verbally at such hecklers, describing them to their faces as "ignorant, ill-bred foreigners" and inviting them to return to their own countries.[9]

Bresnahan and James J. Corbett posed with an Irish flag between them for a photographer. Matty remained conspicuously absent. When he at last appeared, he received a magnificent ovation; the applause lasted for a full minute. Instead of doffing his cap, Matty went over to McGinnity and removed the Iron Man's. McGinnity returned the compliment.

The loginess disappeared, and by the second inning Matty threw with confidence. His breaking pitches, and he meant for the Athletics to see a lot of them, went just where he wanted. Bender gave up five hits on the day. Matty yielded six hits and himself committed two errors, but he also required just four strikeouts to once again shut out the Athletics. In the 27 World Series innings he had pitched, only one opposing baserunner—Schreckengost in game one—had reached third base. In the sixth inning of the final game, three Athletics did safely touch first base: Hartsel made it there on Matty's error, but was forced when Lord hit into a fielder's choice; Bresnahan then rifled a throw to pick off Lord; Harry Davis singled; but Devlin ended the inning by throwing out Lave Cross. In the final three innings the Athletics went three-up, three-down—only one man, catcher Mike Powers, hit the ball beyond the infield.

Matty began the ninth with a 2–0 lead. His confidence wavered slightly with a vague worry that he might somehow "fall down." Lave Cross was the 92nd and last batter Matty faced in the series. Of those 92, he struck out 18, hit one batter with a pitch, walked one, suffered one stolen base, and yielded no hit more serious than a double. The World Series was not yet a tradition, but Matty posted an achievement in the five games played, in terms of three complete games pitched and a perfect earned run average, that continues to stand the test of time.[10]

The Giants bolted for their clubhouse as thousands of their fans swarmed onto the field and clamored for the winners. To an immense cheer Matty and Bresnahan appeared on the clubhouse balcony to unfurl an impromptu paper banner which read:

The Giants
World Champions 1905

Other players tossed their hats, belts, and other articles of their uniforms to their admirers below.

5

TO THE BONE

During the winter Jane became pregnant. No longer would the Mathewsons share an apartment with the childless McGraws. They eventually moved to a seven-room place in Washington Heights, not far from the Polo Grounds. Jane could see, with field glasses, the scoreboard from a window and, when her husband was pitching, started boiling potatoes for supper in the seventh inning. Matty liked a good porterhouse steak after a game. Fancy dishes did not appeal to him; dessert did, though. "His favorite sweet, outside of pie à la mode," said Jane, "was elderberry jam."[1]

McGraw invested some of his now $15,000-a-year salary into a poolroom on Herald Square. His partners included Tod Sloan and a gambler named Jack Doyle. Billiards champ Willie Hoppe appeared at the opening, and among the regulars was a young bookmaker named Arnold Rothstein who, 13 years hence, would cast a shadow on the 1919 World Series. When the McGraws moved to a residential hotel near the Polo Grounds, they were both pleased to make the acquaintance of the Highlanders' first baseman Hal Chase, a young Californian with a captivating way about him, and a moral sense that would cause newspaper sports editor Jim Price to say of him "he has a corkscrew brain."[2]

Harry Pulliam was re-elected as National League president, despite the opposition again of John Brush. Uncompromisingly though not unflinchingly, Pulliam endeavored to end "rowdy ball." Some found the bachelor Pulliam too high strung and romantic in his notions; others expressed admiration for his nerve.

Mike Donlin got himself into jail in Albany, New York, for an incident on a train involving alcohol, a handgun, a diamond merchant, two minor leaguers, and a black porter who refused to be bullied.[3] In Memphis, where the Giants commenced training, the weather was cold and rainy. Among the recruits vying for a place among the veterans was Henry Mathewson, Matty's 19-year-old brother, who at 6 feet, 3 inches and 175 pounds had an athletic physique and a fresh-from-Factoryville personality.

Matty joined camp long enough to pose atop a colossal pushball that the Giants used in a merrier part of their training, but a cold from which he suffered flared into diphtheria and soon he was in a Memphis hospital. When the team went to Nashville for an exhibition, Frank Bowerman remained with him. McGraw felt ample cause to worry for his star. When McGraw was still a boy, diphtheria took within one winter the lives of his mother and four brothers and sisters.[4]

Besides the rain and Matty's health, McGraw had other problems. Donlin's relentless drinking caused the manager for a time to suspend him. Something offended Harry Tuthill so much that the trainer announced he was severing relations with the club, though the relations were later mended. And, in the act of hitting a pitched ball, the backward swing of Henry Mathewson's bat struck Roger Bresnahan in the mouth, damaging several teeth.[5]

John Brush sent to the president of his crosstown rivals a message on the occasion of the Highlanders' home opener. "I wish you luck artistically and financially," he wrote. It was his way of burying the hatchet. Charles Ebbets sought once more to legitimize Sunday baseball in Brooklyn. This time Ebbets argued that, if people by the tens of thousands could take entertainment on Coney Island on a Sunday, they should be able to pay to see a baseball game on a Sunday as well.[6]

Twenty thousand fans congregated for the 1906 opening day ceremony at the Polo Grounds. Tom Murphy, the groundskeeper, decorated the diamond with miniature American and Irish flags.[7] Two cannons boomed, a band struck up, and the Giants strode onto the field with the words "WORLD'S CHAMPIONS" embroidered in large block letters across the front of their home jerseys. The road grays would bear the same immodest statement. Matty, yet ill, appeared wan and weak, though he did make some warm-up tosses to Bowerman. Red Ames pitched the game and won.

Matty did not pitch until May 5, and the fans at the Polo Grounds welcomed him warmly. The same day his brother Henry, no longer on the Giants' roster, pitched a local game in the Bronx.[8] Even without Matty in the rotation, the club had earned a game-and-a-half standing over second-place Chicago. Matty threw well enough for seven innings to leave McGinnity a 4–3 lead, but the Iron Man surrendered three runs in the ninth to give Boston the win. Nine days lapsed before Matty's next start, in Cincinnati. The Reds made nine hits and obtained seven walks, but Matty held on for the victory, thanks to his teammates' five-run rally in the ninth. The next day, as the Giants posted another win in Cincinnati, Mike Donlin broke his ankle sliding into third base. It was a heavy blow. At the time Turkey Mike was leading the league with a .349 batting average.

Matty ended May with a 4 and 1 record, and the Giants yet nipped at the heels of first-place Chicago. But the Cubs, under new ownership, arrived at the Polo Grounds in early June and dropped the Giants into third place with two easy victories. Matty started the third game of the series and failed to finish the first inning; McGinnity relieved and fared as poorly—before the Giants came to bat, they trailed by 11 runs. By the sixth inning, with an 18–0 lead, the Cubs had obviously let up in their effort; even so they scored one more run, which was still one more than the Giants made in the entire game. In a foul mood that began to permeate the organization, John Brush informed the pressbox keeper that he would receive less salary; instead the man quit and thereafter, as sportswriter Joe Vila told it, the new man did not let in as many of McGraw's friends for free.[9]

While his team was yet in reach of the highflying Cubs, and heedless of the situation in the pressbox, McGraw decided to shake up his roster. Cincinnati's new manager, Ned Hanlon, could not get along with his center fielder Cy Seymour; Hanlon and Garry Herrmann were willing to part with Seymour for $10,000 of John Brush's money. McGraw wanted a high-caliber man to replace the injured Donlin and persuaded Brush that Seymour fit the bill. Sam Mertes was traded to St. Louis, along with reserve catcher Doc Marshall, for outfielder William "Spike" Shannon and infielder Dan Shay. How the Seymour purchase made Mertes expendable is unclear, although Shannon at 28 was six years younger than Mertes and having marginally a better season. The very name "Shannon," however, was guaranteed a favorable reception by the inhabitants of "Burkeville," as the seats near left field in the Polo Grounds were called. Mertes refused to report to the Cardinals and claimed that, because he was a Mason, the Irish Catholics on the Giants never cared for him and that he had expected better treatment from John Brush, a fellow Mason.[10] (Mertes did finish the season with St. Louis, but '06 proved his last year in the big leagues.)

Matty saved his team from being swept four games in Pittsburgh by throwing a shutout in the finale. Returning to New York, the Giants rallied by taking seven games in a row from the Reds and Cardinals. In early August a Saturday crowd, as large as any of the last year's World Series, came to see Matty pitch the opener of four games with the Cubs. He did not humble the visitors but pitched well enough to begin the seventh inning with a three-run advantage; when he yielded another run in that inning, McGraw sent Hooks Wiltse to relieve. The victory pulled the Giants within five games of first place.

The series with Chicago resumed the following Monday, and its next two games were marked by controversy. A double-steal attempt was foiled by a close call at home plate making Art Devlin out, resulting immediately in McGraw and much of his team surrounding umpire James Johnstone in angry and prolonged protest. Upon the ejection of McGraw and Devlin, the crowd erupted into a bottle-throwing frenzy. Much time ensued before Johnstone and the other umpire, Bob Emslie, felt secure enough to resume play. The Cubs went on to win 3–1.

McGraw's juices stewed. When Johnstone and Emslie showed up at the ballpark the next day, club officials barred Johnstone from entering—to protect him from the fans, they said. Emslie did go in, thought better of it, and left. The rule book entitled each team, in the event the sanctioned umpires did not appear, to choose among their own players a substitute official. McGraw chose Sammy Strang, and at game time sent his men onto the field. Frank Chance, the Cubs' playing manager, would have nothing to do with what he perceived as a farce and kept his players on the bench. The 8,000 persons in attendance strained to hear Joe Humphreys explain through his megaphone that the Cubs refused to play and that rain checks would be issued. Sammy Strang declared the game a forfeit to New York.

Harry Pulliam cut short his vacation in Sarasota Springs and issued a statement demanding to know if club owners were "a lot of poltroons and dogs [who] eke out their existence solely through the receipts on the New York grounds, and therefore must stand by and see the New York club invalidate the constitution of the National League at will."[11] He suspended McGraw and Devlin, ordered the record to reflect a forfeit to Chicago, and threatened to resign if a clear majority of club owners did not support his actions.

With avid thoroughness, Pulliam obtained statements regarding the Devlin incident not only from umpire Johnstone and Cub catcher Johnny Kling, but also from Joe Tinker, Harry Steinfeldt, McGraw, Harry Tuthill, Cy Seymour, Roger Bresnahan, Frank Bowerman, and even a Mr. Fields. Pulliam concluded that McGraw "used the most villainous language one mortal could" to Johnstone and "well merited his removal." He dismissed the Giants' protest of the forfeited game as "silly and unsportsmanlike." He chided John Brush for "thinking that 'McGrawism' pays, because, like a dog fight, it draws a crowd." Pulliam also announced that, despite his physician's advice that he resign, he would stand again for re-election to his office.[12]

Fresh from three victories in St. Louis, the Giants hoped to redeem themselves in the Cubs' West Side Park. Matty dropped the opener to Three Finger Brown, however, and McGraw soon, if not already, realized the Cubs would not be stopped this year. The Giants did manage to inflict two of the just three losses the Cubs suffered during the entire month of August as the Cubs went on to post a phenomenal 116 and 36 record.[13]

John Brush, now fond of post-season revenue, anticipated a series with the Highlanders. But Frank Farrell, a big stakes gambler who, with former New York City police chief William "Big Bill" Devery, owned the Highlanders, remembered the snub of '04 and spurned any such accommodation. Farrell additionally took satisfaction in that his Highlanders, in another pennant race themselves, outdrew the Giants at the gate by 30,000.[14]

On September 28 Matty had a comfortable eight-run lead against St. Louis at the Polo Grounds. McGraw sent Henry Mathewson, who rejoined the club late in the season, to pitch the ninth inning in relief of his older brother. Except for an error in the field, Henry would have retired the side in order. Matty recorded his final victory, his 22nd against 12 losses, in early October. The next day, the last game of the season, before a few hundred fans at the Polo Grounds, Henry started against Boston. Even with Bowerman behind the plate, the youth yielded 14 walks and hit one batter. McGraw kept him on the mound for the entire game; to his credit Henry struck out two major-league hitters and batted a sacrifice hit.

On October 19, 1906, Jane Mathewson gave birth to a son, Christy Junior. At the time Matty, in the manner of a self-absorbed athlete, was hunting in Michigan with Frank Bowerman. The Bowerman family owned a fruit farm north of Detroit. Matty loved the out of doors, but he does not seem always to have been a successful hunter. A year previously he and Jane did not attend the wedding of their friend Ernest Sterling; in what was to Sterling a personal hurt, they did not even send a gift. Long later Matty confessed that he intended to give the newlyweds a handsome set of knives with handles made of antlers from a deer he himself had slain. Unfortunately he never obtained the antlers.[15]

McGraw sent Billy Gilbert to the Eastern League. Whatever deficiency McGraw saw in Gilbert as a second baseman, he thought to remedy by acquiring from the Reds 38-year-old Tommy Corcoran, who began his big-league career in 1890 as a barehanded infielder in the Players' League. Mike Donlin married a lovely, young, and ambitious comedienne named Mabel Hite and made known his intention to become an actor. "They'll be actors, all right," McGraw predicted. "Bad actors."[16]

In late February Matty and Henry departed by train from New York to Chicago. There they met the rest of the team prior to journeying to Los Angeles, where McGraw arranged to conduct spring training for 1907. Fred Knowles, the Giants' secretary, had contract business yet to settle, and several players found the proposals unsatisfactory. Donlin demanded a $600 raise to his $3,300 salary of the year before and

Jane Mathewson and son, Christy, Jr., in about 1907 or 1908. (National Baseball Hall of Fame Library, Cooperstown, N.Y.)

Matty with Christy, Jr., circa 1915. (National Baseball Hall of Fame Library, Cooperstown, N.Y.)

attempted to sweeten the deal by making the $600 refundable should he become dissipated with intoxicants at any time during the season. Bill Dahlen, Dan McGann, Sammy Strang, and Frank Bowerman balked at the pay cuts offered them, especially as Art Devlin and Roger Bresnahan received raises. Knowles, however, had orders to remain inflexible. Bowerman went back to Michigan, and Donlin left too. Donlin had an additional grievance that management, although paying in full his '06 salary, refused to pay some of his doctor bills for the broken leg he suffered while sliding into base in Cincinnati.[17]

The team practiced at Chutes Park, home of the Los Angeles Angels. Many observers thought the level of play in the Pacific Coast League compared well with that of the majors, and good receipts were anticipated from exhibitions in Los Angeles, Oakland, and San Francisco. From California the Giants traveled to San Antonio to play the St. Louis Browns and then to New Orleans for an exhibition series with the Philadelphia Athletics.

Bowerman came to terms and rejoined the team. Donlin showed up

Frank Bowerman, roughhewn, tough, and Matty's friend, circa 1906. (National Baseball Hall of Fame Library, Cooperstown, N.Y.)

in New Orleans and pinch-hit a triple. McGraw wanted Donlin back in his lineup and offered to pay out of his own pocket the $600 increase the outfielder sought. But a week later McGraw and Donlin quarreled over whether the $600 should be paid prior to opening day or at the end of the season. Donlin left to return to the stage with his wife, and McGraw resolved to do without him.

When the regular season began, Bresnahan caused a mild sensation by appearing behind the plate not only in mask and chest protector but in shin guards as well; modified from those worn by cricket players, these were the first shin guards worn, at least on the outside of the socks, by a big-league catcher. A change in the rule book now allowed only the pitcher to soil a new ball by rubbing dirt into it in order to remove the gloss; any other player who did so would be fined five dollars.[18] That the ball could not receive as much additional scuffing from his teammates had little effect upon Matty. He won his first six decisions, three of them shutouts. By the latter part of May the Giants posted a 24 and 4 record. Nonetheless, as the Cubs came to the Polo Grounds, the visitors from Chicago trailed in the standings by just one game.

A near-capacity crowd came on a weekday to see Matty paired against Three Finger Brown. Spotted an early one-run lead, Matty retired the first nine batters; thereafter a combination of two errors by Bresnahan as catcher, timely hits and daring baserunning by the Cubs, and close calls from the umpires, enabled Chicago to attain a 3–2 victory. Fans threw debris at the umpires throughout the game and were particularly inspired by a Bresnahan tantrum in the ninth inning. A Pinkerton man attempted to calm things by firing his revolver into the air; that only made matters worse, and regular police had to be summoned to restore order.

McGinnity won the next game to regain for the Giants sole possession of first place, and another huge crowd came for the third and final contest of the series. Wiltse started and yielded two runs in the first inning; in the second inning McGraw sent Ames to pitch. In the fifth the manager sent Matty to the mound, but two fielding errors quickly led to two men in scoring position with none out, and Jimmy Sheckard then hit his only home run of the season. Luther Taylor relieved Matty. Hoping to spark a rally, McGraw sent pinch hitters for his pitchers until his entire staff, including McGinnity, took a turn on the mound, but to no avail whatsoever. (Henry Mathewson was no longer one of the pitchers. A mop-up role in an easy victory a couple of weeks earlier marked his final appearance in the major leagues. He remained in New York City, marrying a young woman from the Bronx, finding work, and playing semi-pro ball.) In the clubhouse afterward McGraw tore into Bresnahan for his play. The "Duke of Tralee" was not inclined to take such treatment—he had managerial aspirations of his own—and lashed back. McGraw suspended him for three days.

A trip to Cincinnati in mid-June proved highly injurious. Andy Coakley, now with the Reds, beaned Bresnahan, who fell unconscious and then spent several days in a local hospital before going home to Toledo for an extended recuperation. In the same game another pitch broke Dan McGann's wrist. The Giants held on to win the contest, but the next day Matty lost in the ninth when the Reds rallied with three consecutive hits for a come-from-behind victory.

On July 9 Matty threw a six-hitter against visiting St. Louis, followed four days later by a shutout of the Reds. McGann's arm remained in a plaster cast, but Bresnahan returned to the lineup. Prior to his return, Bresnahan's name was used to advertise a pneumatic head protector which covered the side of the face while batting. Batting helmets or the like, however, were an idea whose time had not yet come, and Bresnahan, upon reflection, decided to disdain the device.[19] His first appearance at the plate came against the same pitcher who had beaned him, Andy Coakley, and he rapped a single.

After the Pirates took two games in a row at the Polo Grounds, McGraw released Tommy Corcoran. On the advice of Dick Kinsella, a scout for the Giants, McGraw reached deep into the minor leagues for a young second baseman named Larry Doyle. Happy to escape the coal mines of his home in southern Illinois, Doyle became a regular and exclaimed, "It's great to be young and a Giant!"[20]

In Cincinnati, Danny Shay engaged some spectators in what McGraw described as kidding but what others called more offensive in nature. An on-duty policeman named Kramer, who just happened to be a former heavyweight prize boxer, told Shay to desist. McGraw intervened saying, in effect, that the umpire was in charge, not Kramer. The officer, or, rather, the former fighter, looked for McGraw after the game. As Joe Vila remarked, neither Harry Tuthill nor Frank Bowerman were around to protect the manager. "He's a wonder," Mike Donlin said of McGraw. "He can start more fights—and win fewer—than anybody I ever saw."[21]

In Chicago in early August the Giants lost four out of five, including another win by Brown over Matty. If it was not obvious before it was now that all the Giants could again realistically hope for was second place. Second place, however, was not enough to hold McGraw's interest; it was said the manager was seen at the race track when he should have been at the ballpark.

McGann, his arm healed, watched an 18-year-old kid named Fred Merkle stand in for him at first base during the last western tour. In late September the Giants exhibited their final tantrums of the season in

Pittsburgh. Before the first game of the series, McGraw threw a cup of water into third-year umpire Bill Klem's face. Klem seemed to let that go; but during the course of the three games, he ejected eight Giants, including four over a single called-strike in a game that also proved Matty's eighth shutout of the year.

The Giants lost nine of their last ten contests. The pennant-winning Cubs outdistanced the second-place Pirates by 17 games. The Phillies, meanwhile, went on a run of their own and hosted the Giants in a season-ending series, of which the Phillies took the first game to clinch third place. In the finale Matty scattered seven hits over seven innings and trailed 3–2, but, by mutual consent, neither team took the field for the eighth inning. The Giants thus meekly accepted their lumps and fourth place.

McGraw had a novel idea for Mike Donlin. After the star outfielder returned to the fold by signing a $4,000 contract, replete with a no-alcohol clause, the manager designated Turkey Mike as team captain for the '08 season in order to encourage more responsible behavior from the sometime vaudevillian. Secure with two years remaining in his own annual salary, McGraw paid scant attention to speculation that John Brush, reportedly dissatisfied with his manager's race-track reputation, intended to replace him with Roger Bresnahan. Instead McGraw negotiated a dramatic trade to reinvigorate his team.

Frank Bowerman would not return. He, along with Dan McGann, Bill Dahlen, George Browne, and pitcher George Ferguson, went to the Boston Nationals for first baseman Fred Tenney, shortstop Al Bridwell, and reserve catcher Tom Needham. McGraw obtained in Tenney a solid personality and performer. At 36, two years older than McGraw, Tenney had spent 14 seasons in Boston, the last three as playing manager. Due to ownerships either unwilling or unable to field a competitive team, the Beaneaters, or, rather, this season the Doves, for new owner George Dovey, had become also-rans, and Tenney, once the baseball darling of New England, had lately heard his share of jeers. Besides his knowledge of the game and aging legs, he brought a sure glove and a still productive bat. With both Matty and Tenney, the Giants now led the league in Baptist-educated college men. In Bridwell, McGraw had an agile and aggressive shortstop to complement Doyle and Devlin.

To emphasize his seriousness about training and about winning a pennant in 1908, McGraw chose Marlin, Texas, as the Giants' spring training site. The New York sportswriters who went with the team, writing more like Ned Buntlines than good journalists, emphasized the saddle horses, mules, and overall rusticity of the place. However, the solid-brick business district of the prosperous and bustling community was well-connected with up-to-date telephone and electric service, and the players roomed comfortably at the modernly appointed Arlington Hotel, where in the adjacent bathhouse they enjoyed the therapeutic hot mineral waters from underground springs.[22]

One young man signed the hotel register as "S. Strang Nicklin." For nine big-league seasons with several teams he had gone by "Sammy Strang," heretofore preferring it to his given name because of the low social status often accorded ballplayers, but from now on the man who, after his ballplaying career, would go to Europe to study concern singing no longer wished to disguise his identity as a major-league utility man. When Tom Needham tried to say something on his fingers to Luther Taylor, Taylor reportedly replied: "Another Bowerman. I bet he has a brogue." Taylor, born in Kansas, could ride a horse like a cowboy and, on a team ride to a barbeque about four miles from town, rode circles around Matty, whose own long legs dangled awkwardly astride his mount. As Taylor and his horse dashed by, Matty's pony sought to accompany them in spite of Matty's best attempts with the reins, and it was remarked that Big Six took his barbeque standing up.[23]

McGraw worked his men hard and infused more new blood. Otis Crandall looked as though he might belong in the pitching rotation, especially since Taylor seemed now a "back number" and McGinnity, coming off, for him, a sub-par year, was suffering from malaria. Temperamental 22-year-old Charles "Buck" Herzog, an infielder from Maryland's eastern shore, struggled to earn a place on the roster. Sammy Strang Nicklin may have eyed him harshly. Veterans in all big-league camps treated the rookies, or "yannigans," with little or no respect, and not a few promising young men became discouraged and returned home. Fred Snodgrass, a youth McGraw had recruited that winter in southern California, found a mentor in Spike Shannon, who took him under his wing and told him what to do and what not to do. Snodgrass believed he would not have made the club otherwise.

When, against Brooklyn, the Giants opened the season at the Polo Grounds, Matty was lifted for a pinch hitter in the bottom of the ninth inning trailing 2–1. The pinch hitter, Merkle, stroked a ground-rule double, and Shannon sacrificed him to third base. The Superbas adroitly fielded a hard hit by Tenney to catch Merkle in a run-down, Tenney hurrying to second on the play. In a private grandstand box Mabel Hite, star of the current hit *The Merry-Go-Round*, watched her husband stride to the plate. On a two-balls-two-strikes count, Mike Donlin hammered the next pitch into the right-field bleachers. Mrs. Donlin clapped her gloved hands exuberantly as her husband wended his way through the crowd swarming onto the diamond to celebrate the victory.

Rocked in four consecutive starts in May, Matty began a resurgence with a four-hit shutout in Brooklyn. By June 20, he had collected 11 victories. Sometimes Matty worked so fast under a hot sun that Bresnahan would walk a little from the plate and pick up and toss a pebble just to slow him down. The Giants, however, stood in fourth place. Cy Seymour, with cramps occurring in his legs, stayed in the lineup despite the team physician Dr. Joseph Creamer's advice to rest. Perhaps Seymour believed this was the best way to avoid the fate of Sammy Strang Nicklin, whose contract was sold to Jack Dunn's Baltimore club in the Eastern League. Luther Taylor, who had seen men come and go and who was smart enough to realize his own career was on the wane, would not be daunted. As rain fell at the Polo Grounds with the Giants trailing in the third inning of a game with the Reds, Taylor borrowed a large pair of rubber boots from groundskeeper Murphy and tramped to the coach's box in an attempt to kid umpire Johnstone into calling the game. Instead Johnstone ejected Taylor to the clubhouse. After the Giants scored five runs to take the lead and before the regulation five innings were complete, Johnstone did stop the contest!

Buck Herzog hurt his wrist and refused to play in one of the Sunday games the Giants scheduled across the river in New Jersey, and McGraw said harsh words to the young man who bolted for home in Maryland. Harry Smith, catching for the Boston Doves, got hit in the arm, and a batboy brought him a cup of water; Roger Bresnahan, batting at the time, intercepted the cup and drank the water. McGraw, chafing to win the pennant, persuaded John Brush to spend $11,000 for the contract of one Richard "Rube" Marquard, a pitcher with the Indianapolis club of the American Association, and from the St. Paul club, for a reported $6,000, McGraw and Brush obtained John "Chief" Meyers, a Cahuilla Indian and a promising catcher.

The Giants climbed in the standings near to the leaders, Pittsburgh and Chicago; so near that, when Pittsburgh beat Boston on the same day the Giants opened a series in Chicago by walloping the Cubs 11–0, the Pirates gained sole possession of first place and the Giants edged into second.

Two days later, on July 17, Matty started against Three Finger Brown. Both men delivered their best. The lone run of the game came in the fifth inning. At one time Joe Tinker had been an easy out for Matty; standing close to the plate with his hands choked-up on the bat, Tinker's right-handed swing—short and quick—was ineffectual against Matty's curve on the outside corner. Tinker, however, had since learned to stand away from the plate, against Matty, with his hands down at the end of a longer bat; in this stance he could factor just enough change in the timing of his swing to pounce on the curve and still hit the fastball.[24] On this day Tinker tagged a two-strike pitch past the outfielder into deep left and took off like a rocket. Ignoring the coach's plea to stop at third,

Tinker continued toward home with a purpose. Bridwell seemed slow to make the relay to Bresnahan, and Tinker narrowly beat the tag. The Chicago fans went wild, and, watching from a roof of a nearby four-story building, a boy became so excited that he fell and broke his neck.

Herzog wired McGraw and asked to come back. Spike Shannon was let go. Moose McCormick, who was, by the way, another Bucknellian, returned, his contract purchased from Philadelphia. Mike Donlin rapped his one hundredth hit on July 13; he was the first batsman in either league to reach that mark, which meant he got there ahead of both Honus Wagner and Ty Cobb. But when the Pirates came to the Polo Grounds later in the month, Wagner connected five times in as many at-bats against Matty, as Larry Doyle unintentionally aided the Pirates in the game with three errors. After his second hit, each time he reached base Wagner gave Donlin, in right field, a taste of his own showmanship. "That's three," he signaled. "That's four." "That's five."[25]

Matty shut out St. Louis at home 1–0. Not only did this represent his 19th victory and seventh shutout with more than two months yet to go in the season, it marked his 22nd consecutive triumph over St. Louis dating back four years. So confident were the Giants in another game of this series with the hapless Cardinals that McGinnity, a lifetime .194 hitter, went four-for-four at the plate; and Donlin, seeming bored, argued himself right out of the game over, of all things, receiving a base on balls. Even solid citizen Fred Tenney got into the act. With Luther Taylor on third and Tenney on first, Tenney sought to divert a throw from Cardinal pitcher Arthur "Bugs" Raymond by running to second base; instead Raymond tried to catch Taylor by throwing to third. Tenney called for time, forsook the successful advance, and ran back to first. He and Bugs just looked at each other. On the next pitch Tenney ran to second again, and this time he stayed there.

The Giants thought they could toy with the Reds just as they had with the Cardinals. In the top of the ninth inning of a game in early August, Hans Lobert singled to Donlin in right field. Turkey Mike, his team ahead 3–0, leisurely played with the ball, tossing it from hand to hand, challenging the speedy Lobert to head for second. Lobert beat the throw, and the Reds went on to load the bases and then take a one-run lead. The Giants managed to tie in the bottom of the inning, and rain resulted in a drawn game. When the Reds won the next day's game, McGraw let his players have it. Had the Giants won these last two contests, they would have been one-half game from first place. The manager could not blame Matty, though. Matty had already won five in a row from Cincinnati this year; if his manager could have looked into the future, McGraw would have seen that, in another remarkable streak, the Reds would not defeat Matty again until well into 1911.

In a streak of a different cast, Three Finger Brown had now bested Matty in their last seven decisions. McGraw employed a different tactic when next the Cubs came to town—he pitched someone else against Brown. Matched with Hooks Wiltse, Brown looked mortal in a 4–1 loss. The game following, Matty beat Orval Overall.

The Giants swept four games in Pittsburgh to take sole possession of third place. In Chicago a forecast of rain threatened to postpone a Saturday game, Matty's scheduled start, into a Sunday double-header. Lest it prove a factor in manager Frank Chance's reasoning concerning the condition of the grounds, Matty volunteered, publicly enough so that the newspapers carried it, to pitch on Sunday if need be.[26] The weather improved enough to render his offer moot, but on Saturday he lost by one run to Three Finger Brown anyway. Wiltse and Crandall lost in Chicago as well. As August ended, the Giants returned east still in first place, albeit just one-half game ahead of the Cubs. Some 40 games remained on the schedule, including more than a few double-headers, but despite the grueling schedule the Giants took satisfaction in knowing that two-thirds of these games would occur at the Polo Grounds.

In Pittsburgh, on September 4, Three Finger Brown faced batter Owen Wilson with two outs and the bases loaded in the tenth inning of a scoreless game. Wilson sent Brown's first pitch past Johnny Evers into short center. The runner on first, Warren Gill, saw that the ball would drop and that the runner on third, his playing manager Fred Clarke, would easily score. Consequently, in accordance with a not uncommon practice of the day—as not uncommon anyway as this sort of bottom-of-the-final-inning victory occurred—Gill did not bother to touch second base. Rather he headed for the clubhouse. As long as the batsman made it to first base safely and the progress of any other baserunner did not appear doubtful, so went conventional wisdom, the run and therefore the victory counted. But Frank Chance, applying a close reading to the rules, had his men ready for just such an eventuality. Even as Hank O'Day, the only umpire, headed from the field, Evers stood resolutely at second base and called to the center fielder for the ball. Joe Tinker pointed out the situation to O'Day, who was drinking a cup of water near the players' bench. Since he had not looked to see whether Gill touched the base or not, O'Day refused to disallow Clarke's run. The Cubs protested. There was no reason, they argued, why they should be obliged to concede the force-out at second base. But Harry Pulliam upheld O'Day's decision saying, "I think the baseball public prefers to see games settled on the field and not in this office."[27]

Matty won his 29th and 30th victories by yielding just one run over a span of 20 innings. In the former, the Phillies got seven hits, but with men on base Matty gave something extra to his pitches; in the latter, a

1–0 victory in 11 innings, Larry Doyle received a severe gash in his leg as Brooklyn's John Hummel sought to break-up a force play. In the two victories Matty garnered 12 strikeouts while allowing just one walk. He would have understood perfectly what Warren Spahn, the great left-hander, meant when he said that the art of pitching is like selling real estate: the secret of success is location. In 1908 Matty would lead the league in games pitched, innings pitched, complete games, wins, earned runs allowed, shutouts, strikeouts, and fewest walks per nine innings.

The Giants, Cubs, and Pirates played better than .700 ball during the first three weeks of September. The Giants led by 3½ games until, against Pittsburgh, Matty failed to notch his 34th win. Owen Wilson led off the third inning with a sharp grounder toward right field. Buck Herzog, playing second base for the injured Doyle, cut the ball off and hurled it to Tenney, catching Wilson by a yard, but Hank O'Day's judgment went one way when it should have gone the other and he called the runner safe. Even Matty stormed in protest. George Gibson moved Wilson to third by stroking a double. It looked like Matty might work out of the jam when the next two batters popped up so meekly that Wilson could not score, but then Fred Clarke rapped a single down the left-field line for two runs. These proved the only hits yielded by Matty during the entire afternoon, but they were enough to give the Pirates a 2–1 win.

The next day, Tuesday, September 22, the Cubs came to the Polo Grounds and swept a double-header with a pair of one-run victories. In the first game Bridwell allowed a baserunner to move from second to third by making the wrong selection on a fielder's choice; the next batter sent another grounder Bridwell's way, which he booted, and the run scored. In the second game, with the bases loaded and two outs in the seventh, McGraw sent Fred Merkle to pinch-hit. Three Finger Brown struck him out.

Thus, on just two days' rest, Matty took the mound in what became one of baseball's most famous games. Jack Pfiester, who won only two more games than he lost on the year for the Cubs, proved on this occasion a worthy opponent. Through nine innings Matty surrendered five hits and no walks; the Cubs' lone tally, thus far, having come on Joe Tinker's fifth-inning home run—the first home run yielded by Matty since the one hit by Tinker two months before. Matty struck out nine Cubs, including, from the heart of the order, Evers and Wildfire Schulte in the ninth. Through eight innings Pfiester had allowed just four hits, two walks, and like Matty only one run. As sunlight waned, Cy Seymour led off the Giants' half of the ninth with a hot grounder coolly fielded by Evers. Devlin singled, but McCormick forced him out at second with another grounder to Evers; Devlin's daunting slide and McCormick's speed averted a double play. Merkle then singled, advancing McCormick to third. The game marked Merkle's first start of the season at first base. It was also the first start, including Sunday dates, that Fred Tenney had missed; his legs desperately needed rest. Bridwell stepped from the batter's box and cast a cautioning look at Merkle, whose lead from first base seemed too eager and too far. McCormick represented the only run that mattered, and Merkle realized that he should keep closer to the bag. Pfiester's first pitch was waist high and over the center of the plate. In the only base hit—because of what it cost Merkle—that he ever regretted making, Bridwell drilled the ball into right center, as umpire Bob Emslie fell on his backside to avoid it hitting him. Bridwell darted for first and McCormick darted home. Merkle, seeing joyous fans already swarming onto the field, got within 15 feet or so of second base, thought touching the bag unnecessary, and instead headed for the clubhouse. As Emslie picked himself up, his partner Hank O'Day—for whom this was, borrowing Yogi Berra's phrase, a case of "*déjà vu* all over again"—ran from his station behind the plate to near the pitcher's mound in order to keep an eye on the impending play at second base.

Obeying Frank Chance's shouted command, center fielder Solly Hofman retrieved the ball and sent it toward Evers. Having heard of the Cubs' protest earlier in the month and recognizing their present intent from the coach's box, McGinnity ran to intercept the slightly errant throw. Chance and some other Cubs surrounded the Iron Man, who then heaved the ball into the stands. Tinker and Harry Steinfeldt wrestled into the crowd after it, and eventually the ball, or some facsimile, got to Evers at second base. Matty afterward told sportswriters that he also realized what was up, caught Merkle by the arm, told him to touch second, and reportedly was willing to swear an affidavit to the fact that he saw Merkle touch the bag. Merkle eventually did swear in an affidavit that he reversed course, made it to second base before the ball did, and stood there until Matty told him to go to the clubhouse. Amid the tumult on the field the umpires conferred. Emslie frankly stated that he did not see whether Merkle touched the base or not, but O'Day concurred with Frank Chance's interpretation of events. Merkle was called out, and therefore the run did not count. Dusk and the fans on the field prevented the game from going on, and by this time it proved a good thing that John Brush had persuaded the police commissioner to augment for the Chicago series the ballpark Pinkertons with regular police. The officers rescued O'Day and Chance from angry fans and then cleared the grounds. Later, emerging from the umpires' dressing room, O'Day told reporters that he considered the game a tie. That evening both umpires received a summons to Harry Pulliam's rooms at the New York Athletic Club.

Cubs' president Charles Murphy railed against McGinnity's interference of Solly Hofman's throw to second base. McGraw said: "There is no set of fair-minded men in the country who would decide the game against us." Fans everywhere debated the rule in question, which stated:

> One run shall be scored every time a base runner, after having legally touched the first three bases, shall legally touch the home base provided, however, that if he reach home on or during a play in which the third man be forced out or be put out before reaching first base a run shall not count. A force-out can be made only when a base runner legally loses the right to the base he occupies and is thereby obliged to advance as the result of a fair hit ball not caught on the fly.[28]

Frank Chance sent his team onto the field at the Polo Grounds at 1:30 the afternoon of the next day in a ploy to continue the preceding game, but the Giants waited instead for the 3:30 start of the scheduled contest; Murphy and Chance thereupon claimed a forfeit to their club of the game played the day before. In the regular game the Cubs rallied to narrow a 5–0 deficit with three quick runs in the seventh. With a runner yet on third base and no outs, McGraw rushed Matty to relieve Wiltse. The Cubs managed another run on a sacrifice fly; thereafter Matty stopped them.

Harry Pulliam endorsed the decision of the umpires by declaring the "Merkle" game a tie and supported this position with a carefully reasoned statement, which he concluded by saying: "My decision in this matter is just as it was in the Pittsburgh decision and as in every other protest that has come before me—to uphold the umpire on questions of fact." Matty's heroics in relief of Wiltse gave the Giants a lead of 13 percentage points over both Chicago and Pittsburgh. The Giants had 15 more games to play, but they dropped a Friday double-header to Cincinnati, that included Rube Marquard's heralded debut in which he was removed after five innings. (Brush reportedly wanted to see some return on his $11,000 investment.) The next day, before another double-header standing-room-only crowd, Matty and Ames recouped the two losses. Tenney contributed both a home run and a triple on legs that obviously pained him. (A decade-and-a-half later McGraw would remark, "Fred Tenney gave his whole heart and soul to the Giants.") In Brooklyn, meanwhile, the Cubs' Ed Reulbach not only pitched both ends of a double-header, he threw two shutouts as well.[29]

The Giants next faced eight meetings with Philadelphia, 13½ games out of the race but still with a respectable .542 winning percentage. The Phillies had on their roster a refugee from the anthracite mines of eastern Pennsylvania, a rookie named Harry Coveleski. The Giants won five of the first seven games with the Phillies, including a pair of victories by

Matty. The two games they lost were each credited to the pitching of Coveleski. Ordinarily five of seven is very good, but concurrently the Cubs and Pirates lost just one game out of a combined 12 played. Consequently, as the Giants prepared to meet the Phillies for the eighth and final time, a loss meant they could tumble into third place, a game-and-a-half behind the leaders. Matty had already won more than one-third of the Giants' 95 victories to date. McGraw now asked Matty, on October 3, to pitch his third game in five days and put an end to the talk of Coveleski as a "Giant Killer." Six thousand persons attended the game in Philadelphia; in Manhattan that many or more waited for news of its outcome at various newspaper bulletin boards. "Ain't it awful, Mabel?" said a voice in the crowd outside *The New York Times* when McGraw, with a two-run deficit to overcome, pulled the gallant but weakening Matty for a pinch hitter in the eighth inning. In the top of the ninth, hopes nevertheless soared as the Giants scored one run and had Moose McCormick on third base with nobody out. Donlin, however, was the first out on a weak fly; then a "nubber" by Seymour led to McCormick being run down between third and home. Coveleski ended it when he struck out Devlin, who allegedly kicked a smart-mouthed youngster on the way to the visitors' dressing room. Another youngster, a red-haired newsboy in New York, said, "I knew it was all up when Matty was taken out."[30]

The Giants had no alternative but to win their remaining three games, all against Boston. Ames and Wiltse won the first two. One more victory would result in a first-place knot with Chicago, which to the Giants made all the more galling Pulliam's decision regarding the "Merkle" game. McGraw could not ask Matty to go to the well once again so soon. Ames therefore made his second start in three days at the Polo Grounds and defeated the Doves, necessitating a one-game play-off with the Cubs to determine the pennant.

The Giants felt that they were being robbed, and the more adamant among them believed that engaging in the play-off would only legitimize the injustice done to them. To resolve an internal dispute whether to participate in the play-off or not, a delegation of team members, with Matty as the elected leader, went to John Brush's sickbed for arbitration. The invalid Brush resided at the Lambs' Club. Besides Matty, the group consisted of Devlin, Bresnahan, Donlin, and Tenney. Off the field, Tenney used a cane to assist his legs, but Tenney's injuries, and even the complaints of the entire team, seemed, as Matty related it, inconsequential before this thin, seriously ill man. Brush refused to advise them what to do. Not wanting to disappoint their fans or leave themselves open to the charge of "quitting," they decided to go on.[31]

Hours before the three o'clock game time, thousands jostled to squeeze into the Polo Grounds. Mounted policemen endeavored to maintain crowd control, as scores of men and boys scaled a 15-foot fence into the ballpark. Spectators congested the grandstand aisles, and women wearing "Merry Widow" hats—a lavish fashion statement derived from a Broadway hit and a constant ballpark complaint from those who had to try to see over them—were asked, and sometimes warned unchivalrously, to remove them. The burgeoning mass in the grandstand and bleachers flowed onto the edges of the field; some found their way precariously to the steep-pitched grandstand roof. Outside, Coogan's Bluff became heavily populated. A policeman came into the clubhouse and exclaimed, "For God's sake, boys, take a lead at the jump. If you don't, there'll be a riot!"[32] Someone else took a more sinister approach at influencing the odds. Amid the tumult, the Giants' physician, Dr. Creamer, perhaps in behalf of some New York gamblers but also perhaps in behalf of John McGraw himself, approached umpires Johnstone and Klem with an offer of a large sum of money to fix the game in New York's favor. The umpires essentially told the doctor to get lost.

Larry Doyle was the first Giant to emerge from the clubhouse; he was hailed loudly. The reception accorded Merkle was palpably cooler. The Giants took their allotted 20 minutes of batting practice. The Cubs, who wisely had made no provocative team demonstration in coming to the ballpark but rather arrived on the elevated train in street clothes singly or by twos, had their own practice cut short when McGinnity strode to the plate, bat in hand, to commence the Giants' fielding practice as the host management made the decision to start the game some 15 minutes early. McGinnity and Chance got into a heated argument in which McGinnity's bat figured prominently. Chance let it be known that, after traveling all this way for one all-or-nothing game, his team deserved a better opportunity to limber up. McGinnity felt otherwise. Players from both clubs intervened to prevent any real violence from occurring, and not long afterward cheers resounded as Matty took the mound.

Bill Klem flamboyantly outstretched his arm and index finger—in a style, it was said, evocative of demanding a beer from a vendor in the stands—as he called Matty's first pitch a strike. The crowd roared as Matty struck out two of the first three Cubs he faced; the other, Evers, grounded to Herzog at second base. Amid an ear-splitting din the teams exchanged positions on the field. Jack Pfiester hit lead-off hitter Tenney in the arm and then walked Herzog. Bresnahan struck out, but, in what seemed to Matty a deliberate tactic, catcher Johnny Kling dropped the third strike conveniently near home plate. Herzog darted uncertainly from first base, encouraged by an anxious voice shouting "Go on!" Actually it was the voice of Johnny Evers, playing deep and behind the runner. Kling's throw to Frank Chance nailed Herzog before he got back to the bag.[33] Donlin's double down the right-field line scored Tenney. After Cy Seymour walked, manager Chance took a slow amble from first base to the mound for a long conversation with his pitcher; when it was over, Three Finger Brown came into the game to face the next batter, Art Devlin, and struck him out.

Chance opened the second inning with a single, but Matty picked him off base. Chance argued long and vehemently with umpire Johnstone before returning to the bench. From the on-deck circle, Solly Hofman threw his bat in disgust. Klem, less tolerant of disrespect then Johnstone, ejected Hofman from the game. Matty then struck out Harry Steinfeldt and Hofman's replacement, Del Howard. Matty did not understand why the Cubs were having such difficulty getting to him. His overworked arm could not develop much speed and his curve would not break.

Joe Tinker led off the Chicago third. It was remarked that, as Tinker stood in the box, Matty surveyed behind him and motioned his outfielders to play further back; if so, Cy Seymour, in center field, refused to take direction and Tinker smashed the ball over his head for a triple. (Matty later denied giving direction to Seymour, saying Cy knew how to play the Chicago batters as well as he did; he blamed instead Tinker's bat, which connected with a curve that failed to break.) Kling then singled Tinker home, and Brown sacrificed to send Kling to scoring position. Sheckard flied to center, Kling not daring to advance from second. Matty did not want to give Evers anything decent to hit, but his pitches did not cross near enough the corners of the plate and he consequently walked him. Schulte doubled down the third-base line to score Kling, Evers pulling up at third. Chance, a right-handed batter, took an "inside out" stroke at the ball and sent it just over Fred Tenney's outstretched glove. The ball rolled into the crowd for a ground-rule double. Even if the crowd had not pressed along the foul line, that splendid piece of hitting would have scored the two runs. Chicago led 4–1. Steinfeldt ended the scoring by striking out.

"Rog, I haven't got anything today," Matty said to his catcher.

"Keep at it, Matty. We'll get them all right," Bresnahan replied.[34]

Matty pitched bravely four scoreless innings more. Brown mowed down the New York batters with his pinpoint control and devilish curve until finally, in the seventh, the Giants cracked the pattern of "three up, three down" to load the bases with none out. Matty hit well for a pitcher, and he hit better when the game was on the line, but McGraw felt it was a necessary recourse, at this juncture of this particular game, to lift him for a pinch hitter. The manager sent Larry Doyle to the plate instead. Doyle had not faced a big-league delivery since he had been spiked a month previously. Matty afterward stated his belief that it was Doyle's

Roger Bresnahan, pictured here around 1908, caught 139 games that year, and with him behind the plate that season Matty posted 37 victories. (National Baseball Hall of Fame Library, Cooperstown, N.Y.)

injury which more than anything else had diminished the Giants' ability to win the pennant. "[I]t broke up the infield of the team at a most important moment," he said. "It takes some time for a new part to work into the clock so that it keeps perfect time again, no matter how delicate is the workmanship of the new part."[35] Doyle popped a high foul ball caught by Kling. Tenney sacrificed a run home, the last run scored by the Giants in 1908. Wiltse, who had a 23 and 14 record on the season, finished the game. The Giants were spent. In the final inning Brown disposed of Devlin, McCormick, and Bridwell with but four pitches.

Bridwell, after Bresnahan perhaps the most "take charge" player in the lineup, was the only Giant to offer congratulations to the Cubs. From one wrathful "krank" in the crowd, Frank Chance received a hard blow to the face, damaging a cartilage in his neck. The Cubs thus knew to leave the Polo Grounds as discreetly as they had come. Matty, 391 innings and 37 victories since opening day, sat disconsolately and alone for a long time in the clubhouse. Toward dusk he left the ballpark for home and Jane. A few fans yet remained by the players' usual exit and gave him a cheer. He tried to speak but could not. He waved and walked away with his head bowed. When he got home he just lay down, too tired to eat.[36]

That night, somewhere on 77th Street between First and Second avenues, a nine-year-old devoted fan, a skinny kid with glasses, cried himself to sleep. That fan, George Toporcer, would one day find himself known as "Specs" and play the infield for the St. Louis Cardinals.[37]

6

CHAMPIONS AGAIN

John Brush reportedly gained a profit on the '08 season of $325,000. About 3 percent of that amount, $10,000, he gave to the players to distribute among themselves. (He rewarded McGraw with a new automobile costing $5,000.) Fred Merkle lost his appetite, could not sleep, and his already gaunt frame took an emaciated appearance. McGraw made it a point to praise the young man, not yet 20 years old. "I could use a carload like you," he said. "Forget this season and come around next spring." McGraw realized the pennant race had not turned solely upon Merkle's base-running mistake. He could with as much or more reason point to Donlin's ill-considered bravado in challenging Hans Lobert to take an extra base, or umpire O'Day's blown call when Herzog had actually thrown out a Pirate baserunner by a good margin, or if the Giants could have beaten Harry Coveleski just once. When Merkle, at his home in Toledo, received his contract for the '09 season, he saw that McGraw had written a $300 raise.[1]

Umpires Klem and Johnstone's accusation of attempted bribery at the Giants-Cubs play-off game became public and would not go away without some kind of resolution. Harry Pulliam, additionally burdened with other matters such as Hal Chase's involvement in an "outlaw" winter-ball league on the Pacific coast, appointed a special committee to investigate the umpires' charges; incredibly, John Brush served as chairman. Brush said that he did not know Dr. Creamer, hired by McGraw, was his employee until he was sent a bill for the doctor's services at the end of the season. Attentive readers of New York newspapers, however, would have recognized from occasional sports articles throughout the season the doctor's name as the Giants' physician. If Brush's statement concerning Creamer's employment is accepted, it is indicative of the incapacitating nature of Brush's illness, and of the extent to which he entrusted McGraw with day-to-day franchise decisions. For whom Dr. Creamer acted as agent when he offered the envelope to the umpires remained veiled, and the National Commission eventually did no more than bar him for life from all major-league parks. Pulliam was not present for the decision, having suffered in February a nervous collapse. The National League owners kept Pulliam on full salary while he recovered, and assigned his secretary, John Heydler, to act as interim president. Creamer returned to his practice (primarily among the city's poor), is not known to have accused anyone of anything crooked, resented big-league baseball for damaging his reputation, and died at the age of 48 in 1918.[2]

Merkle had a ballplaying future. Joe McGinnity and Luther Taylor, in McGraw's estimation, did not—at least not in the big leagues. McGinnity became associated with the Newark club in the Eastern League; Taylor signed with Buffalo. McGraw also believed there was no longer room in the clubhouse for both his temperament and Roger Bresnahan's. He dealt Bresnahan to St. Louis, where Roger would manage his own club; in return McGraw obtained outfielder John "Red" Murray, pitcher Arthur "Bugs" Raymond, and catcher George "Admiral" Schlei.

Back in Factoryville, Matty's younger brother Nicholas, 19 years old, came home despondent from Lafayette College. He had gone to college to be like his famous brother; he went to Lafayette not to be too much like him. Athleticism ran strong in the family and comparisons were inevitable. Many said, whether they actually meant it or not, that Nick showed more pitching promise than Matty at the same age. Hughie Jennings, Detroit's manager and McGraw's close friend, visited his hometown of Scranton from time to time and, once while in the area, offered Nicholas a contract with the Tigers. Gilbert Mathewson, perhaps recognizing what happened to his middle-son Henry's big-league dreams, discouraged Nick from signing at so young an age. At college Nick's behavior became unsteady during his first months away from home. Physically he suffered a case of jaundice; emotionally he succumbed to melancholy. He returned to his parents' home and appeared, slowly, to recover. One January afternoon Nick had what seemed a cheerful conversation with his mother and then went into the barn, left a note, and shot himself in the right side of the forehead with a small caliber revolver. Later in the day Minerva sent Henry, visiting his Baptist home with an Irish Catholic wife and small child, to look for him. Henry found his brother lying, still alive, in the haymow. Nick was carried into the house and a doctor summoned. The doctor could do little more than cleanse the wound and advise that the youth be taken to a hospital in Scranton, where he died.[3]

During the winter Matty gave his name to an insurance brokerage located at 20 Vesey Street in lower Manhattan. After Nick's funeral he

6. Champions Again

went to Boston, coaching baseball pitchers and keeping himself in shape at Harvard University. He remained at Harvard, with McGraw's permission, as the other Giants congregated at Marlin. Mike Donlin once again announced that he preferred vaudeville over baseball, especially since the team of Hite and Donlin earned as much as $1,000 per week on the stage. With John Brush unlikely to accede to Donlin's salary demand of $8,000 for the season, McGraw did not expect to see Turkey Mike in a New York uniform in 1909. After all, $8,000, a salary more than half again what a member of the United States Congress received per year, was also the sum Matty was asking.[4]

Wilbert Robinson, like Hughie Jennings one of McGraw's close friends from their playing days together on the Baltimore Orioles, came to Texas to work with the pitchers and catchers. McGraw also hired Arlie Latham, the irrepressible infielder of the old St. Louis Browns during the Browns' glory years. Latham's acrobatic tumbling pre-dated that of Ozzie Smith by a century. His pranks back then earned him the accolade as "the freshest man on earth," but as far as Fred Snodgrass was concerned Latham was "the worst third base coach who ever lived."[5]

Matty arrived in Texas in the latter part of March. The disadvantage of his late arrival, caused by haggling over money, was compounded by a line drive bruising his hand during training, which kept him from appearing in a league game until May 4 in Philadelphia. In that game he gave up nine hits, four walks, and three runs in six innings as the Phillies went on to win and as the Giants sat in last place with a 4 and 8 record. At the Polo Grounds, fans derided both Admiral Schlei and Chief Meyers as their hearts became even fonder of their missing favorite, Bresnahan. They called for Roger whenever Schlei or Meyers made a mistake. They jeered Marquard as "the $11,000 lemon," and they enjoyed laughing at the reputed alcoholic antics of 27-year-old Bugs Raymond who, so went the joke, caused the ball to move so wondrously by merely breathing on it. McGraw regarded Raymond as "one of the greatest natural pitchers that ever lived" and bent over backward trying to keep him in shape. McGraw's handling of Raymond ran the gamut from persuading him to dry out in a hospital to coming to blows with him on a train, and the manager sent so much of the pitcher's salary directly to Raymond's long-suffering wife that Bugs groused, "Let her pitch."[6]

When the Cardinals came to town a special ceremony honored Roger Bresnahan. Joe Humphreys, described by a sportswriter as "the famous inaudible open-air orator," introduced John Ward, who presented a large loving cup inscribed: "To our pal, Roger Bresnahan, from his New York admirers, Polo Grounds, May 24, 1909." "It was a notable event," said the same writer, "just before the playing of a very bad game of ball."[7] That depended on the point of view. The Cardinals finally snapped what had burgeoned into Matty's 24-game consecutive win streak against them. Matty held them to three runs, but his teammates could not convert seven hits and five walks into more than a single tally.

Matty did not carry the team on his right arm as he had the year previously. No mortal could have. He better economized his deliveries. The tighter the game, the better he pitched; the easier the game, the more he saved his arm for later. He applied a similar logic to his life away from the ballpark, appearing less frequently to play checkers in public and even becoming, except for golf, somewhat of a recluse between starts. "He was ... a little hard to get close to," said Snodgrass.[8]

On July 30 the Giants played for the first time in Barney Dreyfuss's beautiful new million-dollar stadium. Forbes Field, with its visible steel framework painted green, cream-colored brick facing, and tar-and-gravel roof tinted red, had a seating capacity of 24,000 and, under the grandstand, a promenade wider than a city street. Seeking to accommodate their patrons in every way, the Pirate organization assigned maids to the female restrooms. The grandstand faced away from the west; a situation which, when the afternoon sun shone upon the field, caused many ballplayers to adopt the practice of wearing "smoked glasses" when playing there. In Matty's first game at Forbes Field, he suffered three runs scoring on four hits in the first inning; Ames relieved him in the second. Following the loss, Matty's record stood at 15 and 3.[9]

Two nights before the Giants' appearance at Forbes Field, in his rooms at the New York Athletic Club, Harry Pulliam, having returned to his duties as league president, took a revolver and shot himself in the right temple. The bullet put out both his eyes. Somehow he lifted the telephone receiver, then dropped it as he fell upon a couch. The phone signal continued at the club desk until finally an employee went to investigate, finding the dying Pulliam clad only in an undershirt and socks. A doctor was summoned and Pulliam laid into his bed; during the short time remaining to him, he gave no understandable answers to questions, and no note was reported found. His remains were transported to his native Kentucky, near Louisville, for burial. A shock of genuine grief penetrated organized baseball. Many major-league luminaries attended the funeral; among the honorary pallbearers were Ban Johnson, John Heydler, Charles Ebbets, Charles Murphy and James Hart. Pittsburgh's manager Fred Clarke and Philadelphia's manager Billy Murray also attended. From the Giant organization Brush and McGraw were notably absent; only club secretary Fred Knowles was sent to appear.[10]

On his birthday, August 12, Matty won his 18th against three losses. This fifth of eight shutouts on the season occurred in Chicago, as he scattered four hits and walked none. (In a collective pattern of acerbic sportswriting wit that continued to target Fred Merkle, one writer felt constrained to point out that Merkle had touched second base twice in the contest.) The Giants left Chicago five games behind the Cubs. They were also ten games behind Pittsburgh, where they came next to play. During a game in which Matty dueled the veteran Vic Willis, dark clouds threatened ominously in the bottom of the eighth inning as the Pirates tied the score at two runs apiece. With two outs and Tommy Leach dancing from second, Matty walked Honus Wagner to set up the force play. John "Dots" Miller worked a count of two-balls-two-strikes. Miller then sent a liner into right center and it seemed a sure hit. At the same moment the storm broke: lightning flashed and thunder cracked the air. Matty, sensing defeat, hunched on the mound and Chief Meyers threw his mask in dismay. The ball flew nearer to Seymour in center than Murray in right. The lightning disoriented Seymour, who lost the ball, but Murray, hit hat blowing off, ran headlong toward the end of the ball's trajectory, diving and making the catch with his bare hand. Matty thus narrowly avoided a loss as umpire Klem ended the game.[11]

The Pirates won the pennant with margin to spare. In a World Series in which sharpened spikes, or at least the threat of them, figured prominently, Hughie Jennings's Tigers, three-time American League pennant winners, failed in their third consecutive world championship try.

The Giants engaged in an uninspired post-season series with the major leagues' other third-place finisher, the Boston Red Sox. Matty won the opener; thereafter his team dropped the next four games. Less than a thousand persons came to the Polo Grounds to witness the finale. On the season, however, John Brush realized another large profit. Matty, who attracted more people through the gate than anyone else, considered a salary of $10,000 appropriate to himself for 1910. Such a salary, five times as much as a doctor on average earned in a year and seven times as much as an average lawyer, would solidify his and Jane's social standing. He had now played in the National League nine full seasons, and it was reported that he and Jane, shrewd stock market investors, had assets of as much as $50,000. Matty let it be known that, at age 29, he was willing to retire from baseball, if offered an insufficient salary, to pursue instead his insurance and other business interests. He considered a partnership with Ernest Sterling that would have involved importing lumber from Nova Scotia. This venture never materialized. One that did was a collaboration with sportswriter W.W. Aulick, in which Matty lent his name to the first of a successful series of boys' baseball books. With titles including *Won in the Ninth, Pitcher Pollock,* and *First Base Faulkner,* the popularity of the series enabled it to continue until 1916.[12]

Presented with numerous other ways to make money, Matty became adept at rationalizing and accepting them. A safety razor manufacturer offered Bozeman Bulger $100 if he could persuade Matty for $200 to lend his name and face in an advertising campaign. "Is it a really good razor?" Matty asked Bulger. "What difference does it make?" the newsman replied. Before agreeing to the arrangement, Matty got one of the razors and tried it out. "Seems to work all right," he decided. Riders of New York City's public transportation could see Matty's face and name advertising cigarettes. It was a habit in which he personally indulged, but not without some pricklings of conscience concerning how his commercial endorsement might influence others. "Cigarette smoking is likely to be bad for youngsters because they may smoke to excess," he remarked, though not as part of the advertising campaign. "They probably have noticed that I smoke cigarettes. It gives me a lot of comfort. So far as I know smoking never did me harm.... If I found it did affect me I would stop immediately."[13]

During the winter Matty participated, for pay, in a new variation of baseball, an indoor variety, popular at the time. With other professional players, including Hal Chase, he toured different cities in New York State putting on exhibitions. Several of the touring players occupied their spare time at cards for money. Matty just about always recovered a good part of his incidental traveling expenses during any baseball season through his poker winnings. But Chase was said to have been the big winner on this particular expedition. Gabby Street, who the previous off-season gained a measure of immortality by catching a baseball tossed from the top of the Washington Monument and who was a teammate of Chase a few years later, would eventually tell a story of how he once happened behind Chase during a card game with a large pot on the table. Street glanced at Chase's hand and saw three kings. Moments later, with no more cards dealt, Street looked again and saw that Chase's low card had metamorphosed into the fourth king. Chase was too sharp to apply such tricks at the same table with Matty. Both men were bridge players as well and may have found that game more conducive to a congenial relationship. Chase, it was said, could charm women with his own purpose in mind. Jane, Matty's astute bridge partner, was not a woman easily taken in; one can imagine, across a card table, her critical eyes appraising the square jaw, red hair, cobalt eyes, and white teeth of laughing Prince Hal, the man over whom New York fans fawned as much as they did over her own husband and who, unlike her husband, shamelessly worked that affection for all it was worth.[14]

McGraw made changes for 1910. Fred Tenney received his release. Fred Snodgrass and Josh Devore displaced Cy Seymour largely and Moose McCormick entirely in the outfield. Chief Meyers got the lion's share of the catching duties, and, in yet another attempt to preserve Bugs Raymond, McGraw kept as a third catcher Art Wilson. Wilson could not wield a bat like Meyers, but he could handle a spitball and stayed long

Chief Meyers, the Giants' first-string catcher from 1909 through 1915, this photograph is circa 1912. (National Baseball Hall of Fame Library, Cooperstown, N.Y.)

after Bugs was let go. Rube Marquard held on for another year's apprenticeship, as did reserves Art Fletcher and Art Shafer. With so many "Arts" in the clubhouse, Shafer received the sobriquet "Tillie" whether the shy young man wanted it or not. Louis Drucke, from Waco, Texas, won 12 games and struck out 151 batters; unfortunately Drucke's arm had in it just one good big-league season.

Matty tossed a six-hitter in Boston in his first effort of the year, fanning eight and making five assists. On May 2 he faced 29 Brooklyn batters in nine innings en route to a one-hit shutout; in the bottom of the eighth Devlin had cut in front of Fletcher at shortstop to field a grounder that he threw wide and low to miss the out at first base; the official scorer ruled the play a base hit.

Matty did not grumble or sulk when someone made an error. He did not have to. "We'd break our necks for that guy," said Chief Meyers.[15] In late June, Larry Doyle smacked a three-run inside-the-park homer at the Polo Grounds to give Matty a three-run win against the Phillies and to pull the Giants within three games of the first-place Cubs. Doyle arrived at the plate the same time as the ball, made a feet-first slide into the catcher, and, banging his head, had to be helped to the bench. With support like this, Matty had now won more than a third of the team's 33 victories thus far.

By early August, however, Chicago led New York by ten games and was headed to its fourth pennant in five years, though the Giants' second-place finish did not go unrewarded as the organization made peace with their box office rivals and scheduled a post-season series with the Yankees, by which name the Highlanders were now more commonly called. The seven-game series went over well with fans, with more than 100,000 attending. Each Giant received more than $1,000 for the winning effort, in which Matty won three games and finished another. Hal Chase was the Yankee manager, having persuaded team owner Frank Farrell to replace George Stallings with himself late in the season despite the fact that the Yankees were well on the way to a respectable second-place finish behind Connie Mack's Athletics. "God, what a way to run a ball club!" remembered Jimmy Austin, a member of the Yankee team.[16] Under Chase the Yankees plummeted to sixth place in 1911.

Bozeman Bulger wrote a vaudeville skit entitled "Curves" for Matty, Chief Meyers, and actress May Tully. Immediately after the crosstown series they opened as headliners at Hammerstein's Victoria Theatre, located at Broadway and Seventh Avenue. Meyers, recalled Blanche McGraw, had a fine baritone voice and a keen sense of humor, and he performed so well in the show that some of the entertainers kiddingly wondered if he was not really Jewish. Matty, it was said, took to the stage to help overcome his reserve in meeting new people; the $1,000 a week he was reported to have received, for four months in front of the footlights in New York and on the road, had something to do with it as well. The 34-minute skit was full of jokes using baseball expressions, and Miss Tully performed the role of admiring spectator. An exhibition of fancy pitching figured in, and at one point Miss Tully hilariously imitated Ethel Barrymore dramatically breathing "that's all there is; there isn't anymore" after a supposedly daunting batter struck out. The act was a hit, and Matty made fun of his show-business naïveté with comedian Henry Clive. "I can't understand it," he told Clive. "The audience tonight and the audience last night laughed at the same joke." Matty obligingly signed baseballs in every city in which he appeared and often charged against his salary many admission tickets for the starry-eyed boys who flocked outside the theatres just for a glimpse of him.[17]

McGraw told a story about Wilbert Robinson: Always a heavy man, Robinson took on considerably more girth after his playing days were over. One day, in his Giants' coaching uniform, "Uncle Robbie" bent over to pick something up. A fan near the front row shouted: "Say, McGraw, what time does the balloon go up?" McGraw, the spectators and players nearby, everybody but Robbie, laughed.[18]

In spring training, 1911, Robinson gave Rube Marquard special attention. Rube had great stuff. He just did not know what to do with it. Robbie, the former catcher, tutored him how to mix pitches and stay ahead in the count. He made Rube study the strengths and weaknesses of opposing batters. "Now, Rube, you've got to start on the first ball to get the batter," Robbie preached. "Always have something on him and never let him have anything on you. This is the prescription for a great pitcher."[19]

McGraw had gained a rotundity of his own and, in his late thirties, gray hair as well. Matty remained one of the few veteran players who could call him "Mac" to his face. To the others he was "Mr. McGraw." (Behind his back, though, he was often "Muggsy" or the "Little Round Man.") Even after 50 years, in the reminiscences recorded by Lawrence Ritter, he remained "Mr. McGraw" to Marquard, Bridwell, and Snodgrass. (And these were men who had been summarily traded or released by him.) In one thought Bridwell remembered missing a sign and getting called a lot of names by McGraw—McGraw's dugout was famous, or infamous, for the "noise" which came out of it—and the shortstop became so incensed that he threw a punch at the manager and received, in turn, a two-week suspension without pay. In the next thought Bridwell described McGraw as "the kindest, best-hearted fellow you ever saw" and the greatest manager "because he knew how to handle men." He knew how to needle anyway. Once, after Josh Devore stroked a crowd-pleasing triple, McGraw added to his own congratulation: "When I saw you shut your eyes, I never thought you would hit it."[20]

McGraw ran the team with tight reins on and off the field; even Matty was not exempt from the 11 P.M. bed checks. The manager drilled his players in base stealing. Matty remarked that McGraw concentrated on this more than any other aspect of the game. The manager signaled to his batters when to take a pitch, when to sacrifice, and when to swing.

He directed his fielders where to position themselves. He indicated, except for Matty, what pitches he wanted thrown. "You do what I tell you, and I'll take responsibility if we lose," the manager said again and again.[21]

For his own part at Marlin, Matty followed his spring-training regimen of no breaking balls for at least ten days. For one thing, he wanted his arm limber before he attempted throwing breaking pitches; for another, a curveball was of little use to him if he could not make his fastball go where he wanted it. Each year, as he went through the painful process of getting back into big-league shape, he told himself that this spring training would be his last. When a prospect asked Matty for some pitching advice, he would give it. But he made no point of treating newcomers differently than did other veterans. If a prospect sought to prolong the conversation for its own sake, Matty would cut him off curtly. "Listen," he said to one of them, "did you come down here to learn to play ball or with the idea you are attending some sort of conversational soirée?"[22]

Red, white, and blue bunting festooned the great wooden horseshoe of a grandstand for opening day at the Polo Grounds, the air of patriotism enhanced by the day also marking the 50th anniversary of the battle of Fort Sumter. Fred Lieb, a new baseball writer for one of the city's dailies, felt an electric pulse in the cold air for himself and the more than 30,000 others the ballpark could now accommodate with seats in order to make it a full house. Groundskeeper Murphy, according to his own patriotic sense, place small Irish flags at the positions of players with Irish heritage: Doyle at second base and Murray in right. The band played "East Side, West Side, All Around the Town" before striking up "The Star-Spangled Banner." The Phillies, however, beat Red Ames by scoring two runs in the ninth, and the next day they tripped Matty 6–1. The weather stayed so cold that the writer for *The New York Times* wondered why the place should not be called instead "the Polar Grounds."[23]

That night, after midnight, the wooden grandstand went up in flames. The blaze, according to the fire department, started from something like a discarded cigarette smoldering in a pile of debris. A red-orange hue colored the night sky as the ballpark burned uncontrollably for hours. Three firemen were injured and, perhaps more to the point as far as the players were concerned, over a hundred bats were lost. In the morning dense smoke hovered over what remained of the place; later rain put out the last vestiges of fire.

Frank Farrell, to the surprise of many, offered the use of Hilltop Park to the Giants. The receipts from last year's post-season series with the Yankees had done much to mend fences. Hilltop Park did not seat nearly as many as the Polo Grounds, but with nowhere else to go John Brush accepted with gratitude. Brush also, with little time wasted, solidified his land lease at the Polo Grounds site and set in motion plans to build a new stadium to rival Barney Dreyfuss's Forbes Field. When the plans were unveiled in May at a swank restaurant near Grant's Tomb, Bat Masterson, former buffalo hunter, Indian fighter, deputy marshal of Dodge City, and now sports editor of the New York *Morning Telegraph*, whispered archly: "A veritable Eighth Wonder of the World!"[24]

On a Saturday in May, at Hilltop Park, the Giants scored 13 runs in the first inning against the Cardinals. McGraw decided to give Matty the rest of the day off and sent Marquard as a replacement. Rube responded with fastballs that seemed to explode as they struck the catcher's mitt with mostly pinpoint accuracy; he struck out 14 batters over the next eight innings. He gave up a few runs in the process, but finally confidence was instilled into Rube's makeup. And then some. Rube became well-nigh unbeatable.

In St. Louis, in June, Bugs Raymond had his last go-round with McGraw. Raymond, who had professed reform upon his arrival for spring training, had fallen from the wagon with a thud soon after the team left Marlin. McGraw levied another series of fines, and Raymond lamented that his life was "just one fine after another." On the train to St. Louis, McGraw gave what may well have seemed to Raymond his umpteenth final warning. When McGraw sent him to relieve in a bases-loaded situation, Raymond allowed the three Cardinal runners to score, and one more. When Raymond showed up late once again, McGraw, in spite of the pitcher's 6 and 3 record, told him to see the club secretary for ticket money back to New York. "You're through with the Giants," the manager said. When the team returned home, they saw a sign outside a saloon near the Polo Grounds which announced, "Bugs Raymond Tending Bar Here."[25]

Less than three months after the fire, the Polo Grounds reopened for business. The owner intended the new edifice to be called "Brush Stadium," but to everyone else the place remained the Polo Grounds. Construction continued on the upper tier of the concrete and steel grandstand, but already enough seats were available in the lower level to compare in number with Hilltop Park. (The clubhouse and most of the bleacher section had gone undamaged by the fire.) As was his custom, the handicapped Brush viewed the game from the vantage of his luxury automobile parked in the grass, once again velvety and emerald-green, of deep right-center field. Only 6,000 persons came to the occasion, and they seemed more inclined to celebrate yet another return of Mike Donlin to the club than the rebuilt stadium. After an absence from the game of two years, Turkey Mike was signed by McGraw because of Donlin's fan appeal and dramatic flair as a batsman. (There may well have been an element of personal favor in it as well. It got Donlin both some salary and limelight. Turkey Mike's vaudeville career was in decline. Mabel Hite, with her songs and comedy, was still a headline performer, though tragically she was little more than a year away from dying of intestinal cancer. Donlin appeared in 12 games for the Giants in 1911; when the novelty quickly wore off, he was sold to Boston, appearing in another 56 games for them. He batted .316 on the year.) Though upstaged by Donlin, showered with so many wreaths that it seemed to one newspaper observer "as if all the florists in six counties had been raided ... to cull enough posies for Mike," Brush had the satisfaction of seeing Matty shut out Boston 3–0.[26]

As the pennant race tightened, McGraw found fault when Matty played too much golf on an off-day in Pittsburgh with sportswriter Grantland Rice. Larry Doyle remembered the manager summoning the entire team for a meeting. "I want to know right now," McGraw ranted, "which is it going to be, baseball or golf? ... How about you, Mathewson? Which is it going to be?"[27] Doyle also remembered that Matty, who carried his clubs with him on the road in the bottom of his traveling trunk and who could score consistently in the middle 70s over 18 holes, quietly paid his $100 fine, and went on playing golf.

McGraw cracked down as well when too much money changed hands during card games. Cheating at cards would have been unpardonable, but McGraw rather liked larceny as a baseball strategy. His speedsters led the league in stolen bases. (Their 347 total remains a major-league standard.) So much so, it was remarked that they stole the pennant by the seat of their pants—literally. The flannel trousers of Devore, Snodgrass, Merkle, and Murray became so tattered and held together by needle-and-thread mending and even safety pins that McGraw had to wire from Chicago for new uniforms. The Giants may have been the best paid team in baseball, but that did not keep them from grumbling about having to buy their own outfits.[28]

Even Chief Meyers stole 30 bases as he hit .332 and caught in 128 games. At 5 feet, 11 inches and 194 pounds, he swung a huge 48-ounce bat. (Thirty-six ounces is considered hefty for a bat nowadays; Babe Ruth swung a 42-ouncer.) He also let the Giant organization think he was a few years younger than he was in actuality. Born in the same year as Matty, Meyers had not cracked the regular lineup until he was 30. "But when the years started to creep up on me," he later said, "I knew how old I was, even if nobody else did."[29]

Al Bridwell's bat and gritty fielding did not compensate for his slowing legs, especially with Art Fletcher waiting in the wings. Consequently McGraw negotiated another trade with Boston. Bridwell and a youngster named Hank Gowdy went to the team now known as the Pilgrims

6. Champions Again

Matty and John McGraw, around 1920. (National Baseball Hall of Fame Library, Cooperstown, N.Y.)

for Buck Herzog. McGraw did not especially want Herzog's mouth back, but did want his speed and ability at third base. Art Devlin thus entered into a utility role, as Bridwell packed his bags and went to the National League tailenders uncomplainingly. By the third Saturday in July, the Giants stood just two games from first place when Matty notched his 16th victory with a 10–2 gem against the visiting Cardinals. New York fans once again experienced pennant fever. To watch Matty's win, as many as 28,000 had gathered in the Polo Grounds, still rising like a phoenix. One intrepid soul found a perch atop a steel girder.

The Giants split four games in Cincinnati, and Matty lost an opener in St. Louis as he surrendered 11 hits and his teammates committed five errors. McGraw always looked for ways to break negative tension on his clubs. The most commonly told story began with Frank Bowerman superstitiously announcing that he attributed an end of a batting slump to a wagonload of barrels he had seen on the way to the ballpark and wishing similar good fortune to his teammates. Not content to wait for good luck, McGraw went out and hired a teamster for the next day to haul empty barrels in the vicinity where his arriving ballplayers would likely see them. Supposedly the whole team began to hit better. Another time McGraw invited five slumping hitters to his hotel room for dinner and a champagne drunk. The next day, so went this story, the hitters began seeing the ball more clearly. When things got particularly stale, McGraw could call his friend Wilbert Robinson. Robinson, according to how his spirit moved him, divided his time between the Giants and his business interests in Baltimore. During the latter part of the 1911 race, McGraw telephoned and "Uncle Robbie" showed up the next day. "Who's dead around here?" asked the gruff man whom everyone liked, after he had spent a few minutes in the clubhouse.[30] Robbie bought a few rounds of drinks that night, and the team began to relax again.

Charles Victor Faust, a simple-minded man from rural Kansas, attached himself to the club in St. Louis; in his own mind he came as a pitcher, but in the minds of McGraw and the other Giants he arrived as a curiosity and remained with them as a dimwitted bringer of good fortune, for with Charley on the bench the Giants came to feel they improved their chances of winning. Even Matty, who humorously admitted to harboring superstitions himself, referred to Faust as a "really true, on-the-level, honest-to-jiminy" antidote to all kinds of baseball bad luck. The organization provided Faust with a uniform, meals, accommodations, and enough money for barbershop visits and to tip waiters. (Charley, Matty remembered, liked pie with breakfast, lunch, and supper.) Fans at the Polo Grounds, as the Giants continued a long winning streak, relished seeing Charley Faust. They relished it even more when McGraw sent Faust to warm up behind the outfield. At 6 feet 2 inches, and with sunburnt, rugged features, Charley looked like a major leaguer, and his impressive windmill windup imparted probably enough velocity on his pitches, remembered Fred Snodgrass, "to break a pane of glass." His middle name became "Victory."[31]

The Giants announced that they were drawing better than 20,000 persons per game during their August home stand. The organization, nonetheless, still expected fans to return foul balls to the playing field, though coach Arlie Latham called out thanks when someone on his side of the field threw one back.[32] Led by the pitching of Matty and Marquard, by mid–September, as the team prepared for a western swing, the Giants had edged into first place, but they could not shake Frank Chance's Cubs.

In the West, prior to arriving in Chicago, the Giants won nine of 11 games. Charley Faust entertained crowds in every ballpark. In pre-game practice at Forbes Field, in a mock-heralded matchup, Faust took the mound to pitch to Honus Wagner. Wagner dramatically swung and missed at three straight pitches. An even better ovation, though, went to the Giants' regular "mascot," batboy Dick Hennessey, who at first base fielded with aplomb all throws sent to him during the infielders' warm-up.

Marquard boasted about going onto the stage. Red Ames wore constantly, including under his uniform, a good luck necktie given to him by an actress. Matty said the neckwear made Joseph's coat of many colors look like a mourning garment. "I don't change her until I lose," Red announced, and he did not.[33] McGraw used Matty to advantage, both as a starter and as a reliever in tight situations, with the result that the Giants, a day early, arrived in Chicago with a seemingly comfortable first-place lead.

The Giants attended as spectators a Cubs' game against Boston and witnessed a Chicago victory. The Cubs then rattled Marquard 8–0. A wag in the press suggested that Rube could now appear in a popular play called *A Broken Idol*. Matty started the next game against Leonard "Old King" Cole. The erratic Cole could sometimes pitch as badly as anyone in the league, but not this day. Supported by Joe Tinker's two-run double in the third, he held on to beat Matty 2–1. The Cubs and their fans began to believe again, and an off-day gave the Giants time to think about things.

In the next contest, when Jimmy Sheckard rammed a grounder toward third, Buck Herzog speared it with a head-first dive, and, tumbling to his feet, he hurled the ball high and wide over Merkle's head. Merkle, playing on an injured ankle, leaped, caught the ball, and as he landed stretched so that his toe touched the first-base bag. Sheckard was out. With this kind of support, and spotted a two-run lead by a Larry Doyle homer, Red Ames cut short the Cubs' resurgence in a 3–1 victory. (But the margin seemed narrow enough that at different times during the contest McGraw had Matty, Crandall, Wiltse, and Marquard, besides Charley Faust, warmed up and ready.) The next day Marquard shut out the Cubs, 5–0.

The Giants clinched the pennant on October 4, in Brooklyn, with Matty's fifth shutout of the year. McGraw rested Matty during the final week of the season. But at long last, trailing 4–2 in the top of the ninth against Boston and with a thousand fans shivering in the cold at the Polo Grounds, McGraw sent Charley Faust, who had been warming up through all the previous eight innings, into a game. The cooperative visitors worked him for just one hit, a couple sacrifices, and one run. Faust stood in the on-deck circle as the game's final out was recorded, but the Pilgrims remained on the field for him to come to bat, letting him reach first and then wildly circle the bases before tagging him at the plate.

Having outgrown the "postage stamp" of Columbia Park, the Athletics had a new baseball edifice of their own. Shibe Park, named for one of the club's chief investors, was also built of concrete and steel; it was a two-tiered structure with a palatial brick facade. With the Polo Grounds now complete, it would be the first World Series so imposingly hosted in both cities. Accordingly the National Commission ruled that the field had to be kept clear during play—no more ground-rule doubles bounding into a surrounding crowd. Josh Devore dubbed it "the World Serious."[34]

Connie Mack's pitching staff yet included Eddie Plank and Chief Bender. Unlike Rube Waddell, now departed from the big leagues (and within three years, because of tuberculosis, to depart from this life), Mack's leading ace, Jack Coombs, had a sound mind as well as 59 victories in the last two regular seasons to his credit. The Athletics' everyday lineup featured the "$100,000 Infield" of Stuffy McInnis, Eddie Collins, Jack Barry, and Frank Baker. The monetary value referred not to what the tightfisted Mack paid them but to what they were worth.

Both Matty and Rube Marquard signed newspaper deals for ghostwritten articles about the series. McGraw once again outfitted his team in new black uniforms; besides the psychological reminder of the last World Series meeting between these two clubs, he may well have been too embarrassed to send his base stealers out in the tatters that remained of their regular-season garb. George M. Cohan wrote as a lyric "life's a funny proposition, after all," but McGraw reportedly did not see the humor of his celebrity friend placing a bet on the Athletics to win.[35]

In invigorating "hard cider" weather the series opened in New York. The crowd roared at Matty's first pitch, a called strike. The Athletics had a reputation for discerning signs, and in the second inning veteran Harry Davis, substituting for McInnis who missed the series with an injured wrist, correctly anticipated a curveball and sent it to left field scoring a run. Thereafter Chief Meyers kept issuing signs, secluding them from prying eyes as much as possible, but from this point Meyers's signals were bogus. The real signs were coded movements of Matty. (Meyers remembered telling Matty: "Pitch whatever you want to pitch. I'll catch you without signals.")[36] When another Athletic anticipated a curve, he narrowly avoided being hit by a fastball. By game's end, in a 2–1 victory, Matty had dispatched the Athletics with just 94 pitches.

The next day, a Sunday, the Giants attended a testimonial in their honor at a downtown theater. Matty, however, declined the invitation. If the others wanted to dress up in tuxedos and be entertained and applauded with three more games yet to win, that apparently was their business.

Marquard and Eddie Plank had the second game knotted at one run apiece after five innings. In the bottom of the sixth, Eddie Collins punched a double down the left-field line. Frank Baker, who had led the American League in home runs with nine, took a strike and refused to bite on an outside curve. Meyers signaled for another curve—the conventional wisdom is to pitch to a power hitter low and away—but Rube shook him off. McGraw had cautioned his pitchers that Baker was quick enough with the bat to like high fast ones. Marquard elected to challenge Baker with speed. Matty believed that from second base Collins recognized what Rube intended and indicated as much to Baker, though the veteran Baker could also have perceived that, in the context of the brash Marquard shaking off a pitch, the savvy Meyers (besides what McGraw might be calling for from the bench) would not have first signaled for a fastball in this situation. The left-handed hitting Baker pulled the delivery over the right-field wall. The Athletics maintained the lead to win, 3–1.

Whatever McGraw said in the clubhouse afterward remained mercifully unrecorded. Publicly the manager let Rube take the blame for the errant pitch, and the pitcher accepted culpability. Jack Wheeler, Matty's ghostwriter from *The New York Herald*, gave him a voice of unflinching frankness: "Marquard made a poor pitch to Frank Baker.... There was no excuse for it.... We had scouted Baker, knew what pitches were difficult for him to hit, and those he could hit for extra bases. Well, Rube threw him the kind of ball that Baker likes."[37]

Both Matty and Jack Coombs pitched brilliantly in game three. Coombs yielded three hits on the day, two of them in the third inning when the Giants scored a solitary run. All the way into the ninth, Matty threw as though that run was all he would get and all he would need. Frank Baker, in the last moments before he would become ever known as Home Run Baker, fell behind, on curves, two strikes. The same hubris which tempted Marquard the day before in Philadelphia seduced Matty as well. Depending on his ability to get a fastball where he wanted it, he though to cross-up Baker who, conventionally, should have been looking for another breaking ball. When Matty delivered a fast one that stayed high, Baker sent it beyond right field. Suddenly it became so quiet in the Polo Grounds that Fred Lieb thought "those with especially good hearing could pick up the patter of Baker's feet as he romped joyfully around the bases."[38]

Matty felt the strength leave his arm. He had been pitching himself out and had not been expecting extra innings. He remembered a story about a backwoods wedding: An argument arose about the ring, and when it was settled, the bride gazed upon a dead groom, dead father, dead best man, dead preacher, and so on. "Them new fangled self-cockin' automatic guns has sure raised hell with my prospects," she sighed. As he watched Baker circle the bases, Matty said to himself: "He sure has raised hell with your prospects."[39]

The next batter, Danny Murphy, grounded to Herzog, who made

two errors on the play as Murphy advanced to scoring position at second base. Matty, refusing to be rattled, stranded the runner by getting the final two outs of the inning on balls hit too weakly to escape the infield.

In the tenth Matty set the Athletics down in order. In the bottom of the inning, Snodgrass worked a walk and went to second base on a sacrifice. The Giants believed that Baker was why of spikes, and in the first game Snodgrass had nearly torn Baker's trousers off in stealing third. Mack had instructed his pitchers to cut down their motion with Giants on base; in addition the arms of the A's catchers, Ira Thomas and Jack Lapp, gave would-be base stealers plenty to think about. Snodgrass, as Coombs went into his motion, took big leads from second and then darted back before Lapp might throw him out. To Matty's eyes "Snow" was darting back a little too soon. Lapp, anxious to nail the baserunner, failed to cleanly field a pitch. Snodgrass, however, had already turned back to second; by the time he redirected himself and was bolting toward third, Lapp had recovered and the ball was well on the way to Baker. The out seemed sure. The only way to prevent it would be to upend Baker. Once again Snodgrass leapt into the air, his spikes leading; once again Baker planted one knee in front of the bag; and once again Snodgrass tore Baker's trousers—and this time he drew blood as well. Baker held on for the out. Snodgrass heard catcalls even in the Polo Grounds.

In the top of the 11th, errors by Herzog and Fletcher resulted in two runs for the Athletics. In the Giants' at-bat, Herzog doubled and Meyers nearly tied the game once again with a ball deep into the left-field bleachers, but just foul. Herzog scored when reserve Beals Becker pinch-hit for Matty, but the Athletics won, 3–2.

Marquard's ghostwriter, needing little encouragement from Rube, roasted Matty for his pitch selection against Baker. Matty once confided to Grantland Rice that, on a professional level, an alibi was necessary when things went wrong. "You can't afford to admit that any opponent is better than you are. So, if you lose to him there must be a reason—a bad break. You must have an alibi to show why you lost. If you haven't one, you must fake one. Your self-confidence must be maintained.... But keep it to yourself. That's where it belongs. Don't spread it around. Lose gracefully in the open. To yourself, lose bitterly—but learn. You can learn little from victory. You can learn everything from defeat." The tempest brewed by the ghostwriters threatened disharmony on the team. Matty tried to keep it in a teapot. He admitted to Rube, and for the newspaper record, that he had made the same mistake. "I gave Baker a high, fast one. I have been in the business for a long time and have no excuse."[40]

Rain prevented the fourth game in Philadelphia for six days. The lull let sportswriters make more of the Mathewson-Marquard controversy than they would have done otherwise. Besides the need to make copy themselves, some writers resented the nice stipends the ballplayers received for pretending to write articles about the series. (They also vilified Snodgrass for his base-stealing method. One report even had Snodgrass shot by a baseball fanatic, and Snow's parents in California had several anxious hours until the report was corrected. After the hard feelings had waned, and intending no disparagement to either Snodgrass or Baker, Matty remarked that if it had been Red Murray or Fred Clarke stealing against Baker in similar circumstances, Baker would have been cut in half.) A couple of writers filled the void in another way. Hugh Fullerton of Chicago and William Phelon of Cincinnati opened a "modeling agency" in a hotel room and put an advertisement in a Philadelphia newspaper. They instructed the applicants to undress to their petticoats, and then went to work with notepads and tape measures describing and sizing the ladies' figures. "What pretty knees you have!" Phelon would exclaim. "You should be in the chorus of the Follies."[41]

The series resumed October 24 in soggy Shibe Park. Matty struck out the first two batters he faced with six pitches. Collins then singled, and a din of yells, horns, cowbells, and tom-toms accompanied Home Run Baker as he stepped to the plate. Matty struck Baker out, but thereafter he did not fare so well, surrendering ten hits in seven innings. Baker, Murphy, and Barry hit two doubles apiece, and Chief Bender threw a skillful seven-hitter. "The Chief makes the baseball look like a pea," said Josh Devore.[42] The Athletics won, 4–2.

In the fifth game, back at the Polo Grounds, the Giants not only trailed in the series three games to one, they trailed 3–1 going into the bottom of the ninth. Jack Coombs had suffered a pulled groin muscle earlier in the game, and it was now obvious that he was hurt. He downplayed his condition to his manager, saying that he still had his speed, control of his pitches and confidence that he could complete the victory. It looked like he would win, too. He got Herzog to ground to the shortstop for the first out of the inning. Fletcher did manage to hustle to second base on a hit which dropped into short left, but Meyers then grounded to the shortstop for the second out. Many fans rose from their seats to leave as McGraw chose not to pinch-hit for his third pitcher of the day, Otis Crandall. More knowledgeable fans, however, realized Crandall was competent enough with a bat that McGraw had used him 11 times during the regular season as a pinch hitter. Crandall sent a drive that fell between two outfielders, scoring Fletcher. Those who had departed their seats would regret their decision.

During a mound conference Coombs once again prevailed upon his manager to remain in the contest. After all, the next batter, Devore, had been struggling at the plate. Devore waved his bat nervously and then skimmed a single across the left-field grass scoring Crandall. Fred Lieb remembered the fans' exultation after Devore's hit as the greatest display of sheer joy he ever witnessed until Bobby Thomson's pennant-winning home run in the same ballpark 40 years later. The cheering lasted nearly ten minutes, Lieb recalled, and could be heard throughout upper Harlem and the lower Bronx.

In the top of the tenth, Coombs bunted in front of the plate and, despite his pain, beat the throw to first. With Coombs's muscle pull now aggravated, and with the go-ahead run on first base, Mack sent Amos Strunk to run for "Colby Jack."[43] Strunk was stranded on base, and Eddie Plank entered the game to pitch. Doyle doubled down the left-field line; Snodgrass bunted him to third. Merkle flied to deep right, somewhat of a contradiction in terms in the Polo Grounds, where Danny Murphy caught and launched the ball to Jack Lapp. Doyle arrived in the vicinity of home plate ahead of the throw and joined his teammates in a dash for the clubhouse as celebrating fans swarmed onto the field.

Lapp caught the throw and then joined his own teammates as they bolted for the safety of the visitors' locker room. Normally the umpires would have sought their own place of refuge as well, but Bill Klem remained standing at the plate as though expecting something.

"I stood there, awaiting an Athletics' protest, but none came," Klem said afterward. Connie Mack saw that Klem had not given a "safe" sign: Doyle had not touched the plate. But, as the Giants' fans poured onto the field of play, Mack, in the immediacy of the moment, thought of how these fans had considered themselves cheated of a pennant three years before. The Athletics' manager felt there was too much life and limb at risk to argue that the Giants had not yet won the fifth game and decided instead to take his chances on games six and seven.[44]

Mack did not need a game seven. Returning to Shibe Park, Chief Bender after just one full day of rest threw a four-hitter. McGraw was saving Matty for a hoped-for series-winning finale, but in the sixth game Ames, Wiltse, and Marquard combined to yield 13 hits and 13 runs. Things began to fall apart for the Giants in the fourth inning. With two men on base, Jack Barry chopped a bunt which Ames fielded but his throw caromed off Barry's head and into foul territory along right field. Red Murray retrieved and hurled the ball toward second, but the throw went by Fletcher and into left field. Barry ended up scoring on what he intended as a sacrifice bunt. "Nice head work!" someone in the stands yelled through a megaphone; on the bench even Matty laughed as did some of the other Giants.[45] By the time the A's romped for another seven runs in the seventh inning, however, the black uniforms the Giants wore as a symbol of former glory now seemed more like funeral garments.

A controversy occurred concerning World Series money due the players, largely stemming from late-season attendance figures at the Polo Grounds inflated for publicity purposes by club secretary William Gray. Gray had replaced longtime secretary Fred Knowles, who had for reasons of poor health resigned the position. Both Giant and Athletic players demanded to know how, during the series, paid attendances in the packed Polo Grounds were now figured as less than some large attendances had been publicized during the pennant race. At a meeting with representatives Chief Meyers and Harry Davis to resolve the issue, the members of the National Commission browbeat the players into accepting the more modest, and more accurate, numbers. "Do you men think the Commission is trying to steal money from the players?" Ban Johnson asked sourly.[46] William Gray found himself in more hot water when it became known that he had aided scalpers in the speculative sale of large blocks of reserved World Series tickets; John Brush fired him.

For their part, the Giant players voted a series share to former teammate Al Bridwell.[47]

7

But Not World Champions

Havana had become a playground for well-to-do Americans who equated a sense of adventure with money to burn. In November, after the 1911 Series, McGraw took his wife, along with Matty and Jane, and a team of other major leaguers, mostly Giants, married or otherwise, on an exhibition tour to Cuba, with sportswriters and an umpire for good measure. They played on the island against top local professional teams and returned home by Christmas. Some of the players saw the trip as an opportunity to debauch. After two losses, McGraw disabused them of that notion. He invited Josh Devore in particular to either straighten up or take the next boat home. "I didn't come down here to let a lot of coffee-colored Cubans show me up," McGraw said.[1]

During the winter, in a continuation of their World Series collaboration, Jack Wheeler prepared a manuscript under Matty's name for publication in the spring. They chose a title, *Pitching in a Pinch*, that encapsulated Matty's greatest strength as a ballplayer. The editors of *Baseball Magazine*, in making a selection of the "gamest player in baseball," chose the nervous, high-strung, emotionally-troubled Johnny Evers.[2] The editors also could well have chosen the stoical, less troubled characters of Honus Wagner or Eddie Collins, among others, from the elite of players—the ones a good manager always looks for—eager to make a crucial fielding play with their own gloves or to step to the plate with their own bats in a tight situation, a "pinch." By the same token, a relative handful of pitchers, and none better than Matty, had the cool confidence to want to pitch in these same situations. Wheeler, writing in an intelligent, masculine, wry manner, knew the "slant" he wanted to deliver to the baseball public. Fans liked to read about "inside" baseball, and that is what Matty and Wheeler gave them. In the book readers could learn, among other things, why the Giants liked to bunt against Slim

7. But Not World Champions

Sallee, how Josh Devore learned to cope with left-handed pitching, why Fred Merkle preferred to slide head-first into base, and how Bugs Raymond discovered the use of resin.

McGraw made few changes for 1912. Art Devlin went to finish his playing career with the Boston Braves. Outfielder George Burns continued an apprenticeship of practicing hard and mostly sitting on the bench during games. Louis Drucke journeyed north from Texas and pitched just two innings, yielding five hits, a base on balls, and three earned runs, to end his big-league career. The arrival of spitballer Jeff Tesreau, taller than even Matty and thickset, made easier for the manager the decision to release Drucke.

On May 4, at the Polo Grounds, the Giants stole nine bases against Phillies' catcher George "Peaches" Graham, as Matty won the game 4–3. Graham, who had appeared in over 300 National League games over the past four seasons, was not much longer with the Phillies. A few weeks later, Ty Cobb went into the stands at Hilltop Park and physically assaulted a heckler, for which he received an indefinite suspension from Ban Johnson. The trouble with Cobb, said teammate Davy Jones long afterward, "was he had such a rotten disposition that it was damn hard to be his friend." In this case, less from affection for Cobb than to protest not being able to react in kind when fans threw, besides insults, soda and beer bottles from the stands, the Detroit Tigers to a man chose not to play their next regularly scheduled contest which, as it happened, was against the Athletics in Philadelphia. To avoid the financial penalty for failure to show up for a scheduled game, the Tigers' management hastily recruited a makeshift team. Among the recruits was a man named Maharg—Graham spelled backward—recommended for the position by one of the wildcat strikers, Tiger pitcher Sleepy Bill Burns. The makeshift Tigers lost 24–2, and Ban Johnson intervened to limit the strike to just one game. Burns eventually quit playing baseball and made a lot of money in the oil industry of his native Texas. Maharg eked a living as a middleweight boxer and as a factory worker; whether he was also Peaches Graham or not—he denied it in his lifetime and the recurrent assertion has apparently defied proof ever since—Maharg played in one more major-league game, for the Phillies in 1916. In 1919 Burns and Maharg would become instigators in the gambling scheme known as the Black Sox Scandal.[3]

In the National League, club presidents Charles Murphy and Horace Fogel, of Chicago and Philadelphia respectively, grumbled aloud that the Giants would not win so many games if other clubs, especially Roger Bresnahan's Cardinals, made an honest effort against them. On one occasion, after Cardinal pitchers gave the Giants 12 walks in a single game, a reporter remarked that the second-place Cubs would suspect the Cardinals of running a "charitable institution." McGraw and Bresnahan sloughed it off. Not just the Cardinals, no one else could beat the Giants either. Especially no one could beat Rube Marquard. "The reason I'm so successful is because I can beat anybody," the left-hander liked to say. By July 3 Rube notched his 19th victory without a defeat. Even after dropping the next day a holiday double-header, the Giants' record stood at 54 and 13, nearly 15 games ahead of the second-place Cubs.[4]

For his part, against Brooklyn on July 5, Matty won his 11th victory against five defeats. With none of the fanfare Rube's incredible streak was attracting, the 6–1 score marked the 300th win of Matty's career. Or, rather, in a sense, the 299th. For not until the 1940s was it fully realized that Matty won 373 games in his career, not 372 as had been thought. In 1902 the National League did not publish an official compilation of pitching statistics. On May 21 of that year, Matty made a relief appearance in which, after he gave up the lead, his team came back to win; Matty himself scored what proved to be the winning run in the eighth inning. The league credited him the win, but, because Luther Taylor left the game after 6⅓ innings ahead by one run and given the discretion sometimes left to official scorers in those days to determine winning pitchers, it was evidently assumed by most reporters that Taylor had more properly earned the victory. Thus, in popular resources as the *Spalding* and *Reach* guides and Moreland's *Balldom*, Matty was credited with 13 victories in '02, not 14 as the league itself assigned him. Whether in 1912 the July 5 win was number 299 or 300, the achievement attracted virtually no notice in the press. (The error eventually led to Grover Cleveland Alexander believing that he had eclipsed Matty's total victories by one when he retired at age 43 in 1930—only to learn a dozen years later that he had only tied Matty's record.)[5]

About this same time, though, from a boy in rural South Carolina, came by mail an unsophisticated compliment that Jane Mathewson saved through all the days of her marriage and long widowhood. The boy sent with his letter a half dollar for which he wanted to learn from the great pitcher "how to throw your fade-away and in and out-curves ... write me at once please by mail if any more charges.... I have heard of your famous fade-away and would like to know how to throw it."[6]

In August, Matty went a disappointing one-and-five. Also, the jump in Marquard's fastball became mortal again, if not for Jeff Tesreau, who won nearly all his 16 games after mid-July (including the league's only no-hit effort of the season), the Cubs might have overtaken the Giants. As it was, the Giants saw their lead cut to low single digits before Matty began to win again.

He won six games in September for a 23 and 12 record, far from his best. But as Bob Feller observed of the days before relief pitching became regarded as a manly art, and all the more so in Matty's day because rosters hardly exceeded 20 men, a pitcher's true value to his club cannot be determined without taking into account the number of his completed games along with the number of his victories.[7] By these measures of the ability to go out and win games or at least keep them close, Matty was first on his club and second in the league. Moreover, he tied Grover Alexander for most innings pitched, allowed just one walk per nine innings, and was bettered only by Tesreau in earned run average. Offensively the Giants led the league in batting average, stolen bases, and runs scored. In their drive to the pennant, they may have scarcely noticed the passing of Bugs Raymond, found dead in a Chicago hotel room, but they did clinch the league title with time enough to rest and heal their starters before the World Series.

If a criterion of a pitcher's value is complete games, then, for the American League champion Red Sox, Smoky Joe Wood—whose "four-seam" fastball rivaled Walter Johnson's in sheer power—met a high standard. He started 38 games, completed 35, and from all his 43 appearances achieved 34 victories with an earned run average of 1.91. In Tris Speaker, Harry Hooper, and Duffy Lewis the Sox had, in both hitting and fielding, one of the best outfields of the era. In 1912 the Red Sox lineup led their league in slugging percentage and runs scored. The Royal Rooters, baseball's most vociferous fans, quickly familiarized themselves with Fenway Park, in its inaugural season, as they sang, marched, and clamored for their ballplaying heroes in any flamboyant way they saw fit. For the Giants, someone put out the story that Charley Faust, relegated to the bench in street clothes during the regular season, was beckoned home to Kansas by his mythical sweetheart.

McGraw blinked at Joe Wood and decided it was better to risk Tesreau in the first game than Matty; though, to keep the Red Sox guessing, prior to the game he had both Tesreau and Matty warming up. Mayor John "Honey" Fitzgerald of Boston and Governor Eugene Foss of Massachusetts attended as guests of New York's Mayor William Gaynor. A tireless campaigner, "Honey-Fitz" strode alone across the field to greet his fellow townsmen, about 300 in number, seated in the lower grandstand along right field. The Rooters were easy to pick out; they were bedecked in red sashes, waved pennants, and had brought their own brass band with them.

Tesreau was not intimidated by his matchup with the Boston ace, and the Red Sox did not score their first run until the sixth inning. In the seventh a two-out single by Steve Yerkes scored two more runs that put the Sox ahead to stay, as Joe Wood struck out 11 plate-crowding Giants and scattered eight hits.[8]

After a night train to Boston, Matty held the Red Sox the next day to just two earned runs before a raucous house, but his teammates' five errors gave the home team another four unearned runs. It took Matty 25 pitches just to get out of the first inning. Valiant batting, especially by Herzog, Murray, and Merkle, enabled a comeback that took the game through its 11th frame, after which umpire Frank "Silk" O'Loughlin called it a drawn contest because of darkness.

Thomas "Buck" O'Brien pitched a fine game three for the Red Sox; Marquard pitched a slightly better one for the Giants. The Sox trailed by one run in the bottom of the ninth with runners in scoring position and two outs. With fog partially obscuring the playing field, Boston's Forrest Cady sent a drive to right center. It seemed as though both the tying and winning runs would score, but Josh Devore dashed into the fog, caught the ball on the fly, and kept running right into the visitors' clubhouse. The fog prevented most spectators from seeing the catch made, and many left the ballpark in the belief the Red Sox had won, only to read otherwise in the papers. With four umpires covering the game, the play was correctly called. The scene then shifted back to the Polo Grounds where again both Tesreau and Wood pitched well, and once more Wood prevailed. The Red Sox now led the series two games to one.

Hugh Bedient, an 18-game winner and like Joe Wood not yet 23 years old, sent the Royal Rooters into rapture by pitching a masterful performance on Saturday, October 12. In the bottom of the third inning, Matty surrendered back-to-back triples to Hooper and Yerkes, and Yerkes scored on an error by Doyle. Thereafter Matty retired the Red Sox in order, but the Giants could not crack Bedient for more than a solitary run. As soon as the game ended, Bedient bolted for the clubhouse to avoid the fans rushing onto the field to hail him. Matty put on a Mackinaw coat and walked tiredly from the visitors' bench.

The Red Sox boarded a Sunday train for a leisurely return to New York. With this intervening day of rest, they expected Joe Wood to wrap it up on the morrow. But club president James McAleer let manager Jake Stahl know that he wanted Buck O'Brien to start Monday's game. McAleer and Stahl both belonged to an ownership often hard-pressed to make its payments, and McAleer, it has been speculated, may not have really minded the anticipation of another close loss by O'Brien necessitating another game in Boston. The team, however, did not like the decision (it was later said that Joe Wood, expecting himself to pitch, had bet a large sum on the Sox to win the next game) and their attitude soured even more when O'Brien departed after one inning with the Giants ahead 5–0. Marquard won his second game of the series.

If McAleer wished for an extra game in Boston, the thought backfired. Three World Series games, if one included the drawn game, had already been played at Fenway. For the unexpected fourth game the Red

Sox business office, incomprehensibly, sold on a first-come-first-served basis the seats heretofore reserved for the Royal Rooters, who were outraged when they came to the ballpark and found other people in their places. As Smoky Joe warmed his marvelous arm, the Rooters stormed the field as their band played their fight song. It required five mounted policemen to drive them off. Smoky Joe, without a jacket, retreated to the dugout and watched the mêlée. After the prolonged ruckus, when Wood returned to the mound, his arm was dead. The Giants walloped him like a batting-practice pitcher, and Stahl pulled him early. Tesreau breezed to an 11–4 victory.

Ban Johnson tossed a coin to determine which ballpark would host the eighth game. Boston won the toss. (The best-of-seven series should have had its deciding contest won or lost in New York; the coin toss was intended to avoid accusations the series was artificially prolonged to attract one last large gate in New York.) The Royal Rooters, though, boycotted Fenway and compared the Boston police to Cossacks quelling demonstrators in Moscow. Only a crowd of 17,000 attended. Bedient again started opposite Matty and surrendered one run in the third inning. In the Boston seventh, with two outs and two men on base, Stahl sent Olaf Henriksen to pinch-hit for Bedient as Joe Wood warmed up. Falling behind by two strikes, Henriksen, whom Tris Speaker would remember as one of the best pinch hitters ever in the game, refused to swing at two offerings just wide of the plate.[9] Henriksen doubled the next pitch down the left-field line, scoring a run; it was his only plate appearance of the series. After nine innings, the score stood knotted at one run apiece.

In the tenth with one out, Red Murray doubled. Fred Merkle, in a moment that might have at least partially absolved him from the infamy of his base-running error four years previously, singled to bring home the go-ahead run. Joe Wood quashed any more scoring when he struck out Herzog on three pitches and then stopped with his wrist a comebacker by Meyers, retrieving the ball in time to get the out at first base. "How many runs they might have made I'll never know, but that stopped the inning," Wood recollected as an old man. But Wood knew, regardless of what happened next, his presence in the game was over. "My hand was swollen by the time I reached the bench."[10] The Giants needed only three more outs.

Batting for Wood, pinch-hitter Clyde Engle lofted a routine fly ball to center. Snodgrass dropped it. Matty swung his glove in a momentary display of emotion as Engle scampered to second base. Harry Hooper bunted foul and then lined a screamer deep into center field. Snodgrass now made a tremendous running catch and held Engle to third base. Hooper remarked afterward that, 99 times out of a hundred, no outfielder could have come close to that ball and that Snodgrass had robbed him of a sure triple. Matty did not give the next batter, Yerkes, anything decent to hit and walked him to set up the double play. Speaker then popped one up in foul territory on the first-base side—apparently a sure second out. Matty called for Meyers to make the catch even though onlookers thought Merkle, or even Matty, had an easier play. (Meyers thought it was the Red Sox bench that called Merkle off the play.) The Chief lumbered for it but the ball fell just to his right. Speaker went back to the batter's box. "Well," the Texan was remembered to have drawled to Matty, "you just called for the wrong man. It's gonna cost you this ball game." It was bravado that a lesser batsman would not have dared. (Matty seldom spoke to opposing batters; what he replied to Speaker, if anything, is not recorded.) Speaker, however, had recently become the owner of a luxury Chalmers automobile as the American League's most valuable player; he singled to right, scoring Engle to tie the game and moving Yerkes to third,. Matty intentionally walked Duffy Lewis, but Larry Gardner's sacrifice fly ended it.[11]

Matty had pitched with an ERA of 1.57 over 28⅔ World Series innings with two losses to his credit. Snodgrass's "muff" became as notorious baseball fans as Merkle's "bone." (As he had done in '08 so that a good ballplayer would not be ruined, McGraw inserted a raise into Snodgrass's contact for the next year.) The defeat collectively cost the Giant players nearly $30,000 in the difference between the victors' and losers' shares. But Matty evinced no bitterness on the train-ride home; he even sought to deflect blame from Snodgrass: "Any player is likely to make an error," he said. "What really lost the game is that I pitched wrong to Henriksen in the seventh. He was a pinch hitter, and I didn't know his weakness."[12]

John Brush would no longer view games from his automobile deep in center field. He died in November. Ownership of the Giants passed to his distaff heirs and supervision to his son-in-law Harry Hempstead, 43 years old. Hempstead had been managing the family department store in Indianapolis. His first important act was to sign McGraw, said to have spoken movingly at Brush's funeral, to a lucrative five-year contract. At $30,000 annually, the manager would make three times as much as his best player.

David Fultz, a New York attorney and former big leaguer, encouraged ballplayers to organize into a protective association against the excesses of baseball's ownership. About a month before the 1912 World Series, Fultz formally incorporated the Players' Fraternity. Nearly 300 ballplayers joined immediately, and Matty and Ty Cobb, as vice-presidents, lent the stature of their names to the organization. Like Matty, fraternity president Fultz had the benefit of a Baptist college education. He had played football for Brown University, and his seven-year big-league career included part of a season with McGraw in Baltimore and ended when he broke his jaw in a basepath collision with Kid Elberfeld. Fultz was another player whose scruples did not allow him to play baseball on Sunday. Though criticized by contemporaries for lofty idealism, he appears to have been an able and careful lawyer whose positions, in retrospect, can essentially be faulted only for being ahead of their time. Fultz sought restrictions on the reserve clause, higher salaries for journeyman players, improved safety conditions (such as painting outfield walls green so that a batter could better see a ball coming at him), and for owners to provide, not sell, uniforms to their players. He misread, however, in what several years hence proved the fraternity's downfall, the willingness of big leaguers to put their own well-being on the line in behalf of their minor-league brethren. As one baseball executive observed, big leaguers themselves had not that much in common as they were divided into three groups: those on the make, those on the top, and those on the downslide.[13]

Matty at first prominently supported the fraternity and never did go out of his way to oppose it, but within a couple years his name no longer appeared on the fraternity's letterhead among the listing of officers and directors. His relationships with baseball executives were in the main cordial, and his insurance business gave him at least one incentive to keep them that way. Within a few months of the fraternity's incorporation, Matty wrote to Garry Herrmann of the Cincinnati Reds recommending an accident policy to cover the members of that ball club. He offered a cost-saving, two-tiered policy for the seven months of the year which comprised the actual season. For reserve players on the roster, Matty suggested to Herrmann lower coverage "as in the event of accident you would not have as severe a loss as they do not play regularly."[14]

McGraw made a coup by signing Jim Thorpe to a contract. The hero of the 1912 Olympics was already embroiled in controversy, for having once played professional baseball in a low minor league, that resulted in his medals being taken from him. Though the major-league ability of the man described as the world's greatest athlete was unproven, McGraw reasoned that people would pay just to see him take batting practice. In Marlin it became evident that George Burns was ready to replace Josh Devore in the outfield, and the regular season was hardly a month old when McGraw traded Devore, Red Ames, and a young infielder named Heinie Groh to Cincinnati for pitcher Art Fromme. The trade had the saving grace of 23 victories in 1913—that is, when Fromme's wins were added to those of Al Demaree, who joined the Giants late in 1912 and who would, after a respectable journeyman pitching career, become a syndicated cartoonist.

Marquard arrived in Texas late. During a stormy off-season, he had been accused of alienating the affections of vaudeville performer Blossom Seeley from her husband. Despite threats from the husband that he would shoot them onstage, Blossom and Rube went on tour and became famous for a dance called "The Marquard Glide." Rube reportedly sang and danced well, but as an actor was said to be a great left-handed pitcher. After her divorce, they married.

"It didn't work out, though," Rube said many years later. "I asked her to quit the stage. I told her I could give her everything she wanted.

'No,' she said, 'show business is show business.'

'Well,' I said, 'baseball is mine.' So we separated."[15]

Harry Hempstead must have wondered if he could do anything wrong. Not only had he the business reins of a pennant-winning ballclub, but the Yankees brought even more revenue to the family by signing a lease to hold their home games at the Polo Grounds. Hilltop Park, not much to begin with, suffered in comparison with the stadium rebuilt by Hempstead's father-in-law. Considering Frank Farrell's magnanimity in the aftermath of the fire, it seemed an equitable arrangement. Eventually Farrell and his partner Big Bill Devery sold their club to Colonel Jacob Ruppert and Captain Tillinghast Huston.

Brooklyn had a new ballpark as well, Ebbets Field. There, in late April, veteran southpaw Nap Rucker matched Matty through 12 scoreless innings. Things fell apart for Rucker in the 13th and the Giants won 6–0. The Phillies took three straight from the visiting Giants, including, on May 3, a rousing come-from-behind victory against Matty. Led by Red Dooin, Gavvy Cravath, Sherry Magee, Tom Seaton, and Grover Alexander, the Phillies were apparently among the few to take seriously their former president Horace Fogel's accusation of league favoritism toward the Giants; moreover, they were in first place and wanted to stay there. McGraw exacerbated the situation by insulting the Phillies, publicly and otherwise, at every opportunity.

By mid-May, Matty had pitched 47 consecutive innings without allowing a walk. His five victories comprised half of his team's total; the number of the Giants' losses caused them to drift in or near the second division. McGraw had a favorite formula that it would take at least 95 wins to earn the pennant and that Matty would supply 25 of them. It was up to the other pitchers to provide the rest.

They did. During June, for the most part on the road, the Giants won 20 games and lost seven, ending the month in Philadelphia against the team they trailed only slightly in the standings. They swept the series with the Phillies and thereby lifted themselves into first place. Bad feelings erupted after the opener when McGraw, as he headed to the visitors' clubhouse, was attacked by Phillies' pitcher Ad Brennan. Art Wilson and the Giants' other reserve catcher Grover Hartley rushed to McGraw's aid but could not get there before their manager was on the ground and several fans had joined in the effort to inflict physical hurt. McGraw received painful gashes on his chin and right cheek.

Meanwhile, and more coolly, Matty pitched another long streak of walkless innings, 68⅔, accentuated by eight wins in the nine decisions touched by that span. An observer on the Pittsburgh club, Max Carey, in the early seasons of a long career that would mark him as a top-flight outfielder and one of the best lead-off hitters in the game, remarked that, despite 13 years in the big league, Matty never seemed to have to force himself to play. "He either likes it immensely or he is the greatest actor I ever saw," said Carey. "He doesn't take it for granted that has learned all there is to learn and go on piking mechanically. He refuses to get into a mental rut." With his superb control, Matty's fastball did not need to be as fast as it once was in order to fool batters and get them out. Many decades later, television broadcaster and former catcher Tim McCarver would explain: "The ability to get the breaking ball over on fastball counts and to get the fastball exactly where you want it on breaking-ball counts is what makes a successful major-league pitcher."[16]

McGraw negotiated with the Reds for the purchase of infielder Eddie Grant. Harvard Eddie, now an attorney as well as a ballplayer, had once, briefly, been the premier third baseman in the National League. McGraw, demonstrating again that he liked having college-educated men around, wanted Grant for his clubhouse maturity and utility prowess to complement the Giants' mainstay utilityman Tillie Shafer. Grant's New England restraint and quiet humor, according to newspaperman Jimmy Isaminger, caused people to like him better on a second meeting, and better yet on a third. Grant may have welcomed the opportunity to leave Cincinnati. When he had been traded from the Phillies to the Reds, he brought with him from Philadelphia a bride who died several months later. After her death, it was said, Grant was never the same ballplayer.[17]

Matty's walkless pitching streak ended during a 5–0 shutout of the Cardinals in mid-July. He won just seven games and lost six for the remainder of the season. But his team was well ahead in the standings, and he provided McGraw 25 victories.

The Giants once again met the Athletics in the World Series. The Baseball Writers Association, acting on a natural resentment, pulled some strings with the National Commission and nearly prevented a whole contingent of Giants—Matty, McGraw, Merkle, Marquard, and cartoonist Demaree—from making money by putting their names on newspaper articles, ghostwritten or otherwise. But David Fultz put things in clearer perspective for Ban Johnson and the other members of the commission by threatening a liability suit for lost monies and by criticizing the owners, of all people, for demanding that ballplayers disregard contractual agreements.

More serious mishaps, however, befell the Giants before, during, and after the first World Series game. Doyle smashed his car (he had won a luxury Chalmers himself the year before as the National League's most valuable player) into a tree and hurt his right shoulder. Snodgrass's leg yet hampered him from a regular-season injury. Merkle, while making two hits and scoring two runs in the first game, sprained his ankle, which afterward swelled so badly that he required a cane to walk. And in practice before game two, Chief Meyers broke a thumb.[18]

McGraw did not have the bench to compensate for this much damage to his lineup. Eddie Grant had hit just .200 in 27 games, and Moose McCormick mainly had seen action only as a pinch hitter. Concerning the team's catching, Art Wilson's batting average was a couple hundred points lower than Meyers's, and nearly all of Grover Hartley's work had been in the bullpen. McGraw had, though, obtained from St. Louis late in the season catcher "Long Larry" McLean. At 6 feet 5 inches and nearly 230 pounds, McLean was the biggest man, and one of the meanest drunks, in the big leagues. McLean, another case of McGraw's willingness to take on a "bad actor," rewarded the manager's confidence during the World Series by rapping six singles in 12 at-bats and catching errorlessly behind the plate.

Home Run Baker picked up where he left off in the A's last World Series. He stroked three hits in the first game, including a two-run homer in the top of the fifth against Marquard. Rube departed after five innings, as Chief Bender pitched a complete game in a 6–4 victory.

For the second game, in Philadelphia, Matty and Eddie Plank dueled scorelessly for nine innings. Having sent Tillie Shafer to the outfield, McGraw inserted the hobbling Snodgrass at first base to substitute for the more hobbled Merkle. Watching "Snow" struggle down the first base line in the third inning on a hit that should have been easily a double, and then struggle to scoring position on another hit, McGraw sent Hooks Wiltse to run for him. Wiltse spoiled a potentially big inning by getting caught in a run-down between third base and home. McGraw now needed a first baseman and inserted Wiltse there. Matty said that no pitcher fielded his position better, or practiced more at it, than Hooks Wiltse. Wiltse knew what Don Drysdale later knew: A good fielding pitcher who served the right stuff could assist himself with two, maybe three outs, each game. Playing first base is different than pitching, of course, but for the remainder of the game Hooks had 16 chances—13 putouts and three assists—and fielded them all with success.[19]

In the New York tenth inning, McLean led by singling to right. Inserted as the baserunner, Grant advanced to second base on a sacrifice bunt by Wiltse. Matty then singled to left center as Grant scored. After loading the bases, the Giants scored two more runs on a single by Art

Fletcher. In the bottom of the inning, Wiltse very nearly did have an error on what was almost not the final out of the game—a sharp hit by Home Run Baker bounded off Hooks but right into the hands of Larry Doyle, who returned it in time to Wiltse at first base, scoring the out 3–4–3. Matty had another World Series shutout win.

Jack Coombs was injured and could not pitch, so for game three Connie Mack sent a 20 year old named Joe Bush to pitch in the Polo Grounds against the "Ozark Giant," Jeff Tesreau. Born in the same northern Minnesota county as had been Chief Bender, the young man had a pitching delivery that gussied his name to "Bullet Joe" Bush. Bullet Joe won 8–2. Back in Philadelphia the next day, the other pitcher from Crow Tree County threw another complete game that beat by one run the combined efforts of Demaree and Marquard to give the Athletics a 3–1 lead in the series.

McGraw had plans to host a reunion at a New York saloon for his old Oriole teammates on the night of Saturday, October 11. He hoped the party would be aided by a Mathewson victory in game five that afternoon. Eddie Plank, however, pitched a tremendous game, facing 29 Giant batters in nine innings, with only Matty and McLean getting singles. Matty allowed six hits and a walk as errors figured conspicuously in the scoring of the Athletics' 3–1 victory.

McGraw lavished praise on the A's second baseman Eddie Collins, who hit .421 and stole three bases in the series, as "the greatest ballplayer in the world." McGraw's own second baseman hit .150 and was charged with three errors. Matty pitched with an ERA of 0.95 over 19 innings, causing McGraw to say about the 33-year-old right-hander: "He has the greatest heart of any ballplayer I ever knew, and by heart I mean courage. He never quits, and he always uses his head. To show that he is a great money player, he not only supplied all of the good pitching that I got in the series, but he also led the club in batting." The latter portion of McGraw's remark verged on hyperbole, though Matty did have three singles in five official at-bats; McGraw said it in the context of his entire lineup having combined for an anemic .201 average with just five extra-base hits.[20]

Not so magnanimously, drinking too much at the Oriole reunion, McGraw scolded Wilbert Robinson for poor coaching. Uncle Robbie, as much an old Oriole as anyone else, replied that McGraw had committed more mistakes during the series than he had. (In the pressbox there had been a feeling that Connie Mack had indeed "outgeneraled" McGraw, "the little Napoleon," especially in regard to using the sacrifice bunt and the hit-and-run as means to advance baserunners). "This is my party," McGraw told Robinson angrily. "Get the hell out of here." Robinson did so but not before dousing his old, and for the next 17 years former, friend with beer.[21]

For some time McGraw had been organizing with Charles Comiskey a world tour of their respective ball clubs that would begin after the World Series. Their respective ball clubs, more or less. Bona fide Giants Merkle, Doyle, and Thorpe were augmented by erstwhile Giant Mike Donlin; from the Phillies came Mickey Doolan and Hans Lobert; from the Cardinals, Lee Magee and Ivy Wingo. Tris Speaker and Herman "Germany" Schaefer, among others, played for the White Sox. Blanche McGraw accompanied her husband, and Larry Doyle and Jim Thorpe brought with them their new brides. The itinerary would take them to Japan, Australia, Africa, and Europe.

Matty took part in only the American portion of the tour. He was too prone to seasickness to relish the thought of so many days, even weeks, on the open ocean. The voyage might have been an extended honeymoon for Doyle and Thorpe, but Matty had too vivid a recollection of his own honeymoon voyage to wish to repeat that aspect of the experience. McGraw and Comiskey scheduled 34 American dates in 33 days, beginning in Cincinnati and ending in Seattle, in order to ensure that expenses were covered prior to the departure across the Pacific of their large entourage, including, besides the players and their wives, a business manager, two umpires, a doctor, a reverend, Frank Farrell, and others. Matty accompanied them at least as far as Los Angeles. On the way he appeared in several games, including a much ballyhooed matchup against Walter Johnson in Tulsa. When the show stopped in Arizona, he and Jane may have taken the time to visit his stepuncle Albert Doolittle and his wife Kit on their ranch near Winslow. Or maybe the Doolittles came to see them. In a few years, Albert and Kit would become important figures in the very survival of Matty's brother Henry.[22]

8

SOMEONE ELSE'S TURN

The National League ownership thought they had obtained some real window dressing when they elected Governor John K. Tener of Pennsylvania as their new president. Tener had pitched for the White Sox in the 1880s, and afterward met with success in banking and machine politics. The team owners were so pleased to acquire a man of his experience and eminence that they paid him more than twice what his predecessor received. Tener refused to take the office without the understanding that it would not supersede his larger and concurrent duties to the Commonwealth of Pennsylvania. The owners saw no difficulty in this arrangement, since they expected John Heydler, league secretary, to perform the basic, day-to-day executive functions.

While McGraw toured the world, Harry Hempstead agreed to a trade. He sent Buck Herzog and Grover Hartley to Cincinnati for outfielder Bob Bescher. McGraw had a love-hate relationship with Herzog and admired Bescher, probably the league's best base stealer, as a player. The clubhouse, Hempstead could have reasoned, would be a happier place. Hugh Fullerton rated Herzog as the most disliked player in the National League. Other players, Fullerton wrote, "have to wear a respirator to get to his altitude."[1] But if Hempstead thought McGraw would express satisfaction with the deal, he was mistaken. McGraw made it out as a worse trade than it actually was, still claiming years later that it had forced him to make several other trades to strengthen his club again. He was upset Hempstead had not consulted him, for he had long been used to running the baseball operation himself. His immediate and obvious displeasure let Harry know who was the manager, and in the long term the incident provided a convenient scapegoat when the club met with diminished success. Herzog's replacement, 21-year-old Milton Stock, stepped into a no-win situation.

In 1913 an amalgam of baseball clubs calling itself the Federal League located in some big-city markets and somehow, with few high-caliber players, completed its inaugural season. Organized Baseball, meaning the National and American leagues, considered it an outlaw organization. However, since it had not thus far solicited their reserved players, the major leagues ignored the Federals. Many observers assumed the upstart league could not last long anyway, but during the winter the upstarts became infused with rich blood. Investors now included millionaire oilman Harry Sinclair and the Ward Brothers, makers of Brooklyn's Tip-Top bread. With cash on hand and some able baseball executives in employ, the Federal League now actively sought with generous salaries American and National League ballplayers. And since, to Organized Baseball, theirs was an "outlaw league," the Federals claimed they were not beholden to anyone else's reserve clause.

Some big names jumped their contracts, including Joe Tinker, Three Finger Brown, Chief Bender, and Hal Chase. Most of the big-name jumpers were on the downslide of their careers, but people still wanted to see them. The Federal League had an eye for young talent as well, signing exciting newcomers like Edd Roush and Benny Kauff. The rival leagues postured, bid, threatened, and sometimes went to court over disputed players.

The Giant organization, as three-time pennant winners with intentions of a consecutive fourth, kept the Federals from any real penetration of their ranks by signing their champions to two and three-year contracts. The Federals ached to sign Matty, promising him as much as $65,000 to sign for three years. Matty voiced no criticism of players who bolted to the Federal League. Many of them had never received large salaries before, he said, and could hardly be blamed. But he cautioned that what the Federals would promise and what they could deliver might be two different things. He elected to sign with the Giants for another three years. "Every new league is an experiment until it has established itself," he explained. "At my time of life I could not afford to make experiments."[2]

After his shabby treatment from McGraw, Wilbert Robinson took the job as manager of the Brooklyn team, sometimes known as the Dodgers, sometimes yet as the Superbas, and frequently now, in honor of their new manager, as the Robins. Early in the 1914 season, when the Giants came to Ebbets Field, McGraw assigned to Matty the series opener, Matty's first appearance of the year. Uncle Robbie had his first two batters lay down bunts, which they did successfully, and a sacrifice fly advanced the runners. Then Zack Wheat nailed a double. Matty left the game after seven innings, trailing 9–4. More than two weeks later, in just his third start because of so much rain, Matty beat the Brooklyns 4–3 at the Polo Grounds—though really the visitors beat themselves on a throwing error by rookie catcher Lew McCarty which allowed two runs to score. Not one to neglect rubbing salt in a wound when he had the opportunity, McGraw made a point after the game of thanking McCarty on "behalf of myself, Mr. Mathewson, and the other Giants."[3]

In June the Cincinnati Reds came to town with Buck Herzog as manager. The Giants held first place; the Reds, second. A large Saturday crowd welcomed Herzog loudly; in mute counterpoint the Giant management conspicuously refused to host a ceremony and presentation of gifts as they usually did on the first return to the Polo Grounds of a former star. The Giants swept the three-game series. Traveling to Boston for six games with the last-place and apparently once again hapless Braves, the Giants managed, somewhat to their surprise, only a split.

Although McGraw saw things which caused him to voice displeasure with his team's performance, the Giants still won more games than they lost during a July western tour. Matty, helped manfully by his team's bats, raised his record to 17 and 4. When the Giants returned to the Polo Grounds, it seemed obvious the pennant race would occur between them and the Cubs.

The Braves, however, mired deep in the second division on the Fourth of July, by the end of the month had lifted themselves into fourth place. It was heady stuff for the Braves, who had not finished out of the lower division since 1902. Under manager George Stallings, their fifth-place finish in 1912 had been the best in that entire span. (Prior to Stallings's arrival in 1912, they had finished last four straight years.) Like Connie Mack, Stallings wore a suit and tie on the bench. He acted a Southern gentleman off the field; on the field his mouth was as foul, or fouler, than McGraw's. To make the best use of his weak lineup, he regularly played right-handed or left-handed batters according to whether they would face left-handed or right-handed pitching—the strategy, as yet innovative, eventually known as "platooning." His lone star was second baseman Johnny "Crab" Evers, traded from Chicago during the off-season. Stallings's shortstop—and, such was the stuff he had to work with, often his clean-up hitter, with a .246 average on the season with just 33 extra-base hits in 586 at-bats—was young Walter "Rabbit" Maranville. Maranville was Evers's opposite in temperament; he seemed to bring joy, or at least laughter, wherever he went.

The Giants took the first two games of an early August series with Chicago. In the third game Matty yielded two runs in the top of the ninth and lost, 4–3. Meanwhile, Rabbit Maranville's tenth-inning home run against Pittsburgh marked the Braves' ninth consecutive win. By the time the Braves arrived in New York for a three-game series, they had overtaken the Cubs for second place.

"Give me a ballclub of only mediocre ability, and if I can get the players in the right state of mind, they'll beat the world champions," said

George Stallings. "If I'm not a better ball player than that relative of yours [at shortstop], I'll quit," Maranville said to Stallings during their first spring training together. At 5 feet 4 inches and 155 pounds, Maranville let no one intimidate him, unless it was Johnny Evers. Once Jim Thorpe came barreling into second base and Rabbit stood his ground.

"You little shrimp! You blocked me!" Thorpe snarled after the out. He was eight inches taller than Rabbit and had a physique like a Greek god.

"Go back to the dugout, you big ape, before I punch you in the mouth," said Rabbit.

"You sawed off runt!" Thorpe glowered, "I'll kill you for that."

"Yeah? And you're just the guy who can do it," Rabbit snapped back.

Thorpe, so goes the story, trotted off the field grinning.[4]

The Braves won the first two games, cutting the Giants' lead to four-and-a-half. Before 30,000 fans, McGraw sent Matty to burst the Braves' bubble, and Matty dueled nine scoreless innings with George "Lefty" Tyler. In the tenth, Hank Gowdy, whom McGraw had traded to Boston three years previously, tripled a run home. The Giants, in their half of the inning, loaded the bases with none out, but Tyler recovered, with an infield fly and two strikeouts, to maintain the shutout.

About this time Matty gave his name to a magazine article in which he attempted to explain why the Giants had lost three World Series. Only in the case of the 1913 Athletics did he concede that the American League champions had a better team "on paper," though even then he felt the Giant batsmen had faced as tough or tougher pitching in their own league. "The club is McGraw," said Matty. The manager orchestrated all the moves, and the regime obviously worked well enough during the regular season. In the heightened atmosphere of a World Series, however, it seemed to fray nerves. Most of the Giants, said the article, had not the confidence to stand on their own when it seemed only their individual effort might preserve the $30,000 difference between the winners' and losers' shares. After one particularly costly error, Matty recalled the malefactor later confessing: "When I booted that one, I said to myself, 'There goes that new auto I was going to buy.'"[5]

Besides the notorious World Series miscues, Matty described additional blunders such as Fletcher booting an easy play, a wide miss of Murray's normally accurate rifle arm, and Doyle getting duped into a base-running mistake by a ploy as old as the hills. In contrast, he described Connie Mack's men as not only superb athletes but also conditioned to react to situations without strict guidance from the bench. The article may have been intended as both a moneymaker and as a tonic to his teammates, but it could hardly have had a relaxing effect on men who, if they were disposed to fold in a pinch anyway, were now neck-and-neck in a pennant race with a team above whom, on paper, they towered. As candor, the article is a remarkable piece; as balm among athletic egos, it could not have been soothing.

The Giants went nine and nine in the three weeks before they met the Braves again. The Braves went 13 and six. McGraw placed George Wiltse on waivers; no other club claimed him and Hooks looked to the Federal League. Other than McGraw, Matty now remained as the only veteran from the '05 World Champions. During August and early September, mirroring the team as a whole, Matty won only about as many as he lost. Sometimes he pitched as well as he ever did; other times he faltered in ways it seemed he had not before.

The Braves' management painted their ballpark and, while the paint dried, contracted to play the visiting Giants in Fenway. The paint job and rental were more than paid for as the series began with more than 70,000 persons coming to see the morning and afternoon games of a Labor Day double-header. In the morning game Matty took a 4–3 lead into the bottom of the ninth, but, with two men on base, the winning run scored when a low liner from Johnny Evers got by George Burns in left field.

The Giants did romp to a 10–1 victory in the afternoon game, in the course of which Lefty Tyler hit Fred Snodgrass with a pitch. From first base "Snow" thumbed his nose or made some sort of gesture at Tyler. Tyler then pantomimed Snodgrass's famous muff of a fly ball in this same ballpark two years before. When Snodgrass took his position in center field, he made another gesture, this time at the fans. In response the fans threw bottles, and the Giants protested. Boston's new mayor James Curley came onto the field and told umpire Bill Klem that Snodgrass should be removed from the game. Klem declined to take the mayor's advice, though in the ninth inning McGraw did for safety's sake replace Snow with Bob Bescher.

The Giants and Matty had little remaining fire in the belly. The Braves took the pennant by ten-and-a-half games and went on to sweep the Athletics in the World Series. The Giants had to content themselves with a lackluster post-season competition with the Yankees.

Matty put on make-up and appeared before a camera in a Universal Film Company production entitled *The Umpire*. Matty was featured as himself, but, by a magazine description of the story line, that was pretty much where verisimilitude ended. The film does not seem to survive. Ballplayers had become at least somewhat conversant with the money-making engine of motion pictures. Mike Donlin starred in *Right Off the Bat*, a feature film. And the National Commission received annually a nice stipend for the movie rights to the World Series. The players of the 1911 Series balked at not receiving a share of this money, particularly since they had followed management's instruction to pose and otherwise perform for the cameras before each game. The commission responded by inserting into the standard contract a provision requiring a player to lend himself to a certain amount of publicity.[6]

Matty and Jane traveled again in the off-season to Havana with the McGraws. They were the guests of Tillinghast Huston, part-owner of the Yankees. Huston had commanded a company of engineers in the Spanish-American War and, because of his engineering ability as well as the friendship he cultivated with General Leonard Wood, made a fortune in Cuba after the war constructing civil improvements. In keeping company with "Til" Huston, it may have been just as well that Matty's name was no longer included among the leading members of the Players' Fraternity. Huston's paternalistic inclination—and for that matter McGraw's as well, however much he mouthed otherwise—went against the fraternity's grain. When the fraternity sought a charter from the American Federation of Labor, Huston used his influence against it. McGraw said a baseball union would be a fine thing as long as its primary aim was the care of retired players.

Concerning another labor-management issue, in the United States District Court of Northern Illinois—the courtroom of Judge Kenesaw Mountain Landis—the Federal League brought suit against all 16 presidents of the National and American league clubs and the triumvirate members of the National Commission charging them with combination, conspiracy, and monopoly, particularly in regard to their manipulation of the labor of baseball players. The Federal League attorneys must have thought they had chosen the site of their suit wisely, for Judge Landis was not only famous as a trustbuster, but was also known as a baseball fan. (Before becoming a judge, it was told, lawyer Landis once asked for a courtroom postponement so that he could attend a game between Three Finger Brown and Matty.) But, to the Federals' dismay, after the hearing began, Landis expressed dislike of the notion that playing professional baseball was somehow "labor." He warned both sides how far-reaching his decision might be. "Do you realize," he intoned, "that a decision in this case may tear down the very foundations of this game, so loved by thousands?"[7] He urged the opposing parties to reach a settlement while he took the case under advisement. He indicated that he was in no hurry to render a decision, though a decision was what the Federal League most needed so that it might know whether it could survive financially. With a better grip on quality players, the National and American leagues wore down the Federals at an even more vital docket, the turnstile. The Federals eventually settled, and the winning owners would not forget Judge Landis.

In 1914 Matty had won more games than he walked batters. Twenty-four wins, 23 walks, but, with a stellar 17 and 4 record in the latter part of July, he ended the season 24 and 13. McGraw, by his formula, had virtually the required 25 wins from Matty but this time not the pennant. In 1915 Matty's first appearance came in the Giants' fourth game, at the Polo Grounds against the Phillies. He lasted only three innings, giving up four runs, including a first-inning home run by Gavvy Cravath, and at another point walking two consecutive batters. His opponent was Grover Alexander, whose 31 victories would pitch the Phillies to the pennant.

Nearly a month and three starts later, Matty, opposing Cincinnati, took a 6–3 lead into the top of the ninth inning and yielded two more runs before getting the final out, marking his only contribution to his team's seven victories thus far in the season against the three losses credited to him among the club's 14 defeats.

McGraw recognized the need for change. He sent Bob Bescher to St. Louis for pitcher Bill "Pol" Perritt and inserted Dave Robertson to replace Red Murray in right field. McGraw was no longer content with Fred Snodgrass in center, but here he had no replacement. McGraw was convinced, though, that hard-hitting Benny Kauff was the man for the job. Not only could he play ball, Kauff's presumed heritage could answer what the Giant management considered a ticket seller's prayer in a city with one of the largest Jewish populations in the world. The problem was that Kauff already had a three-year commitment to the Federal League, albeit muddied (or so it appeared to those who had an interest in it seeming muddied) by his transfer from Harry Sinclair's Indianapolis franchise to the Brooklyn Tip-Tops. Kauff may have told McGraw that he was not actually signed with the Tip-Tops, and McGraw afterward claimed that Governor Tener encouraged the Giants to pursue Kauff. When Kauff took center field at the Polo Grounds on the last day of April, McGraw found himself in a crossfire between the Federals and his own league. George Stallings, when the expected Kauff made his appearance, had orders not to let his players come to bat. The umpire forfeited the game to New York. Stallings relented to the extent of not disappointing the fans by letting them at least see an exhibition, with Kauff on the bench. The Braves won the game 13–6. Later Governor Tener overruled the umpire and declared the "exhibition" to have been an actual Braves' victory. McGraw was furious, but, as one reporter wrote, "the only things which seem to prevent Benny playing with the Giants are the Constitution of the United States, the traffic rules and regulations, and Hoyle."[8] Kauff was soon back in Brooklyn rapping hits, stealing bases, and collecting sweetened paychecks from the Ward Brothers.

About a week before Kauff trotted onto the outfield grass of the Polo Grounds, far away in France, near Ypres, the Germans lobbed shells of chlorine gas into a four-mile section of line held by French colonial troops. The strange green vapor caused panic among the colonials, who threw down their rifles and fled for the rear. So unexpected and immense was the breach caused by their new weapon that the Germans had not mustered sufficient force to adequately respond to such an opportunity. They were beaten back by Canadians on their flank and by English and Indian troops who arrived to oppose their front. Americans, in the main, clucked at the folly of the war and thanked Providence for having placed an ocean between the New and Old Worlds.

In early July, Matty pitched versus Colby Jack Coombs, their first meeting since the 1911 World Series. Coombs now worked for Wilbert Robinson. For the first seven innings at Ebbets Field, both men showed all the wiles of experience and none of the falling of age. Brooklyn led 1–0 going into the eighth. The magic ended when, with two outs, Matty yielded three consecutive hits, including a triple by Zack Wheat. Coombs preserved his shutout. Writers remarked on the gray edging Matty's blond hair. The Giants were in next-to-last place.

By mid-July the Giants had climbed one notch up the ladder to sixth place, which, at this point in the season, was not yet out of contention, since the league-leading Phillies were just five-and-a-half games ahead of them. If Matty had won only three-quarters of his usual 25-win pace, the team would have been vying for the lead. As it was, even after pitching a shutout of the Cubs on July 16, Matty's record stood at 5 and 6. During the remainder of July he lost three more games. In his first start of August, in St. Louis, Matty began the seventh inning with a 10–0 lead; by the eighth inning the score was 11–9. Tesreau relieved to save it.

Matty was not the only cause of McGraw's frustration. Larry Doyle was hitting the ball well, and a few others were hitting it respectably. The team would, however, make the second highest number of fielding errors in the league. The pitching staff would issue the league's fewest number of walks, but Rube Marquard, having gone 12 and 22 the year before, was winning only about as many as he lost this season—and both of these figures were yet single digits as Rube was failing to pitch deep enough into games for a decision. When the opportunity presented itself, McGraw obtained the contract of another left-handed pitcher, Rube Benton, from Cincinnati. Even with no heir apparent in center field, the manager unconditionally released Fred Snodgrass, who was batting an anemic .191. Snow had no lingering bitterness. "The years I look back at most fondly, and those I'd like most to live over," he said when an old man, "are the years when I was playing center field for the New York Giants."[9]

With the passage of time, Marquard had no bitterness for McGraw either. But not long after the move the acquire Benton—one Rube too many—the 25-year-old (or 28-year-old; biographical research has revealed Marquard was actually three years older than he said he was) found himself placed on waivers. Rube dangled unclaimed by a big-league club until finally Wilbert Robinson decided to take a chance on him with Charles Ebbets's money. Marquard stubbornly and narrowly avoided having to prove himself in the International League before joining Brooklyn and never again won 20 games in a big-league season, but he would pitch well enough to appear as a starter in another two World Series.

Despite all his transactions and tactics, McGraw could not lift his club from the second division. When the team dropped from contention, he lapsed into apathy or worse. McGraw seldom appeared in the coach's box, baited umpires into ejecting him, and, in an ugly incident very late in the season as a last-place finish became a reality, drew a pocketknife on a rowdy fan in Boston.

On August 27 Matty pitched a fine game at the Polo Grounds against the Pirates. He allowed seven hits, one walk, one run, and struck out seven. The 2–1 victory took just one hour and ten minutes to play. It was hit last win of the year. He started and lost three more games, and two relief appearances were inglorious. When he first came to the big leagues, 15 seasons before, he chose New York, a tail-ender club, because he calculated he would have a better chance to pitch there. Five pennants and one world's championship later, he had come to a different opinion. "Traveling with a tail-end club is the poorest pastime in the world," he told Jack Wheeler. "I would rather ride in the first coach of a funeral procession."[10]

In early March 1916, General John J. Pershing with infantry and cavalry pursued Pancho Villa in Mexico. Two hundred miles north of the Rio Grande, the Giants prepared for another campaign of their own. Chief Meyers was gone; he joined Marquard with Brooklyn. The Federal League reached a settlement with Organized Baseball, and not all of the Federal investors were losers. Some received generous compensation, and two eventually joined Organized Baseball ("Mr. O.B." David Fultz liked to call it) as major-league club owners themselves. Besides his $100,000 compensation, Harry Sinclair also dealt the contracts of several Federal players. For $50,000 he sold to the Giants the rights to the baseball services of Benny Kauff, Bill McKechnie, Edd Roush, pitcher Fred Anderson, and catcher Bill Rariden.

Kauff remained a special case. He refused to report to Marlin until he received, besides his regular salary, $5,000 of the purchase price for his contract paid to Sinclair. McGraw saw something in the brash young man that reminded him of the old Orioles. Kauff got the money, not from Sinclair but from the Giants. When he showed up in Texas, Kauff, pockets full of cash, wore expensive clothes and flashy jewelry; he brought a trunkload of bats and a self-proclaimed promise that he was the next Ty Cobb.

Edd Roush arrived less ostentatiously. From small-town Indiana, he did not like New York and he did not like John McGraw; especially he did not like McGraw's manner of cursing at ballplayers. Germany Schaefer, his career at an end as the American League's most whimsical performer, a man whom even Ty Cobb seemed to like, and soon if not already finding employment (wearing his colorful socks and ties) as a scout for the Giants, was, in McGraw's retrospect, the only observer at the time who told the manager that Roush was a better player than Kauff.

Matty's shoulder persistently bothered him—not his right shoulder, but his left one. On a western swing, he visited John "Bonesetter" Reese of Youngstown, Ohio. Not an educated (at least not in the usual sense of the word) physician, the Welsh immigrant, who became an American citizen, had formerly been a steelworker. More than a few ballplayers, Ty Cobb, Eddie Collins, and Honus Wagner among them, came to Reese with their recalcitrant aches and pains which regular doctors could not cure. Reese gave much of his osteopathic-like practice to working-class people in and around Youngstown, but during his long healing career his fame was such that he also treated persons as prominent as Will Rogers and David Lloyd George. Regardless of fame and fortune, he attended his patients on a first-come-first-served basis; the rich and famous had to wait like anyone else. By special resolution, the Ohio medical board declared him a legal physician. Reese told Matty the pain in his left shoulder was actually due to a cracked rib.[11]

Relegated to the coach's box, Matty did not pitch until May 4. By then the team was off to a horrific 2 and 10 start. Matty went the distance against the Braves in this ten-inning game which featured plenty of hits. Fred Merkle tied it in the bottom of the ninth with a home run. In the tenth, Matty surrendered his only walk of the day. The runner advanced when Kauff let a fly ball drop in the outfield, and Hank Gowdy singled home what proved the winning run.

As the Giants experienced a remarkable resurgence, Matty won his first game on May 20, in St. Louis. Only one Cardinal got as far as second base through eight innings; they made a tally in the ninth but could not overcome Matty's four-run lead in what also marked the Giants' tenth straight victory. In Cincinnati Matty saved the Giants' 12th in a row when he relieved in the ninth inning with the tying run on third base, the winning run on first, and one out. The win streak extended to 17 on May 29 when Matty shut out Boston. He had little speed, but his curves broke excellently. The Giants had climbed to second place.

The streak ended the next day in Philadelphia. When the Giants returned to the Polo Grounds from their triumphant road tour, an enthusiastic Friday crowd turned out to see Matty face the Reds. He lasted only three innings as Herzog's team batted him for nine hits, including triples by Heinie Groh, Ivy Wingo, and Hal Chase. In cool 60-degree temperature on June 14, Matty started against the Cubs and lost 4–0 as spitballer Jimmy Lavender threw an imposing one-hitter; all the Cubs' runs scored as the result of errors. A week later, in the rain, Matty relieved Pol Perritt with the score tied against the Braves in the ninth inning. The Braves won it in the tenth on a combination of two singles and a sacrifice fly.

Through the years McGraw had, as a function of his job and sometimes ruthlessly, rid the Giants of players, even crowd favorites, who had outstayed their usefulness in his plans to win pennants. Fans revel in sentiment; managers do not. He had, it is true, found room on his roster for "old" ballplayers like Mike Donlin and Willie Keeler to have a last hurrah or two. But these men were add-ons, and in these cases sentiment was accompanied by good box office. Others, like Joe McGinnity, Frank Bowerman, and Art Devlin, were either released or, so it seemed, offloaded to the Boston Braves. In less than three years only Matty, Doyle, Merkle, Fletcher, Burns, and Tesreau remained as regulars from McGraw's 1913 champions.

Matty had been with the Giants longer than McGraw. No other player had contributed more to the manager's fame and success. No other player, and likely no other man, had more of McGraw's day-to-day respect. With the possible exceptions of Hughie Jennings and formerly Wilbert Robinson, no man was McGraw's closer friend. Though it had become manifest that Matty's great pitching talent was at an end, McGraw was unable to treat him as he would any other ballplayer. McGraw occasionally expressed the thought of Matty one day succeeding him as manager of the Giants. But McGraw was not ready for retirement. He was, after all, just seven years older than Matty, however older he seemed in the flesh. It was, in light of his long subsequent career, against McGraw's grain to go gentle into that good night. Nor was it in his grain to send Matty there.

Garry Herrmann had learned that he did not much like Buck Herzog either, and his team had learned how not to respond to Herzog's hard-driving ways and was, in spite of its manager, nestling cozily in the second division. Herrmann let it be known that Herzog's services were available to other parties. Herzog's personality notwithstanding, McGraw was willing to take him back. Herzog could still play the infield every day with a peppery style and had been undeniably instrumental in three Giant pennants (and would also be a regular on a Giant pennant-winning team again); he also represented the answer to McGraw's dilemma regarding Matty. With Herzog gone, the Reds would need a manager. McGraw told Herrmann that he could have Matty, provided he signed him to a three-year managerial contract for at least $10,000 per annum. Herrmann had not prospered in baseball and Ohio politics without knowing how to trade. The Reds additionally acquired Edd Roush and Bill McKechnie. The Giants received Herzog and outfielder Wade Killefer.

The trade is almost invariably included in lists of the most lopsided trades in baseball history. This may be rightly so, but only if McGraw's friendship for Matty is discounted. The transaction should also be viewed as an exception to the overall rule that baseball business is conducted without more than a manipulative regard for sentiment.[12]

The deal was agreed upon while the Giants were in Chicago. Matty traveled by train to Cincinnati with Roush and McKechnie, who both chirped how happy they were to get out from under McGraw. Matty listened but said nothing, until Roush asked Matty if he, too, was not glad to get away.

"I'll tell you something, Roush," Matty said according to Roush's recollection many years later, "you and Mac have only been on the Giants a couple of months. It's just another ball club to you fellows. But I was with that team for sixteen years. That's a mighty long time. To me, the Giants are 'home.' And leaving them like this, I feel the same as when I leave home in the spring of the year."

Matty went on to express to Roush his appreciation that McGraw obtained for him a manager's job. "He's doing me a favor, and I thanked him for it. And by the way, the last thing he said to me was that if I put you in center field I'd have a great ballplayer. So starting tomorrow you're my center fielder."[13]

9

CINCINNATI

In the summer of 1916, Matty had more on his mind than the end of his pitching career and assuming the managerial reins of the Cincinnati Reds. His brother Henry had contracted tuberculosis and gone to Arizona, near Uncle Al and Aunt Kit, to recover. Henry's wife Marie remained in New York City caring for their four daughters. Marie and the eldest girl, named for Henry's mother, had consumptive symptoms as well; so much so the girl could hardly walk to school. The stalwart Baptist heart of Minerva Mathewson must have felt compassion for her Irish Catholic daughter-in-law when Marie wrote plaintively of her child's illness and her own nervousness and loss of weight. "I've always been a good wife and mother," Marie said. "I don't know what I've done to deserve this."[1]

Henry slept in a tent and focused on the future. The Arizona air seemed to offer hope. He became interested in homesteading a sheep ranch and urged his father to come west so that, together, they could claim a larger acreage. He suspected Jane Mathewson resented the financial help Matty gave to members of his family, but there was no one else to whom Henry could turn. Matty agreed to help with money once Henry got better.

The Reds lost their first game under Matty, in ten innings against the Phillies. Rain dampened the occasion, but the 2,500 persons in attendance represented one of Cincinnati's larger mid-week draws in a long time. Fans gave Matty an ovation during the pre-game practice when he hit fungoes to the outfielders, and they gave him another ovation when he brought the lineup card to the umpire. Edd Roush, playing center, tied the game in the bottom of the ninth with a triple that scored two runs, but he was out at the plate trying to stretch the three-bagger into a home run.

Reds' left fielder Earle "Greasy" Neale was not pleased with Matty's positioning of Roush; he saw center field as more properly his own venue.

When Roush called for a ball, Neale—who earned his nickname for eluding tacklers as a running back at West Virginia Wesleyan—would, without a word, keep right on running toward his teammate. Matty let the two proud young men work it out between themselves. Roush learned how to follow the flight of the ball and keep track of Neale at the same time. Eventually Neale came around. "I want to end this, Roush," he said one day. "I want to shake hands and call it off. From now on, I'll holler."[2]

The middle infield was weak, but the corners were anchored by Hal Chase and Heinie Groh. Chase was still one of the slickest fielding first basemen in the majors—that is, as it was gossiped, when he wanted to be—and this year he was hitting his way to a batting championship as well. Ivy Wingo led the league in sacrifice flies and errors by a catcher. Pete Schneider, a lantern-jawed right-hander from California, turned 21 in this, his third big-league season; he showed enough promise that, during these three years, he was allowed to lose 51 games against a little over half as many victories. Another right-hander, 28-year-old Fred Toney from Tennessee, was so strong it was said he could lift more weight than any two of his teammates, but he had not proven yet that his pitching could win consistently.

Bad weather postponed the series opener when the Reds came to New York. In the rain Matty drove his car from his home on St. Nicholas Place to the Polo Grounds. He entered the Giants' clubhouse and began cleaning out his locker. His former teammates, lounging in their underwear, pretended to take little notice; then three or four of them set up a game of *vingt-et-un* around a plain pine table.

"All right," said Larry Doyle, "get that locker straightened out and sit down with us for a few minutes. We'd like to have you lose one more time before you go."[3]

The next day, a Wednesday, beneath a dark, dismal sky and before 12,000 fans, a horde of moving-picture cameramen recorded Matty's every move. He did not appear to like it. His request that there be no presentation of flowers was disregarded, but he remained adamant that he would give no speech. The Reds for the remainder of the season approached losing twice as many games as they won for their new manager, but this day they pulled out a victory, 4–2.

Mordecai Brown announced that he would pitch the final game of his career on Labor Day in Chicago. It would only be his fourth start of the season, and it just so happened the Reds would be in town. The challenge to Matty was implicit. The Reds were going nowhere, the interest might spark the team, and the enhanced visitors' share of the gate receipts would be appreciated by Garry Herrmann. Matty accepted Brown's challenge with plenty of time for the event to be publicized. Not only that, both men let it be known they intended to pitch complete games.

It was not a pitchers' duel in the usual sense of the term. After five innings the Reds led 6–5. True to their word, neither man would depart. By the time he walked from the mound in the ninth inning, Brown had surrendered 19 hits and trailed by five runs. Chicago's largest crowd of the year gave him a standing ovation. The Cubs rallied for three runs before Matty got the next-to-last out he needed; thus far on the day he had yielded 13 hits, a walk, and a wild pitch, besides obtaining three strikeouts. Manager Joe Tinker sent Fritz Mollwitz to pinch-hit. Mollwitz represented the tying run; he popped out.

"Boys, I thought I could pitch a few more games, but I find I haven't got the stuff any more," Matty said in the clubhouse afterward. "If I ever go into the box again, I will buy every one of you a suit of clothes."[4]

After the season Matty remained in New York long enough to vote in the presidential election. Presumably he cast a Republican ballot. The Republican candidate, the respected jurist and former New York governor Charles Evans Hughes, was, like Matty, the scion of a Baptist upbringing and education. The Democratic incumbent's slogan, "He kept us out of war," proved too persuasive for Hughes to overcome, and Woodrow Wilson was returned for a second term. William Phelon, the bespectacled, balding, and bow-tied Cincinnati sportswriter, who did not believe rooting for the home team interfered with good writing, was anxious to report the actual moving of the Mathewson household to the Queen City, but, prior to attending the league's December meeting in New York, Matty went hunting instead.[5]

At the meeting, held at the Waldorf-Astoria, Matty maintained his reputation as a clotheshorse with suits described as at least a year or two ahead of convention. He soon, if not already, began wearing an elegant white hat that became an off-the-field trademark during his sojourn in Cincinnati. Taller than most men to begin with, the hat served as an attention-attracting beacon. Autograph seekers, though, approached Matty at their peril. "I owe everything I have to them when I'm out on the mound," he once explained to Grantland Rice, "but I owe the fans nothing and they owe me nothing when I am not pitching." This hauteur lessened considerably after Matty entered management and his middle years, and always applied more to adults than youngsters. Jane remembered fondly that, when she and her husband went for Sunday drives in their open-air automobile, boys often added to the occasion by joyously running alongside. And once, during a train stop to change locomotives in Erie, Pennsylvania, a schoolteacher brought 40 boys to the station just for a look at the famous hero. Matty was engaged in cards with teammates at the time. When he heard of the schoolboys, he interrupted the game to step onto the platform to speak to them and to shake their hands.[6]

Matty and Jane about the time he became manager of the Reds in 1903. (National Baseball Hall of Fame Library, Cooperstown, N.Y.)

The Reds' organization was without the services of a single scout, and Matty made sure that void was filled with the hiring of Larry Sutton, a veteran at the trade. Matty's starting outfielders were all left-handed hitters; he hoped to augment them by acquiring right-handed slugger Sherry Magee from Boston. Magee was anxious to leave the Braves, especially after the Braves' management insisted that he take a salary cut, but George Stallings wanted too much in return from the Reds to complete a deal. Matty also heard, as did many others, that Cardinals' manager Miller Huggins had been instructed by owner Helene Britton to put every player on the trading block except Rogers Hornsby. "Hug" was too discerning an employee to thwart Mrs. Britton openly, but, when Matty sat down with Huggins at the league meeting to discuss trades, the Reds' manager learned that more Cardinals than just Hornsby were not available.[7]

Matty did not attend in January the National Commission meeting in Cincinnati, hosted by Garry Herrmann, though the thick-accented Herrmann was famous for his German hospitality served with beer and homemade sausage. The meeting became preoccupied with David Fultz's threatening statement that he had secured the pledges of a large number of major leaguers not to sign their 1917 contracts until certain demands of the Players' Fraternity were met. The demands for the most part were designed to improve the lot of minor-league and fringe major-league players. To sensibilities of a later day, the demands do not seem unreasonable—such as full payment of salary to an injured player and payment of expenses of invited players to and from spring training. But Organized Baseball successfully portrayed Fultz as a "professional agitator," and the dispute became seen in the pubic eye as mere salary ploy on the part of the big leaguers. Herrmann secured Matty's endorsement to the recommendation that players should sign their contracts, get in line, and forget the fraternity pie-in-the-sky. Players themselves did not help their cause much either, as when Heinie Groh said that he would sign his Reds' contract as soon as his own terms were satisfactory. The player revolt never amounted to anything, and as a result the fraternity lost credibility and faded away.[8]

In early March, 1917, 13 Reds departed by train from Cincinnati for Shreveport, Louisiana, the spring training site. Matty laughed at the notion of "thirteen hoodoo," but Billy Phelon, traveling with the club, worried about the inauspicious number as the weather got rainier and colder the farther south they went. Stepping from the train in Shreveport, Matty was greeted by Chase, Groh, and outfielder Tom Griffith. The manager kidded with veterans and talked like a Dutch uncle to the recruits; he spoke affably to everyone else and avoided making predictions. Matty decreed two practices a day: at ten A.M. and two P.M. He planned to leave spring training with an economical 20-man roster: seven regulars, two utility men, three catchers, and eight pitchers. He resurrected a sharp-fielding second baseman named Dave Shean, not in the big leagues since 1912. Two years older than Matty, Shean had been playing for Providence in the International League. A college man from New

England, Shean did not mind prolonging his youth in Rhode Island; he did not mind another chance in the major leagues, either, and would win the job as the Reds' second baseman.[9]

Matty conducted training differently than John McGraw. Running merely for the sake of running became de-emphasized. "Anybody can keep in condition if he wants to," Matty said. "The main thing is to be ambitious and earnest. The rest will take care of itself."[10] The sliding pit was a less important place than it was for the Giants, and when intrasquad games began it was obvious that Matty wanted a bunting game to complement or supersede the hit-and-run. Matty believed Chase was the only bona fide hit-and-run batsman the Reds had; the Giants, he remarked, had five. Three pitchers threw batting practice so that the hitters would see a variety of deliveries, but the manager also warned Hod Eller, trying to make the big league after five years in the minors, not to throw so many curves this early.

In what would become for the Reds' organization another rite of spring, Edd Roush had not yet joined the team. It was part salary ploy, and part opportunity to hunt quail and rabbits and get his Indiana farm planted. Roush, however, by now had to appreciate Matty's most pronounced counterpoint from McGraw: Matty did not yell or berate. Matty put the players on their individual honor. It did not matter, he told them, if they drank, smoked, or kept late hours. All he would do is hold them to the condition that they give their best on the field.

One day, as Fred Toney reached second base during a practice game, a gray-and-white kitten scampered toward him from center field. Someone bobbled the ball and Toney ran to third. "T. Cat," as Phelon put it, advanced with him and Toney was called out, for interfering with the substitution of T. Cat as a base runner. The next inning Toney pitched with the kitten on his shoulder.[11]

The combination of U-boat menace, inept German propaganda, and the interception of a German diplomatic telegram encouraging Mexico to declare war on the United States made American involvement in the European bloodshed ever more likely. Tillinghast Huston, in patriotic fervor and remembering all that the last American war had done for him, had the inspired notion to instruct his Yankee ballplayers in military drill, with bats in lieu of rifles. He persuaded Ban Johnson to institute military practice for all American League clubs. Johnson offered a $500 prize to the best-drilled team. The U.S. Army lent drill sergeants for the purpose, and fans saw drill competitions, lasting as long as 15 minutes, before games. Late in the season a lieutenant colonel officially judged the St. Louis Browns as the best-drilled team in the league.

"What's the use of military training for ball players?" groused Frank Bancroft, the Reds' business manager and a 70-year-old Civil War veteran who had been a big-league, on-field manager the same year Matty was born. "If it took them as long to enlist as it does to sign contracts, the war would be all over before they could start for the front."[12] The previous spring the Reds had lost six of eight games against what must have been a very proud local Shreveport team; this year the Reds fared much better against the locals and on March 24 left Shreveport in high spirits.

En route north the Reds were joined, temporarily, by Ty Cobb. In Texas, the Giants and Tigers had begun a series of exhibition games during which the Giants mercilessly rode Cobb as a privileged character. Cobb, in response and just as mercilessly, slid hard into second base with Buck Herzog covering. One thing led to another and later a fight erupted in a hotel; Cobb pummeled Herzog until the two men were separated. The Detroit outfielder refused to participate in any more games with the Giants. Hughie Jennings came to his star's defense: "I know there are three men—Herzog, Zimmerman and Fletcher—on McGraw's infield who would say or do something in the heat of the game that Cobb would have to resent with his fists or feel that he had not been a man."[13] When the exhibition series was over, the Giant players sent Cobb a sarcastic telegram saying that they were gone now and he was safe to rejoin his team. Cobb raged that they would not have dared such an insult to his face, but he was grateful to Matty for having extended a welcome to train with the Reds and an opportunity, however awkward, to save face. (Though he was no longer with the team, no one's name, other than McGraw's, was so closely associated with the Giants as Matty's; therefore no man could truly be humiliated by the Giants if Matty accepted him.) Cobb seems to have genuinely regarded Matty with respect; he liked connecting his name with Matty's, and, judging from his autobiography, considered himself as having been Matty's friend.

President Wilson asked for and Congress declared war in early April. That did not daunt the spirits of more than 20,000 persons from in and around Cincinnati who in summerlike weather thronged to opening day in one of the most German of American cities. Immigration made Cincinnati almost bilingual. Until the war changed things, German was taught as a second language in all public and parochial schools. Bill Phelon marveled at the paid attendance at Redland Field: "Strange, isn't it, that Cincinnati, one of the smallest cities in the big league circuit, can turn out the biggest crowds on opening day." He described the game itself as "one of the niftiest that I remember seeing in 27 years of opening games. The Reds played on defense as if inspired.... The Cardinals hit savagely ... yet got only four safe ones."[14] Pete Schneider earned a complete-game victory.

The Reds returned the opening-day favor by journeying to St. Louis, out-hitting the Cardinals, stranding 16 of their own base runners, and losing 4–1. From St. Louis, Matty was called back to Cincinnati when Christy Junior was stricken by appendicitis. Hal Chase was left in charge. Christy Junior recovered. But in Factoryville the prognosis concerning Matty's brother was not good. Henry had returned from Arizona to die; he lay in the parlor of his parents' home with cheeks so sunken it seemed apples could have been placed in them.[15]

Bill McKechnie suffered a broken hand, and outfielder Tom Griffith underwent a tonsillectomy besides coping with lingering arm trouble. To compensate, the Reds obtained Jim Thorpe from the Giants. Though he was a right-handed slugger, the acquisition of Thorpe did not solve Matty's problem of a shortage in power from the right side. Thorpe's bat, anomalously, was potent against lefties but not particularly formidable against righties—the word was out that the world's greatest athlete could not hit a right-handed curveball. It was apparent by now that Thorpe would never become a top-echelon baseball player, but his effort was so earnest, even when he ended a rally or muffed a fly ball, that players and fans alike supported him.

Greasy Neale, for a time, played center field again after Roush injured his leg. When the Reds went to Cincinnati in early May, Cubs' manager Fred Mitchell hoped the cold weather might work to the further disadvantage of his hurting opposition. Before just 3,500 fans, Fred Toney and another big man, James "Hippo" Vaughn, both pitched nine innings of no-hit baseball in the same game. The Reds' Larry Kopf on the season would make nearly 18 more errors than any other shortstop in the league, but this day he and his mates fielded all their chances flawlessly. As batters, though, the Reds got only one ball beyond the infield in the first nine innings. (In fact, at that point the Reds had gone 33 consecutive innings without scoring a run.) Thanks to double plays, Vaughn faced just 27 batters through those nine innings, and he appeared to get stronger as the game went on, obtaining the final two outs in both the eighth and ninth by strikeouts.

Larry Doyle and Fred Merkle now played for the Cubs. (McGraw had traded Doyle for Heinie Zimmerman, and Merkle arrived in Chicago by way of Brooklyn.) In the top of the tenth with one out, Kopf singled to right, just beyond second baseman Doyle's reach. Greasy Neale flied out. Then Hal Chase reached first base when the center fielder dropped the ball, Kopf advancing to third on the error. That brought Jim Thorpe to the plate. Chase stole second, but the Cubs were more concerned with the man on third. Thorpe glanced a pitch off his bat, between the plate and the mound. Vaughn retrieved the ball, but Thorpe's speed seemed to preclude the out at first base; so the pitcher tossed the ball to his catcher, another former Giant, Art Wilson. The ball got away from Wilson as Kopf crashed into him and scored. In the bottom of the inning, Merkle nearly tied the game once again when he launched a long ball to left, but Manuel Cueto, a utility player from Cuba, raced back and made the catch against the wall.

Matty's managerial woes nonetheless continued. His left-handed starter Clarence Mitchell pitched so poorly but hit so well that Matty did not lack for well-meaning advice to put Mitchell in the outfield. Roush and Griffith returned to duty, but Jimmy Ring, a pitching newcomer with talent, was hobbled by an infected foot. Journeyman pitcher Elmer Knetzer developed a bad shoulder and was released. Foul tips damaged the foot of reserve catcher Tom Clarke. At times Matty was down to about 15 effectives, with a penurious board of directors behind him not likely to reinforce his roster by purchasing additional contracts. Bill Phelon marveled at all the ways the Reds lost: They could not make or stop a squeeze play; they could not make or stop a double steal; they could not make or stop a hit-and-run; they could not hit or even bunt when needed; and they could not lift a sacrifice with a man on third. On the bright side, Phelon said, the pitching of Toney and Schneider deserved better.

By early June the Reds were in next-to-last place. In Cincinnati, three days following the June 5 date when all American males between the ages of 18 and 45 were obligated to register for the draft, John McGraw got into a post-game, physical altercation with umpire Bill Byron. During the verbal portion of the argument, Byron made a crack that McGraw had been run out of Baltimore before he came to New York. McGraw warned him not to say such a thing again. Byron, of course, did. Groundskeeper Matty Schwab tried to separate the two antagonists and was knocked down for his trouble by Giants' catcher Bill Rariden. McGraw was hustled to the visitors' clubhouse, and Byron went to the umpires' dressing room with blood streaming down his face. The incident cost McGraw a steep fine, a suspension, and, because he could not leave bad enough alone with league president Tener, plenty of unflattering publicity. For his part Rariden sent Schwab an apologetic letter and offered to buy him a new shirt.

Dave Shean split open a thumb on the spikes of a sliding base runner. Loose-jointed pitcher Scott Perry, obtained from the Cubs early in the season and who, Fred Mitchell said, needed an osteopath every time he fielded a bunt, failed to impress Matty and was let go. The Reds' overall pitching, however, began to approach the creditable. Even Clarence Mitchell won some games. The Reds' bats came alive as well and, over just a few weeks, the team's hitting average rose 25 points. In the latter part of June, the team began its longest road trip of the season by taking three out of five in St. Louis and then proceeded to take five of seven from Pittsburgh, bringing the Reds' record to 36 and 37.

The games with Pittsburgh were concluded with a junket to Cincinnati where the absence of a blue law permitted a Sunday double-header on July 1. That same day word came of Henry Mathewson's death at age 30. When they became orphans, Henry and Marie's four daughters were raised for the most part by Marie's family in New York City; the girls were sent for their summers to Factoryville. The sickly Minerva would not live beyond her 12th birthday. Grace, the next daughter, would remember her Uncle Christy driving her and her sisters in his big car to the train station in New York so that they could go to stay at the homes of their grandmother and Aunt Christine. In Factoryville, the elder pair of girls usually went to one home while the younger pair, Helen and Regina, went to the other. The girls called their six-foot-tall Aunt Christine "Aunt Teenie," and became acquainted with store owner George Walton, the only Factoryville man with whom their famous uncle would toss a baseball when he came to visit. In her parlor Grandmother Minerva, as she had done in raising her own children, made sure her granddaughters practiced on the melodeon; Grace remembered her grandmother tapping the top of her head with a spoon and saying "Practice, Grace, practice!" Grandmother Minerva also extracted temperance pledges from her granddaughters. At harvest time the healthy girls were expected to take a place with others employed by their grandparents in the orchard behind the Mathewson house, picking cherries at two cents a quart. The grandmother kept careful tally of, and accepted no stems in, the pickers' baskets.[16]

The Reds climbed to second place. "Not in many, many seasons has a Cincinnati team toured with such dazzling success,"[17] enthused Bill Phelon. Twenty-nine-year-old Mike Regan, getting his first opportunity in the majors, out-pitched and probably would have three times beaten Grover Alexander had not his teammates let two of those games slip away. Roush, Groh, and Chase were hitting the ball at a .300 clip or better. Roush would conclude the season by leading the league with a .341 average; Chase trailed off to .277.

When the Braves came to Cincinnati, Hank Gowdy slipped away to his hometown Columbus and enlisted in the Ohio National Guard; Gowdy would see his share of combat in the war. Eddie Grant and Moose McCormick, at the army camp in Plattsburgh, New York, commenced training to become officers in the expeditionary force to fight in France. Jack Wheeler entrusted the business of his increasingly successful syndicated news service to others while he became an artillery supply officer. Another newspaper friend of Matty's, Grantland Rice, enlisted at age 37 as an infantry private.

By early August the team dropped to fourth place. The fall of Rome had nothing on the Reds, Phelon lamented. George Stallings finally placed Sherwood Magee on waivers. Matty knew Magee as a prickly personality and a powerful hitter, with a batting style not unlike that of Honus Wagner. Magee's former manager, Billy Murray of the Phillies, described him as a slugger willing and able to sacrifice himself with a high one deep in order to get a runner from third to home. (Murray's argument in behalf of Magee was instrumental in bringing about, in 1908, an important rule change that a sacrifice fly should not be charged against a hitter as a time at bat.) Matty still wanted a right-handed hitting outfielder capable of performing more dependably than Jim Thorpe. The Reds assumed Magee's contract; Thorpe went back to the Giants.[18]

Tillinghast Huston announced, not for the last time, that he was considering selling his interest in the Yankees. One thing Huston did for sure was rejoin the army; by the war's end he would be called "Colonel," just like Jacob Ruppert. When Fred Toney won his 20th game, he earned a $1,000 bonus as stipulated in his contract. In the other major league, the White Sox's Eddie Cicotte neared 30 victories and, it was said, a $10,000 bonus promised him, if he reached that plateau, by club president Charles Comiskey. Cicotte missed his last few starts of the season supposedly to rest his arm for the World Series.[19]

Magistrate Francis X. McQuade had a celebrated pair appear before him in his Manhattan courtroom. The Giant organization, happy to flout the state's blue law in so worthy a cause, hosted an official league game with the Reds on Sunday, August 19, with the proceeds to benefit the charity fund of the 165th Infantry Regiment, comprised largely of city men, and known better by its former designation as the "Fighting 69th." Two thousand uniformed soldiers sat among the good-sized crowd, and club secretary John Foster announced that the paid attendance, after expenses, netted $25,000 for the regiment. The Giant organization was not entirely displeased when police felt obligated to arrest the respective managers of the clubs involved. McGraw was used to controversy, but who better to demonstrate what Organized Baseball considered the inherent benignity of Sunday contests than Matty himself, who, now that he was a manager, dressed and acted the part seven days a week, when scheduled on the big-league level, and thus could be described as a convert. (Branch Rickey, when manager of the St. Louis Browns and later as manager of the Cardinals, had Burt Shotton stand in for him on the Christian Sabbath.) Magistrate McQuade, who once had accompanied the Giants to Marlin for spring training, dismissed the charges against McGraw and Matty and instead praised them for what he described as a patriotic gesture.[20]

With a different sort of motive, the Reds continued the long-accepted practice of performing exhibitions on open dates. On a Sunday in Jersey City, with Matty absent, minor leaguers shut out the Reds

8–0. So poorly did the Reds perform that the Jersey City management refused to pay without an argument the visitors' share of the receipts. With Matty present for the next exhibition, the team behaved better. Their reputation, however, preceded them to other places. In Clarksville, West Virginia, for example, local promoters balked at the paid guarantee when they learned that regulars Roush, Chase, Wingo, and others would not appear.[21]

In early September the Reds absorbed eight straight losses, yet held tenuously to the first division by a half game. They finished the season in fourth place with a 78 and 76 record. It was their best winning percentage since 1905. The team won an Ohio series with the Cleveland Indians in six games. It was not a lucrative championship; the winners reportedly earned just $157 each.

The Mathewsons resided in Cincinnati at the Alms Hotel. Matty sold Liberty Bonds in and around the city and reportedly invested heavily in the bonds himself; Hal Chase and Jim Thorpe accompanied him on some of his sales appearances, and he was said to have persuaded Max Fleischmann, on the Reds' board of directors, to buy $50,000 worth. Prior to leaving in mid–November for a hunting excursion in Kentucky, Matty was seen afternoons wearing his white hat at a local race track. He chatted with fans and professed little success as a bettor. "You can almost depend on what a rabbit or squirrel will do," he said, "but I am positive that no man living can tell what a horse will do. For 27 days I have tried my fortunes at the track, and on 25 days out of the 27 I finished with my face on the floor."[22]

Bill Phelon saw a headline, "Reds Parley with Germany," and played with it; he attributed, for one of his columns, denials from Red players. "I wouldn't have time to parley with Berlin even if I wanted to, and I don't," Edd Roush supposedly remarked from his farm. From Hal Chase: "Absolute misstatement, as far as I know. Nothing to it." In light of the war effort, the National League considered limiting their rosters to 18 players. Matty resolved not to worry about the effects of the draft on his team; Chase and Magee were too old, and the younger players were mostly family men with little ones. It was assumed Fred Toney's wife and other members of his family were dependent on his $5,000 salary. "If my government will show me some way that my people can be taken care of, I am ready to go to war tomorrow," Toney said. It became alleged, however, that not only had Toney not lived with his wife for the past three years, she had an independent income of $50 a month as a telephone operator, and that a member of Toney's local draft board had assisted him in perpetrating his fraud.[23]

Bill McKechnie was dealt to the Pirates for cash. Matty thought he made an improvement at second base by obtaining Lee Magee from the

Yankees. No relation to Sherwood, "Magee" was easier to pronounce than "Hoernschemeyer." (Dave Shean, whom Magee replaced, in this year of war, secured a place on the Red Sox roster, and a starting role in the 1918 World Series.) The Hal Chases also made their home in Cincinnati. Just a few days prior to departure for spring training, Mrs. Chase was injured by an automobile as she was crossing a street on a foggy evening. Chase was out of town and did not learn of the accident until some hours later.[24]

John McGraw and Long Larry McLean had an ugly falling out in 1915 which resulted in McLean's exile from major league baseball. Two winters later McLean pleaded with Matty to give him a chance with the Reds. "If you sign me, I will start to train right now and I won't take a drink during the season. Furthermore I would want everybody in America to know that I was on the wagon," McLean said during their long talk. Matty broached the subject in a letter to Garry Herrmann. "McLean is younger than Hal Chase and ought to have three years or more of good baseball in him—*if* he would train." Matty described McLean as easy to manage when not drinking and possibly a good value for a small salary. "I know he would sign with me for considerably less than $2,500. If you want me to tackle the job—I am neutral—let me know at your earliest convenience."[25] Herrmann apparently demurred. In 1921 McLean died in a barroom brawl in Boston.

Matty and members of the team left Cincinnati by a night train on March 10 for Montgomery, Alabama, to which place the Reds' ownership had been persuaded by the local chamber of commerce to conduct spring training. The players stayed at the Exchange Hotel and had locker-room facilities at the YMCA. They could hardly complain. When Matty's entourage arrived, they were greeted by a military band from the nearby army training camp. Thousands of soldiers watched the Reds' daily practice sessions. Camp Sheridan had within its ranks as many as 30 professional ballplayers from various leagues and sent teams to compete with the Reds. Phelon rated the caliber of competition as double A. A chaplain coached one squad; recent big-leaguer Ralph Sharman coached another. Hard dirt infields and chill winds hampered training, though the reception accorded the team by the soldiers and local populace remained warm and cordial throughout. The team then journeyed to Texas to engage Hughie Jennings's Tigers in an exhibition series northward. Against this competition the Reds' two main weaknesses became obvious: the inability to hit a long ball and starting pitching.

The federal court for middle Tennessee would not convene until September. Meanwhile, Fred Toney, out-of-shape but available to pitch, was free on bond facing three separate indictments: violation of the Selective Service Act; violation of the Mann Act, known also as the white slavery law; and conspiracy with one Gladys Strange to violate the Mann Act. Pete Schneider once again got the opening day nod and responded with a one-hit gem against the Pirates. War or no war, 19,000 persons came to Redland Field to inaugurate the season.

Grover Alexander enlisted in the army. From the Reds so did pitcher Mike Regan. The way he figured it, Regan said, democracy would be the prevailing religion of the world when the war was over and that even England would have to admit it for Ireland. The director of YMCA athletic activities for the troops in France sent a public plea for Matty to resign as manager of the Reds and take charge of the recreational baseball forces "over there." Matty was non-committal, even coy, on the idea. Johnny Evers eventually took the YMCA assignment.[26]

In early June the Lee Magee trade looked like a good one. Magee fielded second base magnificently and led the team in batting and baserunning. Toney and Rube Bressler, combined, achieved an 11 and 1 record. The rest of the pitching staff, though, were losing more games than otherwise. "In every defeat," Bill Phelon remarked, "the Reds looked stronger than their conquerors and it was infuriating to the fans to see games dubbed away by blunders mixed with pop flies and failure to take advantage of hits."[27] Greasy Neale drew a league suspension for throwing a punch at a Cub player, three Reds were disabled by injuries, and Chase was described as "indisposed." The team began an eastern swing with just 14 available men, and with nearly 50 games played not one Red had yet hit a home run. (In the American League, Red Sox pitcher and sometime outfielder Babe Ruth would hit 11 home runs by season's end.) Even so, the team kept its record at or slightly better than .500, good enough for third place.

President Wilson ordered the Provost Marshal, General Enoch Crowder, to enforce the Work or Fight Law which required all able-bodied men between the ages of 21 and 31 to either find employment in an essential industry or join the military. Actors and movie-house piano players were among those exempted. Baseball players were not, although Secretary of War Newton Baker gave them until September 1 of the shortened season to make their plans. (Baker extended it further for the players involved in the World Series.) From the Braves, Rabbit Maranville joined the Navy. From the White Sox, Joe Jackson and Claude "Lefty" Williams went to work at a shipyard; their teammate, 31-year-old Eddie Collins, married and a father, joined the Marines.

In the latter part of June, the Reds dropped 10 of 11 games and plummeted to sixth place. At the Polo Grounds, in the final game of an eastern swing, the Giants scored eight runs on nine hits as the Reds made one run on ten hits. Bill Phelon wrote, "They used to say that Buck Herzog's driving methods ruined the team and took the life out of the players—and now it looks as though the mild and courteous ways of Mathewson [have not] received the appreciation that should have been accorded..." Phelon went on to say: "The Red system of machine work and aggression is totally worthless, radically wrong. It gets the hits and then gets no runs. It leaves the bases crowded, game after game. It develops nothing, it amounts to nothing. Other clubs have fun with the Reds by using the bunt and the squeeze and the double steal. The Reds fail to have fun with any of the other clubs."[28]

In Cincinnati, on Sunday, July 14, Hal Chase attended a Presbyterian church service. Three days later Chase approached Pol Perritt and asked him which of the two games scheduled that day he would be pitching for the visiting Giants. Perritt replied that he did not know yet. "I wish you'd tip me off," Chase allegedly said, "because if I know which game you'll pitch and can connect before game time you will have nothing to fear." League gossip had been thick for weeks that Chase was skewing odds and fixing games, and his untimely miscues on the field were causing friction with Red pitchers. Perritt inferred from Chase's remark just such a connotation, warned Chase to stay away from him, and reported the exchange to his manager, John McGraw. After the incident became known publicly, McGraw offered that Chase may have been kidding Perritt: "He is a practical joker and says many things he doesn't mean."[29]

The incident might have remained unknown to the public had not, a week later when the Reds came to Boston, James Costello, a gambler, met with Chase and Lee Magee about a proposition to throw a game against the Braves. According to sworn testimony later given by Costello, Chase and Magee each placed a $500 bet on the Braves to win and assured the gambler that they had "fixed" starting pitcher Pete Schneider. But Sherry Magee went to Schneider with some sort of warning, and Schneider in turn went to Matty and said he did not want to pitch that day, at least not in the first game of the double-header. Matty started Hod Eller instead. The game went 13 innings as Eller, on the mound throughout, pitched a four-hitter. With two outs in the top of the 13th and the score knotted at two runs apiece, Lee Magee nubbed a ball toward shortstop Johnny Rawlings, Rabbit Maranville's wartime replacement; the ball took a bad hop and broke Rawlings' nose. Magee found himself on first base, worrying about the $500 check he had given Costello.

The next batter, Edd Roush, launched a shot into the deep expanse of the Braves' outfield. With Roush barreling around the basepaths for an inside-the-park home run, Magee had little choice but to score. Afterward Magee stopped payment on his check to Costello. Chase let his $500 stand and may have paid some of what Magee "welshed." Costello hung on to Magee's no-good check in case later it should come in handy.[30]

Heavy betting continued to attend the Reds. Opposing players taunted Chase: "Well, Hal, what are the odds today?" The situation could not have been a surprise to Matty. When Jimmy Ring, a year previously, first came to the big league, Matty sent him into a game in Philadelphia as a relief pitcher with the score tied and two runners on base. As Ring prepared to face his first batter, Chase ambled over. "I've got some money bet on this game and there is something in it for you if you lose," Ring related him saying. Ring looked at the 14-year veteran and told him to get away. The newcomer escaped the inning with no more damage but eventually lost the game by one run. The next morning in the hotel lobby, Chase approached Ring where he was sitting and wordlessly dropped $50 into his lap. Ring, who credited Matty with changing his grip on the ball so that he could develop a real major-league curve, went to his manager with what had happened. Matty had faith in the honesty of the young pitcher, but he let the incident lie like a sleeping dog. Now the dog joined the pack of rumors circulating the league.[31]

Greasy Neale had enough. In a practice session at Ebbets Field, Lee Magee seemed to deliberately throw a ball past Neale. Not long later a fist fight between the two men erupted near the bench. The faster and stronger Neale was too much for Magee, and none of the Red players intervened to break up the one-sided contest. Finally Wilbert Robinson and some of his players came over to stop it. Magee looked considerably battered, and Manuel Cueto replaced him in the lineup for the next several days. Matty was not present when Neale and Magee fought, but finally he had enough too. Soon thereafter Chase and his .301 batting average were suspended indefinitely. "Indifferent playing" was rather hopefully given out as an explanation. The Reds responded by taking a double-header from the Giants. It was August 7 and these marked the Reds' first victories in New York all season. The weather was exceedingly hot that day at the Polo Grounds. But umpire Charles Rigler appeared chilled and stunned when, after he called a Reds runner out in the ninth inning of the first game, Matty unleashed a blast of barely restrained verbal fury upon the umpire. It was not that the veteran Rigler, respected as one of the better umpires in the business, had not seen and heard such rage from ballplayers and managers before, but rather that the display was so uncharacteristic of Matty.[32]

"Let's not beat around the bush about this thing," Chase said to reporters. "I'm accused of throwing ballgames for money and trying to bribe other players to do the same." Chase did, however, admit to making what he described as "piker" bets, in amounts of 10 to 20 dollars, always on his own team. Garry Herrmann replied that he hoped Chase would clear himself, but he had six affidavits to the contrary. When the Reds stopped paying his salary, Chase sued the organization.[33]

Home on medical leave—an exploding shell had damaged his eyesight—Lieutenant Harry "Moose" McCormick visited the Polo Grounds pressbox. He created a stir by remarking that soldiers overseas were soured on baseball because of the shirking attitude many players had toward the war.

Thirty-six-year-old Branch Rickey, now a baseball executive in St. Louis, felt that he should do more for his country. He met with Percy Haughton, former Harvard football coach, recently president of the Boston Braves, and currently a major in the army's Chemical Warfare Service. Haughton proposed that Rickey join the army and organize a cadre of respected ballplayers, each to have a commission, to instruct soldiers in the use of chemical weaponry and gas protection.

His pledge of two years ago notwithstanding, Matty threw during practice sessions with the thought in mind of pitching the abbreviated season's Labor Day finale at Redland Field. Instead he followed Rickey into the Chemical Service. The CWS had two other illustrious baseball recruits: Ty Cobb and George Sisler. After Matty departed, the Reds continued to rebound, with Heinie Groh as interim manager, finishing the season in third place. On one occasion, in sweeping the Phillies, they overcame a 7–1 deficit to win. Sherry Magee remarked afterward: "You can't beat a team that won't be beaten."[34]

10

WAR, THEN THE BLACK SOX

Captain Mathewson departed Cincinnati in military uniform. When kidded that Rickey was a major, Matty kidded back that the War Department considered a catcher as outranking a pitcher. He had ten days to take care of personal affairs, get vaccinated for smallpox and typhoid, and report in Washington for orders. His training would take place with the American Expeditionary Force in France. Jane returned to Lewisburg, but not before she accompanied her husband to New York City to see him embark upon a troopship. Matty had accepted his commission on August 24. Three weeks later he and Jane arrived by taxi at the pier. They asked the driver to take their photograph. Matty, in uniform, stood leaning slightly toward his wife and with the facial expression recurrent in his posed pictures—direct, more serene than good-natured, with almost but not quite a smile. Jane clung to his arm and later described the photograph as unflattering to her, for she was on the verge of tears.[1]

The passage confirmed Matty's dislike of seagoing voyages. Influenza and pneumonia on the troopships were far worse scourges than mere seasickness. Branch Rickey on his transit across the Atlantic remembered 130 men buried at sea. The virulent strain of influenza, generally preceding the pneumonia, reached epidemic proportions throughout the world. Upon arriving in France, Matty went first to the American station at Blois ("Blooey" in Yankee parlance), where he could see firsthand the results of General Pershing's stringent officer-fitness program. Officers relieved of duty, for cause, nearer the front came here to the "reclassification camp" to have their cases reviewed and to await the decision whether they would receive duty elsewhere or discharge. At Tours, Matty saw the impressive headquarters of the AEF's Services of Supply, manned by some 2,400 officers and 4,300 enlisted. Pershing, commander of the American forces, believed the entire war effort depended

Matty and Jane as he is about to embark on a troopship for France in September 1918. (National Baseball Hall of Fame Library, Cooperstown, N.Y.)

on logistics. From Tours, Matty traveled to the Chemical Warfare command station at Hanlon Field, near Pershing's own headquarters at Chaumont. Here the influenza and pneumonia which he had been battling confined Matty, beginning on September 29, for ten days in a hospital.[2]

Branch Rickey was also hospitalized in France by the flu and never did see the combat he was willing to face. Grantland Rice did get close to the front lines and what he saw caused him to take refuge in his Christian faith. Receiving a commission and escaping assignment to the army's newspaper, *Stars and Stripes,* Rice reattached to the artillery unit with which he had trained stateside. He watched in awe as young men hurtled themselves in fighting airplanes over France and Belgium, and he watched with aching heart as long lines of walking wounded trudged to the rear after an infantry attack. Some nights, by candlelight, Rice wrote poetry in order to vent what he felt. He found war to be a distillation of all life's troubles, in which the good or bad in a man surfaced much quicker than in ordinary pursuits.

A leading historian of the war wrote that its final year is explained less well by analysis of military strategy than by comparison to a balance sheet.[3] The Germans were expending their divisions with no longer enough men in their nation to replenish their drafts. The British and French were similarly near bankruptcy, except their side of the ledger now received credits provided by the Americans. Previously the brightest Allied hope had been to secure victory sometime in 1919. Now General Ferdinand Foch, the Allied supreme commander, envisioned ending the war in the impending autumn of 1918 and, in order to accomplish this, favored general and simultaneous Allied movements, designed so that wherever his counterpart in the German high command, Erich von Ludendorff, sent his limited reserves those reserves would be needed elsewhere as well.

With hardly time for his soldiers to catch their breath after obtaining a battlefield victory at St. Mihiel, Pershing received orders from Foch to shift his army northward to the Meuse-Argonne. The Americans had only a few days to meet Foch's timetable, and with tremendous improvisation they pressed onward. Not enough of Pershing's divisions had as yet seen real battle, and many thousands of his men temporarily lost their nerve in the mêlée that followed. The dense forest of the Argonne, said Hunter Liggett, commander of the American First Corps, made the Wilderness of Virginia, in which the armies of Grant and Lee struggled in 1864, seem like a park. Liggett described it as a "battle pursued more by the ear and sense of touch than with the eye." By the time the American command ended the fighting to reorganize, there were as many as 100,000 stragglers with which to contend. Liggett, in another allusion to the Civil War, referred to them as "coffee boilers."[4]

The 77th Division, comprising largely men from New York City, was among those that foundered in the Argonne. Major Charles Whittlesey, adhering to Pershing's strict orders to push ahead "without regard of losses and without regard to the exposed conditions of the flanks," led the only battalion of the 77th which made any real forward movement during the first day of the attack. Not a career soldier, Whittlesey was a Wall Street lawyer with an appearance and a moral manner resembling Woodrow Wilson. His men called him "Bird Legs" and sometimes "Galloping Charley." Whittlesey's battalion broke through the German defenses, and lost contact with supporting units in the process. During the night, in accordance with their orders, they held their forward position. The Germans, fearing a large American breakthrough, rushed all available combat troops to the area. In the morning Whittlesey and his men were surrounded. For five days the "Lost Battalion," suffering from exposure and lack of food and ammunition, withstood repeated German attacks. Whittlesey and his officers led magnificently; three of them would earn the Congressional Medal of Honor. A German officer, who had lived six years in Seattle as a salesman, brought to the beleaguered Americans a written appeal for surrender. Whittlesey did not return a reply, nor did he try to keep the existence of the appeal from his men. "You Heinie bastards, come and get us!" was the general tenor of what came from the foxholes.[5]

To the extent the "Lost Battalion" was headline stuff back home, Pershing demanded "vigorous" action for its relief. But American attempts to restore communication with the battalion met with no better success than the German attempts to overcome Whittlesey's men. Finally a strategic flanking action caused the Germans to quit the Argonne altogether. Approximately 800 officers and men had entered the action with Whittlesey. Some 500 had been surrounded. Only 190 walked out.

Company K of the 307th Infantry had been among the units assigned to Whittlesey. Captain Eddie Grant led another company of the 307th, not with Whittlesey. For four days and nights Grant and his men fought desperately to rescue their comrades. On the morning the relief was effected, Grant was so tired he could hardly move; he sat on a log and seemed too weak even to lift a cup of coffee. But when stretcher bearers carried by him his wounded major, Grant, one of the few battalion officers left, was ordered to assume command. The Germans soon thereafter commenced another bombardment, and a shell dropped through the trees killing and wounding more men. "Everybody down!" Grant shouted, not taking cover himself. Moments later another shell killed him.[6]

Matty was in the hospital the whole time the drama of the "Lost Battalion" played out. After his release he remained at Chaumont to attend the CWS Officer Training School. In early November, Matty was transferred to the Gas Offense and Defense Schools. It was here, apparently, that Matty ran into Ty Cobb. The schools were short-term, nononsense affairs in which every topic was covered from details of German artillery fuzes to how to put a gas respirator on a horse. Class work was augmented by practical demonstrations, including donning masks in a gas chamber. One day, according to Cobb, a mistake was made. Lethal gas was introduced into a chamber without the men participating in the drill, including Matty and Cobb, recognizing the hand signal which had been given for them to put on their masks. Cobb said several men died, and that he himself was coughing up matter from his lungs for several weeks afterward; he said Matty also breathed the gas while inside.[7]

Whatever injury Matty's lungs may have received while in training did not prevent him from receiving orders, dated November 11, to report to headquarters of the 28th Division—the "Keystone Division" of the Pennsylvania National Guard—for duty as Assistant Division Gas Officer. The division, having performed a reconnaissance in force the day before, stood poised to resume the offensive toward Metz in a general attack set to begin at 8:30 on the morning of November 11. At 8:10 came word of the impending armistice to go into effect at exactly 11 o'clock. Instead of attacking, the men were now ordered to consolidate their position. Enemy artillery cut loose a barrage; in the division over a hundred more men became casualties. Allied artillery retaliated in kind, firing fiercely until five minutes before the designated hour. Four minutes of silence was followed by another half minute of intense firing. Then all was quiet. Shortly afterward German soldiers approached the American perimeter to trade for tobacco and white bread. American pickets turned them away.[8]

Wearing the red marking on his sleeve that defined him as a staff officer, Matty did not arrive at divisional headquarters, located at Heudicourt, until the fighting was over. He missed it by two days. He collected some souvenirs, including an artillery-shell casing and a German insignia with the words "*Gott mit uns*" upon it. His main duties consisted of gas-warfare instruction to the enlisted men (who at this point had to be less than fully interested) and to inspect German trenches and supply dumps in order to certify gas-safety of entrance. Inevitably came assignment to the division's Advisory Athletic Council. He jotted down his impressions of Metz, from the few hours he spent there, on postcards. He described homemade American flags used by the citizenry to welcome the doughboys—some with as many as eight stars, he wrote. Of a toppled statue of a German ruler astride a horse, he jotted, "Too bad about the horse!"[9]

Branch Rickey and Ty Cobb were both back in the states before Christmas. (George Sisler was training in New Jersey when the war ended.) Matty's contract with the Reds expired at the conclusion of the 1918 season. Garry Herrmann yet needed a manager and was willing to sign Matty again; he sent several cablegrams to that effect, but these were not acknowledged or perhaps not even received by Matty for weeks. For his part Matty sent Herrmann a brief note with little information other than that he was attached to the 28th Division.[10]

In mid–December, CWS headquarters invited officer personnel to provide personal or business reasons which they would like to have considered in the decision whether to expedite their individual return home. Matty responded with a request for a return "on or about January 18th, 1919, in order to resume my former occupation of managing a National League professional baseball club.... Unless at that time, I give assurance of being able to accept such a position, I [would] not find such employment during the season of 1919."[11] Orders effecting Matty's relief were issued on December 26, although they were contingent upon the arrival of a replacement staff officer. Matty spent New Year's in the city of Nancy with Colonel Walter Sweeney, the divisional chief of staff, and a dozen other officers. In mid-January, Matty departed for the military district of Angers and the "Casual Officers' Camp" to await transport home. In February he boarded the ship *Rotterdam* bound for New York.

Upon his arrival, on February 17, it was remarked by the press that he looked as fit and handsome as ever. "I was in New York a great many years and it seems like home to me," he said. "I am under orders to go to Washington immediately, and as I see no further use of instructing anyone how to throw gas, I expect to ask for my discharge and get back to civil life. The only persons I know of in need of gas are umpires."[12]

Baseball history, as it pertains to the 1919 World Series, might be far different had Matty been present at the January 30 hearing before league president John Heydler of the accusations against Hal Chase. Prior to leaving for France, Matty left an affidavit with the league office. Before the hearing, Chase played a trump card by threatening to expose the whole matter in a court of law. Heydler, who came into office on an interim basis after John Tener resigned, and who had only officially received tenure during the recent December league meeting, knew his constituency of club owners wanted the public to see as little of this linen washing as possible. Heydler therefore kept the proceeding closed to reporters. Chase arrived with three attorneys.

John McGraw also came. He was now a part-owner of the Giants with Charles Stoneham, a rich stock and bond manipulator, and with Francis X. McQuade, the same Francis X. McQuade who as a city magistrate had thrown out the charges against managers McGraw and Mathewson for staging a Sunday game. McGraw appeared at the hearing ostensibly as a witness for the prosecution, but, incredibly given the stark difference between the accusations of his tried-and-true friend Matty versus the claims of good-fellow-well-tarnished Chase, McGraw, in effect, sided with Chase. Other witnesses offering testimony, not inclined toward

Prince Hal, were Mike Regan, Greasy Neale, and Jimmy Ring. Pol Perritt sent a deposition. The hearing lasted five hours.

A week later Heydler acquitted Chase. Heydler said the Cincinnati club had been justified in its suspicions because of Chase's "foolish and careless manner both on the field and among players." But the league president also found that no one had corroborated beyond a reasonable doubt the actual allegations, such as whether Chase had indeed sought to corrupt Ring by dropping $50 into his lap. Heydler deflected some blame toward Matty's affidavit itself by describing it as a general complaint lacking in specifics. In the aftermath of the decision, baseball men clung to their own parochial standards of virtue. To Pants Rowland, recently let go as the White Sox manager, Chase remained "one of the greatest hit and run men in the game. He can hit back of a runner any time."[13]

McGraw thought so, too. After the acquittal, he went to see Garry Herrmann. For Chase's services he offered first baseman Walter Holke, catcher Bill Rariden, and the assumption of Chase's unpaid salary from the Reds. McGraw also helped Herrmann, for a second time, find a new manager. When the Phillies fired Pat Moran after a sixth-place finish, McGraw hired him as a coach; Moran now went with McGraw's blessing to Cincinnati as manager.

The Giants' deal for Chase was just a few days old when Matty returned from France. McGraw offered his former star a $5,000 salary as a coach. Matty went to Washington for his discharge, then he accepted McGraw's offer; to reporters he glossed over his trouble with Chase as best he could, saying that to his personal knowledge, apart from what other players said, he only knew with certainty that Chase was guilty of indifferent playing and that no ill-feeling lingered.[14]

Uncertain of postwar conditions, the major leagues agreed to another shortened season with spring training to begin in mid–March. For the first spring since 1908, the Giants trained elsewhere than Marlin. Matty and McGraw departed New York for Gainesville, Florida, and the next day a beaming Hal Chase and several other players boarded a train for the same destination. Pol Perritt, perhaps confused why Chase was now his teammate, remained a while longer at his Louisiana home to tend to some unspecified business.

On the athletic fields of the University of Florida, where the Giants now trained, Matty saw familiar faces. Art Fletcher, now 34, captained the team. The next best thing to being young and a Giant was to be 32 and once again a Giant, though the presence in camp of young Frankie Frisch made the twilight of Larry Doyle's career all the more apparent. Chase and Heinie Zimmerman worked the corners of McGraw's infield. In the outfield reliable George Burns remained in left, flashy Benny Kauff, back from the army, patrolled center, and in his sophomore season Ross Youngs played right. If anything, McGraw was higher on Youngs than Frisch.

Matty worked with a troubled pitching staff. Slim Sallee refused to play for McGraw anymore; he was released and went to Cincinnati. Fred Toney, obtained by the Giants in the latter part of the preceding season, sat in federal prison until May. Pol Perritt continued to drag his heels about joining the team. Ferdinand Schupp would suffer a sore arm. All these ills combined to make Rube Benton's place as a starter more secure, and Jesse Barnes, after a lackluster career thus far, under Matty's tutelage would win 25 games in 1919.

In June the Giants went to Cincinnati. Hal Chase was booed heartily. Matty received a ripple of applause; a year previously, Bill Phelon observed, Matty could hardly walk to the coaching box without cheers. On June 11, trailing the Reds 2–1 in the top of the eighth, Chase strode to the plate with the bases loaded; he lined a sharp one to third baseman Heinie Groh, who touched the bag in time for the double play to retire the side.

It became a pennant race between the Giants and Reds. McGraw sought to improve his roster. He traded Ferdie Schupp to St. Louis for catcher Frank "Pancho" Snyder; from Chicago he obtained pitcher Phil Douglas; and last but not least he purchased a top-notch left-hander from the Braves, Art Nehf, for $40,000 and some lesser players. The transaction for Nehf especially drew the ire of Cincinnati fans who knew their club did not have, or would not spend, that sort of money to buy a pennant. In August, beginning one day after Matty's 39th birthday, the Reds—intending to improve their hold on first place—came to New York to play three double-headers in three days. The Reds swept the first pair of contests, on a Wednesday, before over 30,000 fans. The Giants swept the next day, the second game erupting into a brawl after Adolfo Luque and Rube Benton exchanged bean balls.

For the Friday contests people filled the Polo Grounds to near overflowing. Hod Eller won the first game for the Reds 4–3. The loss gave Matty some satisfaction, at least, in that he had "discovered" Eller and gave him his chance in the big leagues—and in that McGraw, at long last, approached disenchantment with Hal Chase.[15] The timeliness of the first baseman's errors during the series gnawed at the manager, and McGraw sent Lew McCarty to pinch-hit for Chase in the late innings of both Friday games, which the Reds again swept. It was put out to reporters that Chase had sprained his wrist sliding into base, and, from the International League, McGraw obtained George Kelly as a replacement. Chase, however, did remain with the team as a coach and occasional player.

In Chicago, on September 10, with the Giants not yet mathematically eliminated from the race, Heinie Zimmerman told Fred Toney that it would be worth something to Toney not to bear down in his next scheduled start. Toney pitched a couple of innings, thought over the situation, and, though the Giants were already ahead, asked McGraw to take him out of the game. Jesse Barnes relieved as the Giants went on to win handily.

That evening Chase and Buck Herzog, the latter now with the Cubs, had some beers with Rube Benton. Benton later testified before a grand jury that Herzog suggested he, Benton, could make some easy money by throwing the next day's game to Chicago. Instead Benton pitched a complete game victory. Afterward Zimmerman—soon suspended by McGraw, purportedly for missing one curfew too many—remarked to Benton as they passed each other in the hotel lobby: "You poor fish," or some such phrase, "don't you know there was $400 waiting for you to lose that game today?"[16]

During the winter McGraw rid himself of both Chase and Zimmerman by sending them contracts with salaries so low he knew they would refuse to sign. Zimmerman quit baseball and became a plumber. Chase returned to California where the next summer he was corrupting players in the Pacific Coast League. When it suited his purposes in the aftermath of revelations about other crooked ballplayers, McGraw told the press that he had suspected Zimmerman's honesty since Zimmerman's poor play in the 1917 World Series; of Chase he said that he had never been more deceived by a player.

Sleepy Bill Burns, who made a bundle from oil and mining investments in Texas and New Mexico after his lackluster big-league pitching career was over, became highly visible among the Giants and other contending teams during the latter part of the 1919 season. His presence among the players reminded Bill Phelon of a story told by Dick Hoblitzell, a teammate of Burns on the Reds in 1910, who once parted the curtains on Sleepy Bill's Pullman berth and found the Texan cleaning a revolver and reading a Bible at the same time. Burns now showed off his money and feted players to expensive steak dinners as he traveled with them by train. Sleepy Bill talked to McGraw about investing in the oil business and was especially chummy with Jean Dubuc, another former teammate and now a Giants' relief pitcher. But after the Reds clinched the pennant, Burns disappeared from the Giants' view. Burns's friendship would bring to Dubuc a telegram with advice how to bet the World Series and eventual permanent expulsion from Organized Baseball.[17]

Burns and his associate Billy Maharg found the soft spot for which they were looking among the disaffected members of the American League champion White Sox. The White Sox were acknowledged as one of the best teams in baseball and, for all the veteran talent, one of the most poorly paid. Thirty-five-year-old Eddie Cocotte, master of doctoring the ball and making it do wonders, had won 28 games in 1917 and 29 this year, yet Charles Comiskey paid him a salary of just $6,000. Four years previously Comiskey paid $65,000 to the Cleveland Indians for the contract of Shoeless Joe Jackson. Jackson also earned $6,000 a year. Edd Roush, the Reds' leading hitter, made $10,000. Roush had what came to be considered a Hall of Fame career, but never in a single season did he exceed Jackson's career batting average of .356.

First baseman Chick Gandil and shortstop Swede Risberg played with Eddie Collins between them in the White Sox infield. They disliked Collins for his Ivy League education, his marriage into wealth, and his savvy in having brought with him from Connie Mack's Athletics a guaranteed contract when he was sold to the White Sox in 1915. At $14,500 Collins made more than double what Gandil and Risberg did combined. Even the daily meal allowance was a bone of contention; the White Sox received three dollars and the players of most of the other teams, four. Cicotte, allegedly, told Gandil he wanted $10,000 to throw the series: "Cash in advance, and nothing else."[18]

Gandil and Cicotte met with Burns and Maharg at a hotel in New York. Besides Cicotte, Gandil had six other players in the bag: Jackson, Risberg, pitcher Lefty Williams, outfielder Happy Felsch, third baseman Buck Weaver, and reserve infielder Fred McMullin. Gandil told Burns that they would fix the World Series for $100,000. What Gandil did not tell Burns, or for that matter, as what became known of the fix suggests, tell most of his fellow conspirators, was that he already had a negotiation under way with a Boston gambler, Sport Sullivan, for another $80,000.

Neither Burns nor Sullivan had that kind of money, but they knew of a man who did. Arnold Rothstein had come a long way in the decade since he frequented John McGraw's pool hall on Herald Square. Known as "The Big Bankroll," Rothstein's wealth stemmed from gambling houses, protected by Tammany, and from ostensibly legal brokerage firms, known as "bucket shops," which manipulated stocks and bonds, amorally if not illegally. Charles Stoneham, McGraw's partner in owning the Giants, was Rothstein's close associate in the latter ventures, and a frequent and honored guest at the former ones. Through his attorney, William ("The Great Mouthpiece") Fallon, Rothstein would successfully veil from the probings of the Illinois legal system the proof, if it existed, of his direct involvement in the World Series fix. To the main perpetrators of the corruption, however, it did not matter so much whether Rothstein was actually involved as it did that they themselves believed, or could make others believe, that the New York gambler was personally seeking to influence the final result. The aura of Rothstein's name worked as currency in the absence of up-front cash.[19]

On the day before the series began, the White Sox checked into Cincinnati's Hotel Sinton. Matty and sportswriter Hugh Fullerton were also staying at the Sinton. In association with Jack Wheeler's news syndicate, Matty was there to write a copyrighted column about each game. After he retired from pitching, as Wheeler would affirm, Matty insisted on writing by his own hand all the stories under his byline. Fullerton, now in his mid–40s, knew and loved baseball; during his summer vacations from college, he played two semi-professional seasons as an infielder with a team from Olean, New York, in the Iron and Oil League (a league from which John McGraw in his youth had been cut!). Finding his talent for writing about baseball more lucrative than playing it, Fullerton gained prominence with the Hearst newspaper in Chicago, *The Examiner*, and his yearly pre–World Series articles, detailing and analyzing position by position the competing pennant winners, were read nationally. Fullerton picked the White Sox as a much better team. He was not the only one. Bill Phelon remarked that every sportswriter who picked the Athletics to beat the Braves and Willard to beat Dempsey were picking the Sox to beat the Reds.

Fullerton recognized gamblers in and around the Sinton and, aware of stubborn, disturbing rumors concerning the series, made an effort to socialize with his acquaintances among them. The vein of betting advice he received disturbed the newsman, and Fullerton went to Matty's room to talk about it. "Damn them, they deserve it," Matty said bitterly, referring to baseball's leadership. "They whitewashed two players after I caught them with the goods and presented affidavits." The two players meant, of course, were Chase and Lee Magee. Matty and Fullerton were troubled but at the same time not eager to rush to judgment. Anxious either to substantiate or to allay their suspicions, they agreed to mark on their scorecards any plays they viewed as performed with doubtful integrity.[20]

John Philip Sousa's band entertained the enthusiastic, packed house at Redland Field in the festivities prior to the World Series' opening pitch. White Sox outfielder Shano Collins led off the game with a single. Eddie Collins followed him to the plate, as Matty watched with keen interest. The second baseman had played in every one of the Sox's regular-season games, hitting .319 and stealing a league-leading 33 bases. In this situation he could advance the runner to scoring position by either swinging away or laying down a bunt. The former increased the probability of a double play; the latter was the surer choice to get a man in scoring position with one out. Matty reasoned that if the Sox manager, Kid Gleason, figured it as a close game—that is, if Gleason had confidence in Cicotte's ability and intention—he would call for a bunt in these circumstances. Reds' pitcher Dutch Ruether backed Eddie Collins away from the plate with his first offering. Probability is just that. On a one-and-one count, a bunt went back to the pitcher who threw to second base in time to get the lead runner. Collins no doubt took a deep breath as he stood on the first-base bag. In the pressbox Matty and Fullerton may have breathed deeply as well. At least Gleason had faith in his players.

The Reds hit the ball hard, but a sharp defense kept them from getting anywhere on the base paths. During the third inning Fullerton asked Matty if he thought Cicotte was "right." "No," Matty replied, "because if he had his usual stuff the Reds would be making more foul tips."[21] As he took the mound in the top of the fourth, Cicotte paused to regard his fielders, especially his outfielders. With the score tied at one apiece, the pitcher by this time may have realized that he would have to shoulder the responsibility to lose the game himself. The first batter, Roush, launched a high fly to deep center; Felsch raced back and caught it. Pat Duncan then singled over Eddie Collins's head. Larry Kopf batted next and bounded the ball back to Cicotte. Reflexively Cicotte caught the ball, whirled, and threw to Risberg—or it may have been that he hesitated a mere moment. Just as reflexively, Risberg made the force at second and whipped the ball to Gandil—or he may have "short legged" the play just a little bit. When the best-of-nine-games series ended after eight games, Matty and Fullerton found they had marked just seven plays as "suspicious." "Any one of those plays," Fullerton later wrote, "could be explained on the theory that the mistakes were honestly made, as well as on the theory of dishonesty."[22] Umpire Billy Evans called Kopf safe on a close play.

Greasy Neale, on the next pitch, sizzled one over second base. Risberg, displaying quickness and range, intercepted the ball before it penetrated far into center field, though he did not retrieve it from his glove quickly enough to end the inning by getting either Kopf or Neale. Ivy Wingo singled to right; Gandil did not cut off Shano Collins's throw to the plate which failed to precede Kopf's arrival there. Gandil made only one error in the entire series and had the highest fielding percentage of any player who was in the Sox lineup all eight games. His lapse in not cutting off the throw would not appear in the box score, but it did allow both remaining base runners to reach scoring position. Dutch Ruether, rather than defer to the top of the Reds' order in the next inning, tripled to left center, sending the Cincinnati crowd into rapture. A double and a single followed, scoring two more runs. Kid Gleason summoned a relief pitcher. Cincinnati won the game 9–1.

Afterward Matty saw Tris Speaker, now the playing manager of the Cleveland Indians. He asked Speaker about Cicotte and found comfort in the reply. Speaker said Cicotte's last three regular-season performances had been bad, and this was the fourth.[23]

Matty credited Pat Moran's aggressive strategy and told his readers that he felt "a little proud to see the club with which I had been associated making such a good showing. Remember, I have traveled and lived with these men and know them all. The players are showing their gameness in a pinch." He predicted, if Cicotte did not improve, the Reds would take the series in seven games. He also remarked: "I never bet on a ball game, but if we get another warm day tomorrow and Sallee starts for Cincinnati, I think I will get down a little wager on the Reds. The White Sox are supposed to be a great ball club, but no team to my knowledge was ever defeated by so large a score in an opening game of the world series when each contender was trying its best."[24]

Lefty Williams lost the second game for the White Sox. He pitched well, except in the fourth inning when he gave three walks and two hits resulting in three runs. Between the sixth and seventh innings a small airplane buzzed Redland Field. The day before, in a similar occurrence, advertising leaflets had been dropped; today a man-sized figure fell from the plane and onto the field near third base. A policeman dragged the dummy figure to the side and dispelled the crowd's consternation by using it as seat to watch the game.

Three times the Reds attempted a hit-and-run. Two of the attempts ended in double plays. The third resulted in what Matty called "one of the prettiest bits of work seen in the series so far."[25] With one out in the fourth inning and runners on first and third, Moran thought to execute a double steal with the hit-and-run, but catcher Ray Schalk called for a pitch-out and threw the ball hard and straight toward second base. Eddie Collins charged toward home plate ready to intercept the ball, but when he saw that his motion had induced the runner from third to return to the bag, he dropped to the ground and let the ball go to Risberg, who easily tagged out the sliding Edd Roush. (Matty had seen Collins perform a similar play before in a double-steal attempt during the sixth inning of the first game of the '11 Series, only that time Snodgrass was nailed at the plate.)

The White Sox out-batted the Reds ten hits to four but crossed the plate just twice. As for the Reds, it appeared to Matty "rather a remarkable thing for a team to get four hits and four runs in a game in which it seemed as if no part of the plan of attack went through." (Williams had allowed six walks. "He had everything but control," a reporter remarked. "Every Cincinnati runner who scored got to first base on a pass. Williams established himself as the world-series Santa Claus of all time.") Judge Kenesaw Mountain Landis, identified by the press as one of the many celebrities in attendance, generously described the play of the Reds as "the most formidable machine I have ever seen in my years as a fan." Landis added in what seems a humorous vein: "I have learned through years of experience on the bench to maintain a judicial attitude and I promise to do this provided the Reds do not keep making such a lopsided affair."[26]

Bill Burns went to Swede Risberg's hotel room carrying hidden inside his shirt a sop of $10,000 for the corrupted players to continue the fix. On the way Burns met Kid Gleason in the corridor. Things were hectic. There was no day off. Play would resume tomorrow in Chicago. "Hello, Kid," Burns said.[27]

The players in Risberg's room demanded their share of what they thought should have been $40,000 for the two games lost thus far, and Gandil accused Burns of a double cross. Burns denied it; as far as he knew he was acting as middleman for "A.R.'s" money, and he argued that for arranging the deal he was supposed to get one ninth of whatever the players received. The one ninth of the $10,000 was not offered Burns, but, even so, he left the room figuring the scam was still on. If they would not win for Cicotte or Williams, the fixed players told him, they would not win for a "busher" like Dickie Kerr either. Burns either already had or soon would bet all of his own stake on the Reds to win game three.

Kid Gleason described Dickie Kerr, who stood 5 feet 7 inches and weighed 155 pounds, as three inches shy of what an honest-to-goodness pitcher should be. (In his own playing days the 5 foot–7 inch Gleason weighed 160 pounds.) Kerr took 90 minutes to shut out the Reds 3–0. Risberg supported him with several excellent plays on slow rollers, altogether accepting ten chances without an error. Buck Weaver and Joe Jackson had not been present in Risberg's room the day before. By now it was clear to the others that Weaver no longer wanted a dime of the gamblers' money and, though he was keeping his mouth shut, was playing to win. (Weaver evidently never received a dime either.) Eventually Jackson got $5,000 of the corruption, but during the series he batted .375 and was charged with no fielding errors. It seems, however, that as far as Chick Gandil was concerned, the Sox's victory in game three was a tactic to show the gamblers that the conspirators wanted all of the money they had been promised.

That evening Burns suffered in the aftermath of what he called "the crash." The man he regarded as his source to Arnold Rothstein's wealth, Abe Attell, a former featherweight boxing champion, turned out to have conned the confidence man in that Attell had been trading on the unsubstantiated allure of Rothstein's cash as much as Burns had been trading on unfulfilled promises to the players. About 9:30, Burns went to Gandil's room at the Warner Hotel in Chicago; Gandil, Risberg, and Fred McMullin were there. McMullin, according to Burns, told him that there had been a meeting before game three and the players had agreed to double-cross the gamblers just as they had been double-crossed. Once more Burns demanded his share of the $10,000 the players had received through him. Spurned again, Burns told Gandil that he would get even someday.

Gandil's tactics apparently did bring him $20,000 from his other source, Sport Sullivan. This amount he divided equally among Risberg, Williams, Felsch, and Jackson. (McMullin, the reserve, had to wait a while longer.) When it was all over, Gandil is believed to have received from Sullivan another $40,000 of Rothstein's money, withheld until the final series outcome. Eventually Jackson wondered who had done the most double-crossing: Burns or Gandil. Jackson did not know how else to explain the 32-year-old Gandil turning down Comiskey's contract for 1920 and what he heard about Gandil's new home, big automobile, and lack of work in California.[28]

Prior to the eighth game, Kerr won another and Cicotte refused to lie down a third time. This gave the Reds a four-games-to-three advantage. Lefty Williams did not want to lose three World Series starts, but it is suspected, and became part of the legend, that gamblers threatened him or his wife. What is known for sure is that Williams lasted one third of an inning, yielding four quick hits and two runs before Gleason could get Bill James warmed up to relieve him. Williams, a finesse pitcher, had won 23 games in the regular season relying on his curveball. This day, no matter what Schalk may have signaled for, it was apparent to Matty that Williams was feeding only fastballs to the batters. Matty, giving doubt its due in his column, described the pitcher as "hard-worked and ill-used." Williams had, after all, in the 16 innings of his two previous starts "held Pat Moran's boys to four hits [in each contest] and lost because he was wild just before they landed the blows."[29]

Matty preferred to write about a funny incident that occurred in the eighth inning. By then the Reds had a 10–1 lead, and their pitcher Hod Eller got careless. The Sox made some hits, putting men on base. At this juncture more airplanes flew over the playing field. Greasy Neale, understandably given the dummy which had previously fallen from the sky, let his attention drift to the flyers when Gandil smashed one over his head. Neale stood distracted as Roush raced to retrieve the ball. The White Sox scored four runs in the inning. That was all they got.

11

PATH TO GLORY

In 1920, for the first time, women could vote in a national election. Another constitutional amendment prohibited the manufacture, sale, and transportation of intoxicating liquors. Baseball's National Commission resolved officially to stop gambling in all ballparks of both major leagues. Known gamblers, the commissioners promulgated, would be ejected without ceremony. Nonetheless ugly rumors persisted, and Hugh Fullerton advocated in his columns for an investigation of possible World Series crookedness.

The season did not begin well for the Giants. Frank Frisch had an emergency appendectomy. The Yankees, with Babe Ruth in their lineup, outdrew in paid admissions their landlords at the Polo Grounds. Matty, despite a lingering case of what was diagnosed as bronchitis, filled-in as manager while John McGraw sat out suspensions for abusing umpires. McGraw hired Johnny Evers as a coach, dealt Art Fletcher to the Phillies for Dave Bancroft, and in effect promised more change when he designated Larry Doyle team captain for the "time being."[1]

In June, Matty was called to testify at a jury trial in Chicago. Lee Magee, who went to the Cubs after his year on the Reds, was released before the 1920 season began. Though his 1919 numbers were respectable, no other club picked him up. Magee knew why and, at age 31, did not care to be thus deprived of his livelihood. He threatened to "blow the lid" unless signed by some big-league club; when that did not happen, he got a lawyer and sued.

The judge of the case ordered the Chicago Club to make specific its causes for dissatisfaction with Magee. Cubs' president William Veeck answered that, in February, Magee confessed to him and John Heydler that he, Magee, had conspired to fix with Chase the game in Boston. Matty, in his testimony, explained his suspicions of the honesty of Magee's performance during the game in question, particularly poor fielding throws and how in the 13th inning Magee had disregarded a steal sign after reaching first base on the ball which broke Johnny Rawlings's nose. Frank Costello, the Boston gambler, described under oath how Chase and Magee each bet $500 on the Reds to lose. "Chase's check went through all right," Costello said, "but Magee stopped payment on his." In his defense Magee countered that it was the sharpness of his hit which broke the Boston shortstop's nose and that, prior to Roush's game-winning home run, he stole second base after all. It was Chase, Magee averred, who double-crossed him by placing the money against their own team. After three days of testimony, the jury took 45 minutes to decide that Magee had no claim. During the trial no issue was raised concerning the recent World Series. Organized Baseball, for the moment, breathed easier and congratulated itself on exiling a corrupt player.[2]

Matty's "bronchitis" did not get better. On June 23 at the Polo Grounds, he vented his frustration, and got out of his coaching duties early, with a first-inning tirade against the umpire, a tirade that seemed to have no basis. By early July he was rediagnosed, and found to have tuberculosis. Once, in what now to them seemed many years ago, Larry Doyle and Matty in a spring training incident got into an argument over some beer Doyle may or may not have drunk; another time Matty embarrassed Doyle by refusing to speak to some of Doyle's friends who had come a long way to see him pitch. Now, in a hotel room in New York, the friend Matty told first about the diagnosis was Doyle. Soon thereafter Matty quietly quit the Giants. After his absence was noticed by members of the press, he informed them that he was going to the Adirondacks for treatment. He speculated that eventually he would go to Arizona and become a rancher.[3]

Babe Ruth thrilled the nation as he hit 54 home runs—the previous high mark was 27 hit by Ned Williamson in 1884. In August, as Matty's condition worsened, John McGraw got drunk on bootleg whiskey one night at the Lambs' Club and into a fight with a fellow member. Then he mixed it up with two other Lambs who were trying to get him home safely, and he slightly fractured the skull of one of them. It took Arnold Rothstein's lawyer, William Fallon, to get McGraw out of the resulting legal scrape. Fallon soon had more work; for in September, at long last, a Cook County grand jury convened to consider the 1919 World Series. Philadelphia sportswriter Jimmy Isaminger looked up Billy Maharg, working as a laborer in a Ford plant. "We were all double-crossed by Abe Attell," Maharg was quoted as saying, "and I want everybody to know the truth."[4] Newspapers across the country picked up the story. During the eventual trial, in the following summer of 1921, Bill Burns, admitting he had an ax to grind with the indicted players, proved the prosecution's most effective witness.

In adults pulmonary tuberculosis may remain asymptomatic two years or more after initial infection. Symptoms do not usually manifest until after the lung has become lesioned enough for the lesions to appear on x-rays. A cough, at first occurring only in the mornings as a result of phlegm forming during sleep overnight, gets more severe as the disease progresses. Eventually the infected individual coughs to rid the lung, or lungs, of yellow, purulent mucus. When the turberculosis bacteria reach sufficient mass, the person suffers fever, malaise, and weight loss.[5]

Jane Mathewson nursed her husband in a semi-darkened room of an apartment in Saranac Lake, New York, a community nestled in the Adirondacks and which ministered to consumptives, drawn to the place by the international reputation of the Trudeau Sanatorium. At times Matty's fever approached 105 degrees. Jane cooled his forehead and read to him accounts of the 1920 World Series between Brooklyn and Cleveland and of the ongoing grand jury investigation in Chicago. Scores of letters from fans and well-wishers arrived at their Saranac address daily, and she read these to him as well. By November, Matty's temperature fell to normal for brief periods, and his strength revived to the extent that he could walk a few dozen steps before returning to his bed. His physician, Dr. Edward Packard, cautioned Matty not to talk more than necessary and refused to allow him to leave the apartment until he put on some weight.[6]

Dr. Packard had personal faith in the Adirondack air to have a healthful effect on lungs infected by tuberculosis; nearly a decade before, as an intern in a New York City hospital, he had contracted the disease. The mountains, since the time of Ralph Waldo Emerson, were known as a place where consumptives could either reinvigorate or, at least, die in relative breathing comfort. Robert Louis Stevenson came in 1887; Branch Rickey in 1909. Dr. Packard took the cure sufficiently to remain in Saranac as a Trudeau staff member, eventually entering private practice; he married and became a father. Dr. Packard took the cure sufficiently to remain in Saranac as a Trudeau staff member, eventually entering private practice. Three years younger than Matty, he earned his degrees at Syracuse University (while there he was a member of the varsity crew); during the war he served stateside as a major in the army medical corps.[7]

In December, Matty suffered a setback when a lung collapsed. Dr. Packard inserted a tube into Matty's chest to drain fluid. Rumors circulated, and the doctor, though declining to go into detail, felt obligated to tell the press that Matty was not dead. Visitors remained prohibited and the patient confined to his bed. Dr. Packard described Matty as "doing as well as can be expected under the circumstances." The collapsed lung was beyond cure, but the doctor considered the other lung as potentially healthy. "Matty suffers great pain when coughing." Packard said. "This is an indication of a drying-up process and is viewed with favor and adds to his chances of recovery."[8]

The December setback may have occurred as a result of a deliberate collapsing of the lung by Matty's doctor. Artificial pneumothorax, or collapse therapy, was an infrequent, risky procedure involving the insertion of a hollow needle between the ribs and application of slightly pressurized air into the chest cavity. By the 1920s the procedure had few advocates remaining; these supporters continued to believe the operation could prolong life for gravely ill consumptives. It was described as an action of last resort or the choice of the desperate.[9]

Matty and Jane resided in their rooms, at the Santanoni Apartment House for Health Seekers, for more than a year. ("Santanoni" was an ellipsis for Saint Anthony.) The elegant residence, a New York reporter remarked, "would do credit to Riverside Drive, a smiling, friendly house, belying in its every stone its reasons for existence." Emotional depression at times seemed a worse adversary than the tuberculosis. Dr. Edward Livingston Trudeau, founder of the sanatorium and who lived with the disease in his own lungs for more than 40 years, called its effect upon the spirit "the grip of the tiger." Matty diverted his mind by brooding instead over chess and checker problems. He also found refuge in the essays of Charles Lamb.[10]

When summer came Dr. Packard permitted Matty to take half-hour automobile rides. The country roads carried traffic in bootleg whiskey from Canada—in 1924 Abe Attell was arrested in Plattsburgh, about 50 miles northeast of Saranac, on just such a charge. Prohibition or no, it was not easy to convince tubercular veterans from the war, or other consumptives, that a man or woman staring death in the face should not have a stiff drink if he or she wanted. John McGraw telephoned from time to time as the Giants fended off the Reds, Pirates, and Cardinals to win the 1921 pennant. On the occasion of Matty's 41st birthday, a reporter's request for an interview was granted. A week had lapsed since the Black Sox acquittal. The reporter sought Matty's opinion of the scandal and brought up an incident, early in the trial, when Kid Gleason and some of the "Clean Sox" visited the courtroom and jocularly fraternized with the defendants. The visit caused a great deal of adverse editorial comment. "In a way it was only natural," Matty replied. In explaining, he said that a fellow employee would condemn the act of a defaulting bank teller but not equally abhor the individual. "I don't think Gleason and the rest ... wanted to see their former comrades sent to the Penitentiary.... They would not have been human if they did.... As to fraternizing—the soldiers who fight hardest are most willing to shake hands and be friends when the war is over. It is only far from the firing line that the battle to the last man idea has any strong hold." Overall, Matty observed, "Nobody can kill the game of baseball except the public."[11]

The Mathewsons moved from the Santanoni to a large, handsome house not far from the Trudeau Sanatorium and near to the larger and even more handsome home of Dr. Packard. Christy Junior enrolled in the local high school. Matty was sometimes glimpsed downtown; he went for haircuts and occasionally to the lobby of the St. Regis Hotel to play checkers, finding one local match memorable enough that he sent an account of it to the checker columnist of the Syracuse *Post Standard*. On his automobile rides into the country, Matty took his shotgun and looked for grouse. When he thought he recognized a promising place, he got out of the car and slowly walked into the field to flush the birds. Jane loyally described him as a good shot who never fired "except upon the wing."[12]

In New York City on September 30, the Polo Grounds hosted a benefit game for Matty, organized by Fred Lieb. The scheduled match between the Giants and Braves was preceded by an "old-timers" contest featuring, among others, Frank Bowerman, Roger Bresnahan, Joe McGinnity, Billy Gilbert, Chief Meyers, and George Wiltse. The souvenir program sold for a dollar; inside Hugh Fullerton wrote: "The test of a man is not that his friends like him as it is that his foes respect him. [Matty] played straight, he played hard, he asked no odds and when he was beaten he was first to congratulate the victor." Ring Lardner contributed a "You Know Me, Al" letter:

> Well Al I guess the old boy was some pitcher and had everything and I remember one time when I give St. Louis two hits and shut them out and Gleason says to me you looked like Matty in there today. So I says maybe I will be as good as him before I get threw. So Gleason says no you wont because Matty uses his head. Well I says I can use my head to. Yes says Gleason as a hat rack.[13]

Eighteen thousand persons attended. Some of the retired veterans, such as Art Devlin and Fred Tenney, had put on girth since their playing days; others, like Moose McCormick and Red Murray, showed (in a different sense) that as athletes they could still cover a lot of ground. The old-time Giants beat the 1921 regulars 2–0 in a five-inning game that featured plenty of paunch, easy pitching, and good humor. Rain cut short the regular game to just one inning, though only 4,000 fans asked for a refund. Lieb had consulted with an insurance agent who showed him an historical table of how often it rained in New York City on the day of the scheduled benefit, and who advised a $25,000 policy in the event of bad weather. Lieb thought it a gamble worth taking, and the resultant good publicity caused the insurance company to ungrudgingly make payment. The entire effort, from both the attendance and the insurance policy, netted for Matty nearly $55,000.[14]

By their third summer at Saranac, Matty had recovered sufficiently so that he and Jane walked daily into woods and fields. Upon the summer solstice, they began recording a list of wild plants and flowers. For each venture into nature they sought to find at least one wild plant, new to them, and learn its name and something about it. Jack-in-the-pulpit, a spiked flower partly covered with an arching veil and with a root known as the Indian turnip, was the first entry. Blue gentians were Matty's favorite flowers.[15]

Matty threw the ceremonial first ball when the Saranac Lake team inaugurated its 1922 baseball season against Plattsburgh. He became active in the affairs of the local American Legion post, proudly wearing a legion pin in his lapel. He created a board game called "Big Six" which enabled baseball aficionados to pursue the pastime seated around a table. When another reporter was allowed to visit, the newsman was obliged to photograph Matty and two friends playing the board game in the sunshine of a well-tended backyard. Manufactured by Piroxland Products of New York City, the game was available postpaid for $2 east of the Mississippi and for $2.50 west of the river.[16]

On August 9, 1922, Matty and Jane made a dozen wild-plant entries into their log with the notation that these were found in Factoryville, where they had journeyed to visit his parents. Three days later the plant log would end with over 170 entries. Matty's enigmatic smile was back and so was most of his weight, though he walked slowly and with a cane. Lines etched his face—like his father it was apparent his features would age with handsomeness. His eyes, remarked an observer, had both the shadow of death and the light of returning health in them.

He played checkers with his father. "Checkers saved me up there," he said. He sat on the porch steps and looked at trees he had planted when a boy. His mother's chickens pecked in the yard. Henry's daughter Regina, eight years old, brought flowers to her uncle for him to identify. In tall grass behind the house, Matty found a big spider web with the spider waiting patiently in the center; he poked the web with a blade of grass and then watched the spider shake the web threateningly. "Do you suppose he is trying to frighten me?" Matty asked.[17]

The Giants again won the pennant and again faced their tenants, the Yankees, in the World Series. For the opening game former New York governor Al Smith, who had been instrumental in making professional baseball on Sundays legal in the state, threw out the ceremonial first ball. Judge Kenesaw Landis, now the sole commissioner of both major leagues (his new office having replaced the three-man National Commission), had struck a chord of startling probity for his administration by banishing all eight Black Sox from professional baseball. ("Regardless of the verdict of juries, no player who throws a ball game, no player that entertains proposals or promises to throw a game, no player that sits in conference with a bunch of crooked players and gamblers where the ways and means of throwing games are discussed, and does not promptly tell his club about it, will ever play professional baseball," the judge said.) When Landis, at the World Series opener, appeared in a bunting-laden box shortly before game time, he was accompanied by a ramrod-straight, faultlessly groomed man in a gray business suit and pearl-gray felt hat. Many in the crowd thought the judge's guest was Matty. Instead it was a man often regarded as the nation's most eligible bachelor, General John J. Pershing. Eventually Matty was recognized by people in the stands as sitting in the pressbox, where he had come to take notes for newspaper articles. He was described by a fellow reporter as broad-shouldered and bronze as a Texas Ranger. "Stand up, Matty, stand up!" fans cried. Matty posed for photographers—his face registering everything from gravity to laughter—but he refused to stand up.[18]

The Giants took the series in four games. (Five actually, if the one is counted that was called in the 10th inning because of darkness, even though the sun was yet fairly high in the sky. Judge Landis was so irate that he ordered all proceeds from this particular contest to go to charity.) John McGraw delighted in telling the world that his pitchers held Babe Ruth to a .118 average in 17 at-bats.

Boston in 1922 had both last-place major-league teams. Red Sox owner Harry Frazee had committed the unforgivable sin of peddling Babe Ruth to the Yankees in order to finance a Broadway musical. The Braves' owner, George Washington Grant, had perpetrated the lesser misdeeds of selling Art Nehf to the Giants and Rabbit Maranville to the Pirates. Grant suffered so many financial worries, remembered Fred Lieb, that he balked at donating his share of the gate receipts for Matty's testimonial game. Regarding his ownership of the Braves, Grant let it be known that "I will sell anything I have but my family, if I get my price."[19]

Judge Emil Fuchs of New York took Grant's statement at face value. The son of Orthodox Jews from Germany, Fuchs, a prospering attorney who included the New York Giants baseball club among his clients, had grown up in the settlement houses of Manhattan's Lower East Side, derived his title from past service on a municipal court, and never quite put behind him the fact that he once successfully defended Arnold Rothstein from a murder charge. Fuchs led a group of investors in meeting Grant's price. They included James McDonough, a New York banker, Albert Powell, a millionaire dealer in coal and New England real estate, and, for the prestige of his name if not for his money, Christopher Mathewson. Chosen president of the club by the new stockholders, Matty said that he would rather have been the on-field manager but his health would not stand it.

Judge Fuchs neither sought nor wanted money from Matty, offering instead, should things work out, the opportunity to buy—at the original purchase price—all or as much of the judge's own interest in the team as Matty should one day want. "The thought struck me that perhaps if he were actively connected with baseball again that the environment he loved might give him an added incentive to fight his way back to health," Fuchs wrote in his memoirs. "I told him not to assume any financial burden. The opportunity would always be there ... if the club was successful. I was always glad I did not permit him to assume that additional worry."[20]

Jane advised against the offer, and Dr. Packard argued that seclusion, rest, and the air of Saranac would prolong Matty's life; otherwise, the physician warned, Matty placed his survival in jeopardy. But Jane, recognizing her husband's determination, relented. "If it's your desire to go back to the game of your youth and affection," she told him, "go ahead." In accepting Fuch's business proposal, Matty confided to the judge, "I would rather spend another two or three years in the only occupation and vocation I know than to linger many years up in Saranac Lake."[21]

Besides the franchise purchase amount of $350,000, the new owners would pay additionally as much as $80,000 annually to rent their ballpark from James Gaffney, a former Braves' owner. Braves Field, built in the heady aftermath of the miracle of 1914, had a seating capacity of 40,000. The team drew well when contending; the trouble was developing a team of contenders. The salaries that George Grant paid made the team seem like Devil's Island to most established major leaguers. Fred Mitchell stayed as manager, and the club had two distinguished veterans in Hank Gowdy and Rube Marquard. Billy Southworth, the right fielder, was the only stand-out player for whom the future did not seem either a short-term or an uncertain thing. Dick Rudolph, like Gowdy a remnant of the 1914 season, coached the pitching staff.

Matty, riding a crest of good publicity, made well-received speeches to the Boston Chamber of Commerce, City Club, and the Newsboys' Union. The team acquired another distinguished veteran in Stuffy McInnis, whose $14,000 salary was considered too rich by the Cleveland Indians. A native of Gloucester and a local favorite during four years with the Red Sox, McInnis, coming off a good year and just 32 years old, was a worthwhile investment not only as a player but also as a gate attraction and symbol of an in-good-faith effort to field a creditable team. The organization also had fond hopes for Harvard infielder Arthur Conlon. (So did Harvard.)

Judge Landis attended the Braves' 1923 home opener as Matty's special guest. Soldiers, sailors, and marines, accompanied by a military

Matty with Kenesaw Landis and Emil Fuchs at the Braves' 1923 Opening Day. (National Baseball Hall of Fame Library, Cooperstown, N.Y.)

band, drilled and expended blank ammunition in boisterous, and smoky, pre-game festivities. Matty felt well enough to parade with the other dignitaries to the flag pole in deep center field for the raising of the national colors. Judge Landis, soon thereafter, donned a catcher's mask and glove, Mayor James Curley took a bat, and Governor Channing Cox threw a pitch that Curley missed and Landis somehow caught. Despite the gay ceremonies, the stands, in the cold weather, were filled only to half-capacity. The Braves would lose this and the following next three games to the Giants, including a double-header on Patriots' Day.

Jacob Ruppert built a grand, new baseball edifice in the Bronx where 60,000 fans congregated on the Yankees' opening day, and Babe Ruth made the place his own by walloping a game-winning home run. Charles Stoneham sought to keep up with his former renters by lavishing money to enlarge and improve the Polo Grounds. Twenty-five thousand came to watch the Giants open their home season against the Braves. Again Judge Landis participated in an expansive pre-game ceremony featuring an abundance of political figures. Matty sat in a box near the Braves' bench; the crowd clamored for him. Landis approached the box and magisterially refused to take no for an answer. Matty climbed over the rail and onto the field, his action prompting a prolonged and enthusiastic ovation. McGraw embraced him, and Matty remained on the field while Landis presented World Series rings to the Giants. As he slowly returned to the box, an erupting second ovation palpably belonged less to the defending champions than to Matty. If that was not sentiment enough, Marquard stood as the Braves' starting pitcher. Many in attendance, while the Braves held a slender lead, pulled for the visitors. An eighth-inning rally, however, drove Marquard from the mound and enabled the Giants to win, 7–3.

In mid–May the Braves stood unimpressively in sixth place. Matty and Judge Fuchs plunged into treacherous waters and negotiated a trade with John McGraw. Hank Gowdy and pitcher Johnny Watson went to New York in return for Jesse Barnes and catcher Earl "Oil" Smith. Barnes had won 20 games in each of the two seasons Matty had been a coach with the Giants; Watson and Smith were "bad actors" and players whom their respective clubs were glad to cut loose. Boston fans remained sensitive on the issue of transactions between the Giants and Braves; so much so that, from the day the new ownership was announced, Matty and Fuchs made it a frequent point to deny publicly any collusion with McGraw and Stoneham. Since Gowdy, though only 33 and despite former glory, was considered by Boston sportswriters as about "done" anyway, the transaction received from the local press the benefit of the doubt in that the Braves, in this case at least, seemed to get as good as they gave. The trade also enabled the venerated Gowdy an opportunity to play for a contender once again.

The trade notwithstanding, by late June the Braves hovered in or near last place. Several players voiced to reporters their unhappiness about manager Fred Mitchell, and when the Braves visited the Polo Grounds—as the Giants drove to their third consecutive pennant—Oil Smith allegedly went after McGraw with a bat for depriving him of World Series money. The malcontents in the Braves' clubhouse received a message from their management either to stop griping or to begin thinking about a career outside big-league baseball. Rallying, if such it can be termed, around Southworth and McInnis, and thanks to rookie Joe Genewich who pitched in September as well as anyone in the league, the team had the "distinction" of losing 100 games and at the same time avoiding last place thanks to the Phillies, who lost 104.

Hugh Jennings, now a Giant coach, was rumored as a replacement for Mitchell. Matty denied it, but the rumor mill persisted. Frank Chance was also mentioned as a possible manager, as was former Giant George Burns, now playing for the Reds. John Foster, the Giants' secretary and a newspaperman himself, remarked to some of his chums in the pressbox that in no way would it be Frank Chance. The Peerless Leader, Foster said, was too blunt a man for Matty. Foster was not so certain about the quiet and reliable Burns; it depended on whether Matty wanted a man whose sense of strategy resembled McGraw's. Rabbit Maranville's name also came up, but no one who knew Matty took seriously that notion.[22]

Matty returned to Saranac for the winter, but not without negotiating another trade with McGraw. McGraw felt ready to try Travis Jackson at shortstop. This made Dave Bancroft available. While keeping Fred Mitchell in the organization as its chief scout, Matty wanted Bancroft as the Braves' playing manager. A superb fielder and a switch-hitter with a batting average exceeding .300 in the Giants' three successful pennant drives, the 32-year-old Bancroft was a valuable performer. McGraw, at first, wanted Joe Genewich included in the deal, but pitching talent with a future was too rare a commodity on the Braves' roster and Matty declined to part with the right-hander. Billy Southworth, veteran pitcher Joe Oeschger, and some cash went to New York for Bancroft and outfielders Casey Stengel and Bill Cunningham. John Foster expressed no surprise at Matty's choice; he described Bancroft as reserved to the point of taciturnity and might have added that, like Matty and Judge Fuchs, Bancroft was an expert auction bridge player. (Blanche McGraw in her memoirs recalled the Bancrofts fondly, remembering her husband at home laughing with Bancroft perhaps more than with any other player and describing Bancroft's wife Edna as "the best of company.") McGraw bragged about sending Bancroft to the Braves in order to help his old friend Matty. The 33-year-old Stengel remarked after he got the news: "The paths of glory lead only to the Braves."[23]

In Saranac, Harry Hull, a rugged individual, civil engineer, and friend of the Mathewsons, purchased a corner lot at the intersection of Old Military Road and Park Avenue. As a young man Hull came to Saranac for his health; a relapse brought him back to stay. He would design and build on the corner lot the first home Christy and Jane Mathewson, after 20 years of marriage, intended to own for themselves. From their current residence down the street, Matty and Jane could watch their friend display his thoughtfulness and skill in the construction. Hull laid the foundation of the two-and-a-half-story, colonial-style structure into a man-made knoll, evoking a dignity-of-place to an already attractive setting. The entry of the completed house featured a large hall and a broad, J-shaped staircase with solid cherry railing. Stair risers, an inch-and-a-half shallower than the convention, accommodated a man with one useless lung and the other damaged. The hall led to spacious living and dining rooms; imported Italian tile adorned the fireplace. Expansive porches, a feature of Saranac's "cure cottages" where consumptives sat and breathed the open air, balanced the exterior sides. Christy Junior commenced his studies at Bucknell; even so, the house had five bedrooms and three baths.[24]

Matty, in December 1923, interrupted his stay in Saranac to attend the league meeting in Chicago. While there he spoke against the practice of paying bonuses over and above players' regular salaries. The practice made owners seem generous, he said, but it also enabled them to begin the next year's negotiation with the player at a significantly lower level than if the bonus had been factored as salary. Matty's recommendation would have acted to increase the long-term expense of salaries solidly based on past performance, with a compensating savings of eliminating the possibly greater short-term extravagance that bonuses represented. He may not have persuaded his fellow executives, but they received his remarks cordially and welcomed him among their rank.[25]

The Braves' salaries collectively increased to over $200,000 during the first year under the management of Mathewson and Fuchs, compared to the $80,000 it had been in the last season under George Grant. Even so, Matty acquired among his ballplayers a reputation for tightfistedness, especially on the matter of limiting them to the specified amount of their per-day meal money. Judge Fuchs endeavored to maintain his law practice while at the same time acting as the club's vice-president. Two years older than Matty, short, heavy-set, deliberate in his polite and suave manner, there seemed to some a cultivated hint of menace in Fuch's courtesy. But there was no menace in the former city magistrate when it came to baseball. In spring training Fuchs occasionally put on a uniform to play catch. When Matty needed rest, the judge himself ran the organization, and his less pecuniary-minded exuberance sometimes exceeded what Matty considered better judgment. "What difference does it make?" Fuchs asked when some of the players, recognizing a softer touch when they saw one, attempted to get him to intervene in their behalf on the matter of daily meal money.

Matty usually prevailed, including on the meal money. His attention to financial detail was such that John Wheeler, a dozen years after their collaborative publication of *Pitching in a Pinch*, still received annually from Matty a carefully figured check for Wheeler's share of the previous year's book royalties. In 1925 Wheeler received a check for $86.[26]

As far as Judge Fuchs was concerned, Joe Genewich, money, and any infielder the Cardinals might like were available if Branch Rickey would just part with Rogers Hornsby. The judge seems to have been serious in the offer, but made it after Rickey had turned down $200,000 and four players from the Giants for Hornsby. Rickey demurred on the Giants' proposal because one of the players was not Frank Frisch.[27]

It was obvious to those who attended the December league meeting that Matty was not a cured man. Yet he felt well enough to go to spring training in St. Petersburg, accompanied by Jane, whom a member of the press described as Matty's ever-faithful nurse and "presiding genius."

Jane's presence, as she meant it to, made it difficult for others to impose too strenuously upon her husband's time and energy. Later in the year Dr. Packard worried publicly, again, that Matty's "recovery depends on freedom from cares and worries and any excitement would jeopardize his health." Though when pressed for more information, the doctor backed down and said that Matty was "all right."[28]

The Braves went south without a single contractual hold-out, due largely to management's more generous attitude toward salaries. It was also recognized, by those who wrote copy for a living, that Matty did none of the club's contract negotiating in the newspapers. Burt Whitman, capable, affable, and so long in the business that he would have the distinction of being one of the few Boston sportswriters for whom Ted Williams ever said kind or respectful words, remarked that Matty believed a ballplayer's popularity was a big asset and it did no good to haggle publicly over money and risk diminishing that popularity.[29]

Matty encouraged college men with talent to try out for the big leagues. "The college man has helped professional baseball, and baseball of any kind has helped the college man." He cautioned, however, "If you cannot make the big leagues, give it up. Do not stick through your best years in the minors." It was advice that Art Conlon followed. The Harvard man's prospects as a second baseman diminished when James "Cotton" Tierney was obtained from the Phillies, and Conlon sought Matty's opinion whether he should remain with the Braves or accept a proffered business opportunity. "Although I am sacrificing the club's equity in your contract in telling you this," Matty told Conlin candidly, "I believe it is in your best interest to accept the business opportunity."[30]

Art Devlin joined the coaching staff, and Joe McGinnity, who the summer before at age 53 pitched for a team in the Mississippi Valley League, was invited to Florida as a guest. Manager Bancroft, after spending the winter at his home near Lake Superior, preached against carelessness in getting sunburned, and Matty made certain the pitchers did not throw curveballs too early. Given the spaciousness of Braves Field, the overall strategy of Matty and Bancroft was to develop a young, fast team. Under Bancroft's leadership the club would lead the league in fielding, and they would score 129 runs fewer than any other team. Brooklyn's Jack Fournier would lead the league with 27 home runs. The entire Braves lineup would hit 25.

Bancroft played shortstop with daring and flair. He could make the back-hand play of a hard grounder, even on the edge of the outfield grass, and with his strong right arm still throw the runner out at first base. He knew when to cut off throws and when only to pretend. He ran the entire defense from his position, and he was unsatisfied with his infield counterparts. John Kelleher, picked up on waivers before the season began when the incumbent third baseman Tony Boeckel was killed in a car accident, was let go. Bancroft then tried Ernie Padgett at the "number five" spot. At second base Cotton Tierney also disappointed the manager; Tierney's fielding and hitting were such that he was encouraged to get eyeglasses like Specs Toporcer, the Cardinals' infielder.

It was Bancroft, though, who misjudged a screamer, hit by Walter Holke in Philadelphia, which struck him in the lower abdomen and caused appendicitis-like symptoms. He went to New York for an operation. The appendix was healthy, but the surgeon did find a small intestinal tumor; the doctor removed them both. It looked like Bancroft, recuperating at Emil Fuch's summer home, would be out the remainder of the season. Dick Rudolph assumed the managerial role.

In Bancroft's absence the team resumed its losing ways as easily as before. By late July the club had fallen once again in the standings to in or near last place. Matty and Judge Fuchs got rid of some players, signed others, but nothing helped. Poor crowds made Braves Field seem cavernous; in a gesture to those faithful who did come, home plate was moved closer to the grandstand.

In early September, Matty and Bancroft watched Dazzy Vance, the Brooklyn strikeout king, pitch a three-hitter against the Braves. Matty observed that Vance now threw both his fastball and his curve (described by Rube Bressler as "like an apple rolling off a crooked table") with exactly the same motion. Bancroft said: "A couple years ago all I had to do was to watch the fingers on Dazzy's pitching hand as he went up on his backswing and I knew what was on." Bancroft added that this tip-off did not work anymore.[31]

On September 10 the Giants beat the Braves 22–1 in the first game of a double-header. Bancroft could not only be taciturn, he was tough too. It was reported that during his operation he declined a general anesthetic for a local one, but the Braves' poor pitching and porous infield play was more than he could stand. He put on his uniform and inserted himself in the lineup for the second game, which the Braves managed to lose by just a mere eight runs.

The Giants won their fourth consecutive pennant. This time their World Series opponents were not the Yankees but the Senators, led by Leon "Goose" Goslin and longtime ace Walter Johnson. "The Big Train" no longer had such a consistently fearsome and overpowering fastball, but he pitched well enough to win 23 games during the regular season. This year marked Johnson's 18th in the American League, all with the Senators, and his first World Series. Fans across the country, including many New Yorkers, were pulling for him. The series went seven games.

In the finale, with President and Mrs. Coolidge looking on, the Senators' playing manager Bucky Harris used three pitchers through eight innings to keep the score knotted at three runs apiece. In the top of the ninth, amid tumultuous shouts of "Walter! Walter!" Johnson—who had already suffered two complete-game losses in the series—entered the game and pitched four innings of scoreless relief. In the bottom of the 12th, with one out, Muddy Ruel lifted a foul to the left side of home plate. Hank Gowdy tossed his catcher's mask aside—or so he intended. As he followed the ball's descent, Gowdy stumbled over his mask and missed the catch. Reprieved ("like a sinner forgiven," he called it), Ruel then doubled.[32] Travis Jackson fumbled the next ball put into fair play, a hard grounder hit to his right by Walter Johnson, allowing Johnson to reach first base as Ruel remained on second. Earl McNeely then hit a ball over the third baseman's head, scoring the winning run.

The World Series had increased in value since Matty's last appearance in one and Gowdy's misplay was quickly labeled a "$50,000 muff." Matty witnessed the game—it was noticed he now wore eyeglasses—and that night he had dinner with Fred Lieb on the train back to New York. Prohibition notwithstanding, Matty enjoyed an occasional drink with fellow reporters, a fraternization, Jack Wheeler attested, Matty as a player never enjoyed with newspapermen. Lieb remembered chatting about many things with Matty during this particular evening, but the conversation always seemed to go back to Gowdy and the play the catcher had missed. The man who had been on the mound for Merkle's failure to tag second base and Snodgrass's drop of a fly ball ruminated that Gowdy's error was well nigh unforgivable.

Sunday baseball remained illegal in Boston, Pittsburgh, and Philadelphia. In Boston, Judge Fuchs and others worked energetically for repeal of the baseball blue law. It was said some persons in Boston already profited from Sunday baseball: those politicians receiving "seed money" to support it. The judge termed these political hacks "Jesse James boys without horses" and resisted the "hold-ups." He felt certain the advent of Sunday baseball was too popular to prevent and therefore inevitable. (In Boston it took place in 1929.)[33]

Cotton Tierney was traded to Brooklyn for Bernie Neis, a nimble outfielder whose muscular 5 foot 7 inch frame caused him to be described as a "minor Hercules." Stuffy McInnis's contract, one of the highest in the league, was not renewed. Matty considered making an offer for the Giants' solid-hitting outfielder Irish Meusel, but evidently thought it unwise to press with local fans the issue of Braves Field as a home for McGraw's cast-offs.

Rain plagued the early going of the 1925 Braves' two-a-day workouts in St. Petersburg. Matty again journeyed south, though obviously frail. "He loved to play checkers with the old-timers." Judge Fuchs remembered.[34] The judge's son, then a boy, recalled years later that

Matty, blindfolded, on one occasion in St. Petersburg played at least eight checker opponents simultaneously and beat them all. When Matty caught a cold, he returned to Saranac for rest and not to Boston for the season opener. The judge, with the assistance of club secretary Edwin Riley, now handled the executive matters.

The big news in baseball was Babe Ruth's "stomach trouble," which kept him off the playing field. Babe or no Babe, home-run balls flew into bleachers and beyond at a tremendous rate, even though Thomas Shibe of the A.J. Reach Company, manufacturer of baseballs, assured the public: "It is the very same sphere, the yarn, cork and leather being the same quality as in previous years."[35]

Not everyone believed Shibe. The Braves took three straight games from the visiting Giants and lost the fourth on an eighth-inning home run by Frank "Pancho" Snyder. Not just any home run but the first ever to sail completely out of Braves Field, clearing the wall in left field, with a slightly favoring wind, by some 15 feet and falling onto the tracks of the Boston and Albany Railroad. (When Braves Field was built 10 years previously, Ty Cobb stood at home plate and remarked: "No home run drive will ever go over that fence.") A few weeks later Bernie Neis hit a ball in the same direction even farther than Snyder. "I must have muscles in my hair," remarked the compact left fielder.[36]

Jimmy Welsh, a rookie, would hit .312 and, from the Braves' right-field position, top the league in outfield assists. In his enthusiasm to do well, after a game in May, Welsh had a semi-pro player hit fungoes so he could practice catching fly balls in the Braves' "sun field"—but, in so doing, Welsh turned his ankle and missed some starts. The team as a whole stumbled as well; in the latter part of May it had threatened the first division from fifth place, but by July 4 it was mired once again in last. Fans taunted Bancroft with cries of "Get a ball club!" Fred Mitchell drummed for fast, young, talented ballplayers; though it seemed—Jimmy Welsh being an exception—the organization was trying the youngsters at the major-league level too soon.

Recognizing what Branch Rickey, through Cardinal control of several minor-league teams, was accomplishing in the development of young players, the Braves acquired the nearby Worcester club in the Eastern League. Like the Cardinals, the Braves were not rich in cash and could not afford to outbid wealthier competitors for the best talent from independent minor-league organizations. Casey Stengel was sent to Worcester as both president and manager with the mission of developing players for the parent organization. It proved more responsibility than Stengel was ready to assume at this point in his life. When he became restless to accept a chance to manage elsewhere, Stengel, as manager, wrote a letter to Stengel, as president, asking for his release. President Stengel granted the request, congratulating himself on his new position. Judge Landis offered to declare the transaction null and void. Judge Fuchs declined. "If that's the way Stengel works," Fuchs said, "let him go. We'll be better off without him."[37]

The Braves won three games in Brooklyn and took a double-header at home from the Cardinals. On July 10 Larry Benton, a 27-year-old right-hander who, in his third season with the club, was finally coming into his own, shut out the Reds 1–0. The team remained in last place, but some observers began to remark a change in the players' attitudes. Rabbit Maranville, now the Cubs' manager, was among those who saw it: "The big improvement in the Braves, to my way of thinking, is the way the boys are fighting for Banny. This is what helps a team rise above itself—that fighting and hustling stuff."[38]

In Saranac, Matty kept abreast of progress, or lack thereof, through reports and charts sent to him. Andy High joined the club from Brooklyn; what Wilbert Robinson would receive in return depended on how Bancroft evaluated the infielder's ability to perform at third base everyday. For the waiver price of $1,500 the Braves obtained from the Athletics yet another youngster, Walter Gautreau, whom Bancroft would try at second base. At 5 feet 4 inches, "Doc" Gautreau stood five inches less than Bancroft and two inches less than Andy High; Gautreau weighed 130 pounds, but he fielded with panache, and Bancroft blessed him by saying that he never had to tell the newcomer anything twice. Gautreau had the additional credentials of hailing from Cambridge and Holy Cross. Fans came in droves to see him, and just about anything he did brought applause. On Saturday, August 29, 32,000 fans came to "Gautreau Day" at the ballpark, witnessed the presentation to the honoree of a new automobile, and saw "Doc," from the lead-off position in the lineup, rap three hits in a double-header. On September 1, Gautreau's two singles figured in the scoring as Larry Benton outpitched Grover Alexander 2–0, in a game in which the Boston crowd had the further delight of seeing manager Maranville ejected by umpire Bill Klem. The victory lifted the Braves out of the cellar.

Judge Fuchs, likely taking a cue from Matty, promised all the players new suits of clothes if they could stay out of there. Attendance figures indicated the Braves organization would actually make money on the year. The club continued its rise and ended the season in fifth place. As the World Series between the Senators and Pirates was about to begin in Pittsburgh, Matty, weakening in Saranac, approved the completion of the Andy High deal with Uncle Robbie. Jess Barnes, a pitching workhorse who for the second consecutive season had given the Braves over 200 innings, center fielder Gus Felix, and catcher Mickey O'Neil would go to the Robins for catcher Zack Taylor, utilityman Jimmy Johnston, and outfielder Eddie Brown. In Pittsburgh, Judge Fuchs and Uncle Robbie verbally sparred, good-naturedly, about who got the better of whom in the transaction and went to Ring Lardner to arbitrate their dispute. "It is my opinion you both got stuck," replied the writer.[39]

Soon after the trade was announced, pneumonia claimed what was left of Matty's working lung. Jane stayed by his bedside in the new house Harry Hull built for them. Dr. Packard attended him as well. Matty's condition deteriorated so rapidly that Christy Junior was not able to return in time from Bucknell. The man who had lived in the shadow of death for five years recognized his end.

"I am at peace with God and man," Matty said to Jane. "I have had a beautiful life. Don't grieve. We have had our share of God's blessings." He instructed that his burial take place in Lewisburg, near the university. "That's where I first met you," he told his wife.[40] He died about 11 P.M. on October 7.

Earlier in the day Judge Fuchs watched as Walter Johnson struck out ten Pirates in the Senators' opening-game World Series victory. Late that night the judge was playing bridge with reporters in the Hotel Schenley. A newsman from one of the Boston papers entered the room, interrupting the merriment. "Silence, gentleman, I have some bad news for you," the reporter began.[41]

The next day when the Pirates in white and Senators in gray assembled in two lines near home plate, each player wore a black mourning band on his left arm. Beneath a bright autumn sky the chattering and cheering capacity crowd at Forbes Field became hushed, and a woman with an operatic voice sang "The Star-Spangled Banner." The flag was lifted to the top of the pole in deep center field and then lowered, in memory of Matty, to half-mast. The wave of grief which passed over the crowd was palpable. Among them, John McGraw tried to hide his tears and Hughie Jennings wept openly.

Matty's body was carried by train to Lewisburg and taken to the home of Jane's mother. A wealth of flower arrangements, from across the country, were given for the funeral. One from a former battery mate said simply, "Mathewson and Bresnahan." Jane was particularly touched by those who knew Matty well enough to send blue gentians. John McGraw, Dave Bancroft, and Emil Fuchs served as pallbearers, as did Braves business associates Edwin Riley and Albert Powell—and, from the days long before when Matty's mother made them buckwheat pancakes on Sunday mornings, Ernest Sterling. The burial took place on a Saturday. Bucknell had a football game at home that afternoon. Kick-off was delayed until Matty lay in the grave.

People venerated him, editorialized the New York *World*, "not because he had a hop on his fast one, not because he struck out hundreds of batters, not because he was cool in the pinches, or because he made a game fight against a mortal disease, but because, before anything else, he was a gentleman. Like Corbett in boxing and Camp in football he made us feel that he stood for what the game could be if all those associated with it were like him. He was a vindication of our love for sport."[42]

Epilogue

Judge Fuchs took over as the Braves president. Dave Bancroft left the organization after two seasons more. Things got so bad in 1929 the judge decided they could get no worse if he made himself manager. Under Fuchs the Braves won 56 games, six more than they won under Jack Slattery and Rogers Hornsby in 1928. The Braves did become respectable on the field in the early 1930s, under manager Bill McKechnie, but fell to the bottom again in 1935. The judge described himself as nearly a millionaire when he arranged the purchase of the Braves and nearly a bankrupt when he departed from the ownership more than a decade later.

John McGraw managed the Giants into 1932 and died of cancer two years afterward. In his office at the Polo Grounds he kept just two photographs of players: one of Ross Youngs, the other of Matty—favorites who both preceded him in death. Blanche McGraw never married again. When in 1957 the Giants played their final game in New York, she was among the last persons to leave the Polo Grounds. She carried roses.

Minerva Mathewson survived her eldest and last living son by four months. In her will she forgave her husband the $500 loan she lent to Gilbert just before they married and which he never repaid. The remains of Minerva and Gilbert are buried in unmarked graves near the stone of her mother and father.

Christy Junior graduated from Bucknell with a degree in electrical engineering. He pursued beautiful women and a career in the Army Air Corps. While serving in China in 1933, he took his bride of two weeks aloft in his plane. The plane crashed, his wife was killed, and he lost a leg. His mother had journeyed to China for the wedding; she remained to nurse him back to enough health so that he could cross the Pacific and then the continent to continue his convalescence at Walter Reed Hospital. He recovered, married, divorced, and married again. During the Second World War, despite his artificial limb, Christy Junior returned to active duty as a trainer of pilots. After the war he went into business in Texas, where in 1950 he was killed by a gas explosion that occurred in his home. He had no children.[1]

Jane Mathewson also never remarried. She invested wisely the money left to her by her husband, and her wealth increased during the long years of her widowhood. She resided for more than two decades in the home built by Harry Hull. In 1939 she attended the ceremonies in Cooperstown which memorialized her husband as one of the first five players to be enshrined in the Hall of Fame. The others, Babe Ruth, Ty Cobb, Walter Johnson, and Honus Wagner, were present to witness the honors accorded them.

After her son died, Jane returned to her family residence in Lewisburg. She, as a mentor, became friends with a young lady who lived on the same street. When the attractive young woman received a gentleman caller, Jane would leave a note advising the young man to treat her friend well. She signed the notes "Mrs. Christy Mathewson." Jane died in 1967.

NOTES

Chapter 1

1. George Capwell's will and the resulting judgment are recorded in the office of the Registrar of Deeds and Wills, Wyoming County, Pa. That Nelson Doolittle was a clergyman is recorded in the Clinton township census.
2. Correspondence with Rev. Garford F. Williams of Nicholson, Pa., who has done historical and genealogical research concerning this area of Wyoming County.
3. Henry Mathewson filed for divorce in Wyoming County in August 1874. The divorce was granted in August 1876.
4. *Clinton Township Census of 1880*. Albert is listed as age 15; Benjamin as 13. Nelson Doolittle's age is recorded as 75.
5. "Mathewson's Folks"; Sterling, "Christy Mathewson as Man and Boy"; and a visit to the home graciously allowed by Darren Maria. Melodeon: reminiscence of Grace Mathewson Van Lengen, Minerva's granddaughter through son Henry. Stained glass: reminiscence of Betty Phillips, Minerva's granddaughter through Edith Christine.
6. $500 loan: will of Minerva I. Mathewson, dated 11 January 1926. Real estate to Janette: deeds transferred 25 June 1887 and 14 October 1887. House purchase: deed transfer completed in 1889 between Rachel V. Knapp and husband to Minerva I. Mathewson. These are recorded with the Registrar of Deeds and Wills, Wyoming County, Pa.
7. Christy and Jessie sneak some cake: reminiscence of Keith Wrigley, Jessie's son.
8. CM, "How I Became a Big-League Pitcher." "Old Charley": *Boston Globe* 17 Jan 1926.
9. CM, "How I Became a Big-League Pitcher."
10. *Boston Globe* 17 Jan 1926.
11. Sterling, "Christy Mathewson as Man and Boy." For these and other quoted details of CM growing up.
12. For what Anna Held performed: William C. Young, *Famous Actors and Actresses on the American Stage* (New York: Bowker, 1975).
13. CM, "How I Became a Big-League Pitcher."
14. Frank Stanton's recollections are recorded in a series of letters written in 1945–1946 to Kenneth B. Rhone, editor of *Grit Magazine*; the letters are in the Mathewson file at the Bertrand Library. Following his graduation from Bucknell, Stanton served as athletic director at Dennison University, earned a law degree in 1908, practiced law in Cleveland, and was elected mayor of Chagrin Falls, Ohio. He died in 1960 at age 82.
15. *L'Agenda, 1900* (Lewisburg, 1899). A Bucknell yearbook.
16. Edmund Morris, *The Rise of Theodore Roosevelt* (New York: Coward, McCann & Geoghegan, 1979), 477. Eventually, as president, Roosevelt saw his error and called for football reform.
17. Others, including Virgil "Ned" Garvin and Andrew "Rube" Foster, have been variously credited with teaching CM the "fadeaway." The matter was thoroughly researched by Dick Thompson, who made a presentation entitled "Matty and His Fadeaway: The Origins of a Legend Reexamined," offered at the SABR national convention in June 1995.

Thompson's conclusion coincides with CM's own article, "How I Became a Big-League Pitcher," in supporting David Williams as having shown CM the pitch in Honesdale. Thompson also revealed that CM's manager at Taunton, Ray Kellogg, played 39 games at second base for the New York Giants in 1901 under the name Ray Nelson. With apparently an assist from SABR founding member Keith Sutton, Thompson additionally pointed out that in 1898 the Honesdale team was known as the Reds and in 1899 as the Eagles. For CM with Honesdale: Sutton, *Wayne County Sports History*.

18. On throwing curveballs: Jordan, *Pitching*; Jansen and Jansen, *Craft of Pitching*; and John Montgomery Ward, *Base-Ball: How to Become a Player* (Reprinted, Cleveland: SABR, 1993). Also Thorn and Holway, *Pitcher*; and McCarver and Peary, *Baseball for Brain Surgeons*. On throwing the fadeaway: CM, "How I Became a Big-League Pitcher."

19. Fastball in on right-handed batter: Stanton's recollections for *Grit*. "Drop ball": CM, "How I Became a Big-League Pitcher." CM watches first major league game: *Boston Globe* 2 Feb 1923. "How I Became a Big League Pitcher," however, relates a conflicting "first major league game" incident in which CM, enroute to Taunton, waited outside the players' gate at the Polo Grounds and cheered with others when Amos Rusie appeared in street clothes.

20. For quoted conversation from the day of the Penn-Bucknell game: John F. Smith's letter dated 30 April 1950, contained in Mathewson file at the National Baseball Museum. Smith's letter describes CM signing with and playing for Norfolk, as well as CM's decision to go to the Giants.

21. Stanton letter, 24 August 1945.

22. Smith letter.

23. The Smith letter has CM winning his first start, 6–5; Al Kermisch, a SABR researcher, provided additional information to the author indicating that CM won 7–5. Smith recollected CM winning 21 games for Norfolk; Hannan, in "Christy Mathewson's First Baseball Contract," stated CM went 20-1-1; Kermisch researched 19 victories with two defeats, but the point of CM's pitching success is the same.

Chapter 2

1. "Fadeaway": CM, "How I Became a Big-League Pitcher." Radbourn, Welch, Hubbell: Thorn and Holway, *Pitcher*. "Pitching it ten or twelve times...." CM, *Pitching in a Pinch*. Bulger quoting Davis: *Boston Globe* 17 Jan 1926.

2. CM's debut: *NYT* 18 Jul 1900; Mayer, *Christy Mathewson: A Game-by-Game Profile*; and a description contained in the Mathewson file at the National Baseball Museum. Joe McGinnity was the winning pitcher for Brooklyn and the first National League batter CM struck out.

3. Wagner's "groove" and Chesbro's welcome: CM, *Pitching in a Pinch*, 8–9, 43.

4. Walter Camp: *Collier's Weekly*, 22 December 1900. Jane at Female Institute: Bucknell Alumni Office; for details of her personal appearance: Betty Cook, "Athlete—Soldier—Gentleman," and Blanche McGraw, *Real McGraw*, 190.

5. CM, "My Life So Far."

6. Bucknell's academic year is recorded in the college catalog and yearbook. CM's transcript indicates he did not participate in the third term of either his sophomore or junior years. He likely left the "philosophical course" of study, designed for completion in four years, for the "eclectic course" which had no definite time span.

7. Mack and $50: *NYT* 4 Apr 1901.

8. The environs of the Polo Grounds are derived from copies of drawings provided by the Ballparks Committee, SABR.

9. CM's first three losses of '01 came from the Cardinals. Tom Padden scored the winning run in the first and third losses, besides ending the middle loss with an unassisted double play.

10. Morris, *Theodore Roosevelt*, 724.

11. "Matty": Lieb, *Baseball as I Have Known It*, 145. Arthur Macdonald, "Statistics of Baseball," *Scientific American*, 1 May 1915. Paul Dickson in *Baseball's Greatest Quotations* (New York, Harper, 1991) includes this exchange between unknown players, recorded by writer Frank Graham, in regard to CM: FIRST PLAYER: How big do you think that big kid is? SECOND PLAYER: Six feet. FIRST PLAYER: He's the biggest six you ever saw—a big six."

12. *L'Agenda '02*, 188.
13. *NYT*, 17 Apr 1902.
14. "Well, well, well!" is identified in Stark, *Year They Called Off the World Series*, 72; he is also remarked upon in McGraw, *Thirty Years in Baseball*, 85.
15. "Fading idol" and "no great improvement:" *NYT* 22 May, 14 Jun 1902. "I cannot win with them behind me!" and Hendrick's allegation: Blanche McGraw, *Real McGraw*, 184–5. For Horace Fogel's perspective when CM's arm went limp during the '02 Memorial Day game: *TSN* 8 Jun 1907.
16. "Good umpires are born...." Quoted in Alexander, *John McGraw*, 81. "Cheese": Fleming, *Unforgettable Season*, 97, 113.
17. For the details surrounding McGraw's connivance to come to New York: Alexander, *John McGraw*.
18. CM learns from McGinnity: McGraw, *Thirty Years in Baseball*, 141–42. McGraw quoted: *NYT* 18 Jul 1902.
19. *NYT* 30 Sep 1902.

Chapter 3

1. Cook, "Athlete—Soldier—Gentleman."
2. *Lewisburg Saturday News*, 7 Mar 1903.
3. Sher, "Christy Mathewson" ("He was terribly ill all the way down." Jane is quoted). Blanche McGraw, *Real McGraw*, 190–91.
4. Blanche's appearance: Alexander, *John McGraw*, 82. Polo Grounds seat: *NYT* 6 Nov 1962.
5. *NYT* 6 Sep 1903.
6. Silver dollars: Alexander, *John McGraw*, 105.
7. CM's checker playing: Blanche McGraw, *Real McGraw*, 192; John McGraw, *Thirty Years in Baseball*, 142. Poker playing and fine: Mann, *Branch Rickey*, 102; CM, *Pitching in a Pinch*, 51.
8. *NYT* 18, 19 Apr 1904.
9. Mann, *Branch Rickey*; *TSN* 3 Sep 1904; besides Tenney and Rickey, *TSN* mentions Togie Pittinger and Kaiser Wilhelm, both pitchers, who also would not play on Sundays.
10. Mordecai Brown quoted in Stark, *Year They Called Off the World Series*, 120–1. Dizzy Dean quote: Dickson, *Baseball's Greatest Quotations*.
11. Stark, *Year They Called Off the World Series*, 160.
12. CM, *Pitching in a Pinch*, 106.
13. Klaw and Erlanger's: *NYT* 3 Oct 1904; *TSN* 15 Oct, 26 Nov 1904. Blanche McGraw, in *Real McGraw*, put the amount brought in for the players by the event as $25,000; *TSN* described it as $10,000; Donlin quoted as saying each player netted $429.
14. McGinnity, Donlin "sore": *TSN* 1 Oct, 26 Nov 1904. The 1 Oct *TSN* lists the salaries of CM and McGinnity as $4,000 for the '04 season; Luther Taylor, who recorded 27 wins for the club received $3,000; McGraw is listed as earning $10,000 for the season with a $2,500 bonus for winning the pennant. The *NYT* 25 Jun 1905 lists salaries and average incomes for various professions: a member of Congress received $5,000 per year; a lawyer on average earned $1,500; a doctor, $2,000; a clergyman, $750.

Chapter 4

1. *TSN* 31 Dec 1904.
2. Clubhouse: *NYT* 16 Apr 05. According to Seymour, *Baseball: The Golden Age*, the Giants scheduled a starting time of 4:00 to accommodate Wall Street patrons; early or late in the season, because of daylight, the first-pitch time was adjusted. In 1912 the Giants changed their regular starting time to 3:30. Other clubs began their games at 3:00 or 3:30.
3. "Sis": Blanche McGraw, *Real McGraw*, 205.
4. Schacht, *Clowning Through Baseball*, 3.
5. Brush and McGraw offer a World Series: *TSN* 2 Sep 1905. The eventual gross receipts of the first four games were divided as follows: 60 percent, players' pool; 10 percent, National Commission; 30 percent, between the two club managements. The players' pool came to $27,394.88—75 percent to the winners (*NYT* 14 Oct 1905).

6. *NYT* 10 Oct 1905, for this and following quotations from the World Series' first game.
7. Pitching strategy, Seybold: *TSN* 28 Oct 1905.
8. Late breakfasts: *Boston Globe* 24 Feb 1926. Logy: *TSN* 28 Oct 1905.
9. *NYT* 15 Oct 1905. Dickson, *Baseball's Greatest Quotations*.
10. "Fall down": *TSN* 28 Oct 1905. Five years previously Lave Cross, playing for Brooklyn, had been the first major leaguer to get a hit, a single, off CM.

Chapter 5

1. *Boston Globe* 24 Feb 1926.
2. Alexander, *John McGraw*, 119. Price quoted in Lieb, *Baseball as I Have Known It*, 97.
3. *TSN* 17 Feb 1906.
4. Pushball: *NYT* 18 Mar 1906 (photograph). CM in hospital: *NYT* 22 Mar 1906. Diphtheria and McGraw: Alexander, *John McGraw*, 11.
5. Bresnahan's teeth: *NYT* 28 Mar 1906.
6. Brush to Gordon: *NYT* 15 Apr 1906. Ebbetts: *TSN* 16 Jun 1906.
7. Groundskeeper Murphy is referred in sources variously as "Tom" or "John"; Joseph Durso's *The Days of Mr. McGraw* features a photograph of him.
8. Henry: *NYT* 5 May 1906.
9. Pressbox keeper: *TSN* 16 Jun 1906.
10. "Burkeville": Brush, "The Evolution of the Baseball Grandstand." Mertes, Masonry: *TSN* 21 Jul 1906.
11. *NYT* 8 Aug 1906.
12. Statements, "McGrawism," physician's advice: *TSN* 25 Aug; 1, 8 Sep 1906.
13. Cubs' August record; losses to Giants: Donald Honig, *Baseball's 10 Greatest Teams* (New York: Macmillan, 1982); *NYT* 10, 20 Aug 1906.
14. Comparative attendance: *TSN* 20 Oct 1906.
15. Christy Junior: Alumni Office, Bucknell University. CM's own name in college records appears as "Christopher Mathewson, Jr." Gilbert's uncle thus perpetuated his name to a third generation.
Hunting trip to Michigan: *TSN* 19 Jan 07; also an unattributed newspaper clipping at the National Baseball Museum (written in first-person narrative of Jane Mathewson reminiscing at the time of her husband's induction into the Hall of Fame) states that CM was hunting in Michigan with Bowerman at the time of Christy Jr.'s birth. CM's "My Life So Far" includes a photograph with the caption "Deer hunting in Michigan."
16. Blanche McGraw, *Real McGraw*, 212.
17. Train departure: *NYT* 24 Feb 1907. Contract difficulties: *TSN* 16, 23 Feb, 2 Mar 1907. Donlin's doctor bills: *TSN* 2 Feb 1907.
18. Thorn and Palmer, *Total Baseball*. The following year, 1908, the rule was amended to proscribe the pitcher from defacing the ball as well.
19. *TSN* 25 Jul 1907 states Bresnahan wore the head protector; *NYT* 13 Jul 1907 states he did not.
20. Chambers, "Young and a Giant."
21. Donlin: Graham, *McGraw of the Giants*, 32.
22. *Marlin: 1851–1976* (Waco, Texas: Texian Press, 1976).
23. Fleming, *Unforgettable Season*, 26, 27.
24. Tinker's batting: CM, *Pitching in a Pinch*, 1–4.
25. Fleming, *Unforgettable Season*, 139.
26. Possible postponement in Chicago: The rule, promulgated in 1906, authorized "the captain of the home team" to be the sole judge in determining the fitness of the playing field for beginning a game; after play commenced, the decision to suspend play, and to resume play, belonged to the umpire (Thorn and Palmer, *Total Baseball*).
27. Fleming, *Unforgettable Season*, 213.
28. McGraw quoted in Alexander, *John McGraw*, 134. Rule quoted in Fleming, *Unforgettable Season*, 261.
29. Fleming, *Unforgettable Season*, 278. Pulliam's decision was upheld at an evidently rancorous meeting of the league's board of directors. For a letter dated 23 Sep 1908 from R.D. Emslie to Pulliam: *The Baseball Research Journal*, Vol. 22, 1993. McGraw on Tenney: *Thirty Years in Baseball*, 188.

30. *NYT* 4 Oct 1908.
31. CM, *Pitching in a Pinch*, 194–97.
Brush's illness has been described as *locomotor ataxia*, known also as *tabes dorsalis*, a syphilitic disease with a prevalence, in the early part of the twentieth century, indicated by the number of newspaper advertisements for remedies promising its cure; it was considered in the diagnosis of most spinal cord problems. The disease is marked by symptoms of fleeting, sharp pains, especially in the legs, and often leads to severe walking problems and loss of position sense; as it progresses, the disease can cause severe back and abdominal pain, including vomiting, loss of leg reflexes, and reduced ability of the pupils to constrict with light. *Harrison's Principles of Internal Medicine*, 12th edition (New York: McGraw-Hill, 1991).
32. *TSN* 5 Nov 1908.
33. Deliberate tactic: *Pitching in a Pinch*, 137–8. CM described how Evers tried to distract baserunners when Kling was catching: "If the Jew had thrown that time, he would have had you," he quotes Evers as saying—and, if the runner paused to return a remark, Tinker could be on the way to intercept a throw from Kling and to make a tag. When Kling dropped the third strike against Bresnahan, Evers, playing deep and behind Herzog, according to CM, shouted for the runner to "Go On!" (On whether Kling was actually Jewish: David W. Anderson, "John Kling, Cub Stalwart," *National Pastime*, Number 21, 2001.)
For a manager who relished the stolen base as both tactic and strategy, McGraw's selection of a lead-off hitter for his lineup often seems jarring, as in this game with the selection of Tenney, who at this point in the season could barely walk, let alone run. Yet Tenney batted in the lead-off position much of the season; Bresnahan, who though a catcher was a fast runner, was another McGraw favorite in the lead-off spot.
34. CM, *Pitching in a Pinch*, 202.
35. Ibid., 269.
36. Bridwell: CM, *Pitching in a Pinch*, 135; Fleming, *Unforgettable Season*, 320. CM's exhaustion: unattributed newspaper clipping of Jane Mathewson's reminiscences at National Baseball Museum.
37. Ritter, *Glory of Their Times*.

Chapter 6

1. Brush's profit, other money details: *TSN* 22 Oct 1908; Alexander, *John McGraw*, 139. McGraw quote: CM, *Pitching in a Pinch*, 205.
2. Anderson, *More Than Merkle*, 215–17.
3. *Tunkhannock New Age Republican*, 14, 21 Jan 1909; "Mathewson's folks"; conversations with Grace Mathewson Van Lengen, Henry's daughter. Grace, born in 1910, remembers sensing that Gilbert and especially Minerva did not comfortably reconcile to her mother Marie's Catholicism. Perhaps in an attempt to win Minerva's acceptance, Henry and Marie named their first child, born in 1908, after her.
The local newspaper cited Henry as the person who found Nicholas; whether Marie and little Minerva were with him is not mentioned. Grace, who as a child and as an adult was close to Jane Stoughton Mathewson, spoke a slightly different version of the events surrounding her uncle's suicide, described to her years afterward by Jane, in which CM, not Henry, found Nicholas in the haymow. The written accounts do not record CM being in Factoryville at the time.
4. Insurance business: Homer Croy, "'Christy' in the Swivel Chair," *Baseball Magazine*, March 1909. CM's salary, at Harvard: *TSN* 18 Feb, 11 Mar 1909. Congressional salary, and other contemporary average earnings: *NYT* 25 Jun 05.
5. Latham: Tiemann and Rucker, *Nineteenth Century Stars*; Ritter, *Glory of Their Times*, 94.
6. McGraw quote: McGraw, *Thirty Years in Baseball*, 19. Raymond quoted in Thorn and Holway, *Pitcher*, 19.
7. *NYT* 25 May 1909.
8. Ritter, *Glory of Their Times*, 96.
9. Forbes Field: *TSN* 1 Jul 1909; J. Edward Supple, "The New Ball Park at Pittsburg," *Baseball Magazine*, July 1909.
10. *TSN*, 5 Aug 1909.
11. Murray's catch: *TSN* 2 Sep 1909.

12. Salary demand: *TSN* 21 Oct 1909. Nova Scotia: Sterling, "Christy Mathewson as Man and Boy." W.W. Aulick collaboration: *TSN* 13 Jan 1910. Once a letter from an admiring boy found its way across the country to CM with no more than a large "6" addressed on the envelope (Cook, "Athlete—Soldier—Gentleman").
13. Razor blades, cigarettes: *Boston Globe* 17 Jan, 24 Feb 1926.
14. Indoor baseball and Chase's card-playing: *TSN* 20 Jan 1910. Additionally on Chase: Kohout, *Hal Chase*; Lieb, *Baseball as I Have Known It*; James, *Historical Baseball Abstract*, 337–342; Richard Scheinin, "The Story of Hal Chase" (*San Jose Mercury News*, March 1993).
15. Ritter, *Glory of Their Times*, 176.
16. Ibid., 83.
17. *Variety* 29 Oct, 5 Nov 1910. $1,000: Seymour, *Baseball: The Golden Age*, 118. Signing baseballs and buying tickets: Cook, "Athlete—Soldier—Gentleman."
18. McGraw, *Thirty Years in Baseball*, 153.
19. CM, *Pitching in a Pinch*, 220–21.
20. Ibid., 113.
21. Ibid., 127.
22. Ibid., 214.
23. *NYT* 15 Apr 1911.
24. Lieb, *Baseball as I Have Known It*, 38.
25. CM, *Pitching in a Pinch*, 229; Ritter, *Glory of Their Times*, 97.
26. *NYT* 29 Jun 1911.
27. Sher, "Christy Mathewson."
28. In Ritter, *Glory of Their Times*, Fred Snodgrass remembered 1911 as "the year we had to buy our own uniforms."
29. Ritter, *Glory of Their Times*, 179.
30. McGraw, *Thirty Years in Baseball*, 198.
31. CM, *Pitching in a Pitch*, 233; Ritter, *Glory of Their Times*, 103; Schechter, *Victory Faust*.
32. Foul balls returned: *NYT* 18 Aug 1911.
33. CM, *Pitching in a Pinch*, 236.
34. Lieb, *Baseball as I Have Known It*, 82.
35. "Life's a funny proposition…." David Ewen, *American Popular Songs* (New York: Random, 1966).
36. Ritter, *Glory of Their Times*, 181. Meyers realized that when Harry Davis coached third base and shouted to the batter "It's all right," a fastball was being predicted, usually correctly.
37. CM quoted in Lieb, *Baseball as I Have Known It*, 79.
38. Lieb, *Baseball as I Have Known It*, 80.
39. CM, *Pitching in a Pinch*, 282.
40. Rice, *Tumult and the Shouting*, 46. *NYT* 18 Oct 1911.
41. Lieb, *Baseball as I Have Known It*, 81.
42. Ibid., 82.
43. So nicknamed because he had played ball at Colby College.
44. Lieb, *Baseball as I Have Known It*, 83.
45. CM, "Why We Lost Three World's Championships."
46. Lieb, *Baseball as I Have Known It*, 41.
47. CM, *Pitching in a Pitch*, 303.

Chapter 7

1. CM, *Pitching in a Pinch*, 115.
2. F.C. Lane, "The Gamest Player in Baseball," *Baseball Magazine*, September 1913.
3. Jones quote: Ritter, *Glory of Their Times*, 41. Makeshift Tigers game: *NYT* 19 May 1912.
4. "[C]haritable institution": *NYT* 30 Aug 1911. Marquard quote: Ritter, *Glory of Their Times*, 13.
5. For a complete explanation of the tangled web concerning 372 or 373 career victories: Joseph M. Wayman, "The Matty-Alex Tie," *Baseball Research Journal*, Number 24, 1995.

6. Boy's letter: CM collection, Keystone College.
7. Bob Feller, with Bill Gilbert, *Now Pitching* (New York: Birch Lane, 1990), 134.
8. Hugh Fullerton's article in *NYT* 6 Oct 1912 mentions the Giants' plate-crowding, as well as other tendencies.
9. Carmichael, *Greatest Day in Baseball*, 65. Speaker refers to the Giants' Moose McCormick as also one of the game's best pinch hitters.
10. Green, *Forgotten Fields*, 15.
11. Ritter, *Glory of Their Times*, 150. CM seldom spoke to batters: *Pitching in a Pinch*, 15.
12. CM quoted in Sher, "Christy Mathewson."
13. David L. Fultz, "The Baseball Players Fraternity and What It Stands For," *Baseball Magazine*, November 1913; "The Facts About the Baseball Players' Fraternity," *Baseball Magazine*, December 1913; C.P. Stack, "David L. Fultz, President of the Baseball Players' Fraternity," *Baseball Magazine*, February 1913. CM's support of fraternity: editorial, *Baseball Magazine*, January 1913. The statement of big leaguers divided into three groups is attributed to Garry Herrmann in Seymour, *Baseball: The Golden Age*, 225.
14. CM's letter to Herrmann: Mathewson file, National Baseball Museum.
15. Ritter, *Glory of Their Times*, 16.
16. *Literary Digest*, 23 August 1913. McCarver, *Baseball for Brain Surgeons*, 112.
17. Eddie Grant: *TSN* 31 Oct 1918.
18. Giant injuries: *Spalding Official Base Ball Guide of 1914* (Cleveland, 1914).
19. Wiltse's fielding practice: CM, *Pitching in a Pinch*, 208–9; Drysdale: Dell Bethel, *The Complete Book of Baseball Instruction* (Chicago: Contemporary, 1978), 59.
20. McGraw's remarks about Collins, CM: *NYT* 12 Oct 13.
21. Alexander, *John McGraw*, 170–1; Kavanagh and Macht, *Uncle Robbie*, 53.
22. World tour: *Spalding Guide of 1914*; Moreland, *Balldom*; McGraw, *My Thirty Years in Baseball*.

Albert and Kit Doolittle are mentioned in letters from Henry Mathewson to his mother retained in the possession of Henry's daughter.

CM and his wife did not return to Factoryville for the November wedding of his sister Christine to Walter Branning of Scranton. Tall, athletic, musically talented, imposing in appearance, this daughter of Minerva Capwell Mathewson waited until her 29th year for marriage. The ceremony took place in her parents' home (*Tunkhannock Republican New Age* 20 Nov 1913). The marriage of CM's other sister, Jane, brought apparently little joy to her family and it would seem not much, for long anyway, to Jane herself. Leroy French was remembered by the family as having clever hands; he was an expert telegraph key operator and a dandy musician. He was probably a lot of fun as a suitor, but as a husband his weakness for alcohol appears to have ruined both himself and his wife. Leroy and Jane French had no children; the surviving recollections of them come from two of her nieces, after the passing of many years.

Chapter 8

1. *NYT* 4 Oct 1912.
2. CM, "My Life So Far."
3. *NYT* 5 May 1914.
4. Walter Maranville, *Run, Rabbit, Run: The Hilarious and Mostly True Tales of Rabbit Maranville* (Cleveland: SABR, 1991), 81–82. This work, edited by John Holway, includes an afterword by Bob Carroll entitled "Who Was Rabbit Maranville?" from which this story is derived.
5. CM, "Why We Lost Three World's Championships."
6. "The Umpire," *Baseball Magazine*, December 1914. *Right Off the Bat: American Film Institute Catalog, Feature Films 1911–1920* (Berkeley: University of California, 1988); Rob Edelman, "Mike Donlin, Movie Actor," *Baseball Research Journal*, Number 30, 2001. In *Right Off the Bat*, a purported biography of its star, as a boy Mike Donlin saves from drowning a girl from a wealthy family, as a young man woos her but is considered unsuitable by her family because he works as a mechanic and plays bush-league baseball, is kidnapped by gamblers before a game, and escapes just in time to hit the winning home run. In the crowd, it just so happens, is John J. McGraw (also appearing as himself) who signs Donlin to a contract with the New York Giants.

7. *NYT* 27 Apr 1915.
8. *NYT* 1 May 1915.
9. Ritter, *Glory of Their Times*, 116.
10. CM, *Pitching in a Pinch*, 52.
11. CM visits Reese: *NYT* 16 Jul 1916; Reese information provided by Mahoning Valley Historical Society. Also, David W. Anderson, "Bonesetter Reese," *Baseball Research Journal*, Number 30, 2001.
12. The trade is also tainted by Herzog marring his subsequent career with gambling. As a starting second baseman, Herzog belonged to McGraw's pennant-winning club of 1917; McGraw later expressed doubt of the honesty of Herzog's play in the World Series.
13. Ritter, *Glory of Their Times*, 225–26.

Chapter 9

1. Henry and Marie Mathewson: letters possessed by their daughter Grace Mathewson Van Lengen.
2. Ritter, *Glory of Their Times*, 226. Neale and West Virginia Wesleyan: "Earl Neale Football Player Extraordinary," *Baseball Magazine*, December 1919.
3. "Sentiment and 'Matty.'"
4. *Cincinnati Enquirer* 5 Sep 1916.
5. CM stays long enough to vote, goes hunting: *TSN* 16, 23 Nov 1916. Besides writing for the *Cincinnati Times-Star* and contributing to *The Sporting News*, William Phelon was also associate editor of *Baseball Magazine*; prior to his Cincinnati years, he worked for the *New York Morning Telegraph* and the *Chicago Tribune*. For sketches of Phelon and Hugh Fullerton: "Chicago's Baseball Writers," *Baseball Magazine*, September 1908.
6. Suits, hat: *TSN* 21 Dec 1916, 8 Nov 1917. Rice, *Tumult and the Shouting*, 48. Cook, "Athlete—Soldier—Gentleman."
7. Reds hire Larry Sutton as scout: *TSN* 21 Dec 1916. Interest in Magee: *TSN* 22 Feb 1917. Discussion with Huggins: *TSN* 28 Dec 1916.
8. CM does not attend, endorsement: *TSN* 11 Jan, 22 Feb 1917.
9. *TSN* 1, 8 Mar 1917.
10. *Boston Globe* 24 Feb 1926.
11. Reds at Shreveport: *TSN* 15, 22, 29 Mar 1917.
12. *TSN* 22 Mar 1917.
13. *TSN* 5 Apr 1917.
14. *TSN* 19 Apr 1917.
15. Christy Jr.'s appendicitis: *Cincinnati Commercial Tribune* 21 Apr 1917. Henry's sunken cheeks: family remembrance.
16. Reminiscence of Grace Mathewson Van Lengen. Mathewson cousin Alvie Reynolds provided the recollection of CM throwing a baseball to George Walton. Walton made such an impression on Grace that, when she became a wife and mother, she made it a point, when visiting Factoryville, to show Walton her own firstborn.
17. *TSN* 19 Jul 1917.
18. Magee's batting style: CM, *Pitching in a Pinch*, 18. Billy Murray on Magee: John Thorn and Pete Palmer, *The Hidden Game of Baseball* (New York: Doubleday, 1984), 22; Tom Simon, "Sherry Magee," *Baseball Research Journal*, Number 30, 2001.
19. Toney: *TSN* 16 Aug 1917. Cicotte: Asinof, *Eight Men Out*, 21–2.
20. That McQuade went with the Giants to Marlin is mentioned in a letter from CM to McQuade dated 13 December 1921 (Mathewson Collection, National Baseball Museum).
21. *TSN* 6, 13 Sep 1917.
22. Liberty bonds, racetrack: *TSN* 1, 15 Nov 1917.
23. Headline, Toney quotes: *TSN* 6 Dec 1917, 10 Jan 1918.
24. Mrs. Chase: *TSN* 7 Mar 1918.
25. Letter dated 6 January 1917 from CM to Garry Herrmann (Herrmann Papers, National Baseball Museum).
26. Regan: *TSN* 16 May 1918. YMCA: *TSN* 9 May 1918.
27. *TSN* 6 Jun 1918.
28. *TSN* 4, 11 Jul 1918.
29. Church service: *Cincinnati Enquirer* 18 Jul 1918. Chase: *TSN* 29 Aug 1918. McGraw: *TSN* 22 Aug 1918.

30. *TSN* 10, 17 Jun 1920; *NYT* 8, 9 Jun 1920.
The Reds collectively breathed easier in the second game as Schneider pitched a 5–0 shutout; behind him his teammates made two double plays and a triple play. Lee Magee went 2 for 5.
31. *TSN* 22 Aug 1918, 17 Jun 1920; Allen, *National League Story*. CM teaches curveball: *TSN* 1 Jan 1920.
32. Brawl: *Cincinnati Commercial Tribune* 6 Aug 1918. "indifferent": *TSN* 15 Aug 1918. Umpire Rigler: *NYT* 8 Aug 1918.
33. Chase quote, Hermann reply: *TSN* 22 Aug, 5 Sep 1918.
34. CM practicing: *TSN* 8 Aug 1918. Sherry Magee: *TSN* 29 Aug 1918.

Chapter 10

1. *TSN* 5 Sep 1918; Sher, "The Immortal Big Six."
Among business taken care of prior to departing overseas, CM instructed that the dividends from his investments be directed to his account at the Lewisburg Trust and Safe Deposit Company. His stocks included those of the Union Pacific, Northern Pacific, Southern Pacific, Pennsylvania, and the Atchison, Topeka and Santa Fe Railroads, American Smelt and Refining, U.S. Steel, and Westinghouse Electric (Mathewson Collection, Miller Library).
2. CM's movements are derived from his personal military records (Mathewson Collection, Miller Library).
3. Liddell Hart, *Real War*, 422–23.
4. Liggett, *A.E.F.*, 208–09.
5. Joe McCarthy, "The Lost Battalion," *American Heritage Magazine*, October 1977.
6. *TSN* 31 Oct 1918.
7. Cobb, *My Life in Baseball*, 189–91.
8. Edward Martin, *The 28th Division in the World War*, Volume 5 (Pittsburgh, 1924).
9. Mathewson Collection, Miller Library.
10. Cobb, Sisler: *TSN* 19 Dec 1918. Herrmann receives little word from CM: *TSN* 5, 26 Dec 1918. Cablegrams: newspaper clipping of Jane Mathewson's reminiscences, Mathewson collection, National Baseball Museum.
11. Mathewson Collection, Miller Library.
12. *NYT* 18 Feb 1919.
13. Chase hearing: *NYT* 6 Feb 1919, *TSN* 13 Feb 1919, and John A. Heydler, "A Defense of the Hal Chase Affair," *Baseball Magazine*, December 1920. Rowland: *TSN* 6 Mar 1919.
14. *TSN* 27 Feb 1919, *NYT* 8 Mar 1919.
15. CM discovers Eller: *NYT* 7 Oct 1919.
16. *NYT* 24 Sep 1920, *TSN* 30 Sep 1920. Benton seems to have remained cozy enough with the gamblers to get some "inside dope" on the 1919 World Series. The grand jury was told that Benton mentioned to the Braves' Art Wilson and Tony Boeckel that Chase had given him a tip which netted $3,800 on the series' first two games. Benton denied it, saying that if he made some money it was because he bet the Reds on merit.
17. *TSN* 8 Jan, 30 Sep, 11 Nov 1920.
18. Veeck, *Hustler's Handbook*, 260.
19. Burns's testimony during the Black Sox trial renders his connection to Abe Attell, the false-dealing, supposed emissary from Rothstein, less shadowy. Because comparatively little light was shed during the trial on the purported connection between Sullivan and Rothstein, concrete evidence detailing how, or whether, Gandil received the $80,000 from Sullivan is elusive.
20. Hugh Fullerton, "Baseball on Trial," *The New Republic*, 20 October 1920. "Damn them....": *TSN* 7 Oct 1920.
21. *NYT* 2 Oct 1919.
22. Fullerton, "Baseball on Trial."
23. For more on Cicotte's pitching performances at the end of the 1919 regular season: Al Kermisch, "From a Researcher's Notebook," *Baseball Research Journal*, Number 23, 1994.
24. *NYT* 2 Oct 1919.

25. *NYT* 3 Oct 1919.
26. Ibid.
27. *NYT* 21 Jul 1921.
28. Joe Jackson, "Transcript of Testimony before Cook County Grand Jury," 28 September 1920, obtained through SABR. Also Joe Jackson with Furman Bisher, "This Is the Truth," *Sport Magazine*, October 1949.
29. *NYT* 10 Oct 1919.

Chapter 11

1. *TSN* 17 Jun 1920.
2. *NYT* 8, 9 Jun 1920; *TSN* 10, 17 Jun 1920.
3. Doyle moments: "Sentiment and 'Matty'"; Lieb, *Baseball as I Have Known It*, 146. CM tells Doyle of sickness: Sher, "The Immortal Big Six."
In a Friday double-header a few days before CM's absence was noticed in the press, Doyle played second base, the *NYT* reporter observed, in the manner he had 10 years previously—and at the plate on the day Doyle hit two home runs, a double, and three singles (*NYT* 3 Jul 1920).
4. Quoted in Asinof, *Eight Men Out*, 168.
5. *Merck Manual of Diagnosis and Therapy* (Rahway, New Jersey, 1992).
6. *TSN* 25 Nov 1920.
7. Dr. Packard: biographical information provided by Saranac Lake Free Library and Historic Saranac Lake.
8. *NYT* 22 Dec 1920.
9. Taylor, *Saranac.*
10. James K. McGuinniss, "'Nobody Can Kill the Game of Baseball Except the Public' Says Matty," New York *Evening Telegram*, 14 Aug 1921. Taylor, *Saranac*, 131.
11. McGuinniss, "'Nobody Can Kill the Game of Baseball Except the Public' Says Matty."
12. *Syracuse Post Standard* 25 Apr 1921. Grouse hunting: *Boston Globe* 24 Feb 1926.
13. Testimonial game program: Mathewson Collection, Historic Saranac Lake.
14. Lieb estimated CM received $45,000 from the testimonial. CM, in a letter dated 21 December 1921 to Judge McQuade, thanked him for the receipt of $54,000 from the "'Matty' fund" (Mathewson collection, National Baseball Museum).
15. The wildflower log in the possession of the National Baseball Museum. Blue gentians: *Boston Globe* 24 Feb 1926.
16. CM's Legion label pin is among his mementos given to Keystone College and is visible in photographs of him during his Braves presidency. John J. Daly, "Matty the Miracle Man of Saranac Lake," *Baseball Magazine*, August 1922.
17. Cullen Cain, "Matty's Fadeaway Does a Comeback," newspaper clipping in CM file, National Baseball Museum.
18. *NYT* 5 Oct 1922. Landis quote: Dickson, *Baseball's Greatest Quotations*.
19. Lieb, *Baseball as I Have Known It*, 142. Grant quote: *TSN* 1 Mar 1923.
20. Fuchs and Soini, *Judge Fuchs*, 24.
21. Ibid.
22. Jennings as possible manager: *TSN* 12 Jul 1923. Foster on Chance, Burns: *TSN* 25 Oct 1923. Maranville: *TSN* 31 Jul 1924.
23. Foster on Bancroft: *TSN* 29 Nov 1923. Blanche McGraw, *Real McGraw*, 283. Stengel quote: Kaese, *Boston Braves*, 195–6.
24. Gallos, *Cure Cottages.*
25. *TSN* 20 Dec 1923.
26. *Literary Digest*, 26 Dec 1925.
27. Kaese, *Boston Braves*, 199.
28. "Presiding genius": *TSN* 7 Feb 1924. Dr. Packard's statement regarding CM's health arose during a court case, with CM named as defendant, arising out of an automobile accident; he is quoted from an affidavit introduced to a judge in Norwich, New York (*NYT* 8 Oct 1925).
29. *TSN* 13 Mar 1924. Ted Williams with John Underwood, *My Turn at Bat* (New York: Simon & Schuster, 1969), 108.
30. Cain, "Matty's Fadeaway Does a Comeback." Fuchs and Soini, *Judge Fuchs*, 41.

31. *TSN* 11 Sep 1924. Bressler: Ritter, *Glory of Their Times*, 208.
32. Carmichael, *My Greatest Day in Baseball*, 62.
33. Fuchs and Soini, *Judge Fuchs*, 63. Also, William E. Brown, Jr., "Sunday Baseball Comes to Boston," *National Pastime*, Number 14, 1994.
34. Fuchs and Soini, *Judge Fuchs*, 42.
35. *TSN* 30 Apr 1925.
36. "The World's Greatest Baseball Park," *Baseball Magazine*, August 1915. Kaese, *Boston Braves*, 197.
37. Kaese, *Boston Braves*, 198.
38. *TSN* 30 Jul 1925.
39. Fuchs and Soini, *Judge Fuchs*, 32.
The trade substantially improved neither club; the best that might be said of it is that Brown would lead the league in hits the next year, and in 1929 Branch Rickey and the talent-laden Cardinal organization thought well enough of Andy High to make him their regular third baseman.
40. Ibid., 48.
41. Kaese, *Boston Braves*, 199. Judge Fuch's and Harold Kaese's accounts vary in the details of the identity of the reporter who entered the room and the wording of what was said, but the gist is the same.
42. Quoted in "Taps for 'Matty'—He Played the Game," *Literary Digest*, 24 October 1925.

Epilogue

1. Newspaper clippings from the *Adirondack Daily Enterprise* pertaining to CM's death and CM Jr.'s China tragedy, kept in the Adirondack Room, Saranac Lake Free Library. Also a letter dated 30 January 1944 from Major Christy Mathewson, Jr. to Captain Arnaud C. Marts in the Mathewson collection, National Baseball Museum.

BIBLIOGRAPHY

Adams, Glenn D. *A History of Keystone: The Academy and the College.* Factoryville, Pennsylvania: Boston Camera, 1990.
Alexander, Charles C. *John McGraw.* New York: Viking, 1988.
Allen, Lee. *The National League Story.* New York: Hill and Wang, revised edition, 1965.
Anderson, David W. *More Than Merkle: A History of the Best and Most Exciting Baseball Season in Human History.* Lincoln: University of Nebraska Press, 2000.
Asinof, Eliot. *Eight Men Out: The Black Sox and the 1919 World Series.* New York: Holt, Rinehart, 1963.
Benson, Michael. *Ballparks of North America.* Jefferson, North Carolina: McFarland, 1989.
Boston Globe, 1923–1926.
Brush, John T. "The Evolution of the Baseball Grandstand." *Baseball Magazine*, April 1912.
Carmichael, John P., editor. *My Greatest Day in Baseball: Forty-seven Dramatic Stories by Forty-seven Stars.* New York, 1945.
Census of 1880, Clinton Township, Wyoming County, Pennsylvania. A copy is maintained by the Wyoming County Historical Society. The location of Factoryville businesses and residences are indicated on a census map.
Chambers, Bill. "Young and a Giant." *The National Pastime*, Number 13, SABR, 1993.
"Chicago's Baseball Writers," *Baseball Magazine*, September 1908.
Cincinnati Commercial Tribune, 1916–1918.
Cincinnati Enquirer, 1916–1918.
Cobb, Ty, with Al Stump. *My Life in Baseball: The True Record.* Garden City, New York: Doubleday, 1961.
Cochrane, Mickey. *Baseball: The Fan's Game.* Reprint, Pittsburgh: SABR, 1992.
Cohen, Richard M., David S. Neft, Roland T. Johnson and Jordan A. Deutsch. *World Series.* New York: Dial, 1976. An inning-by-inning resource about World Series games.
Cook, Betty. "Athlete—Soldier—Gentleman." *Union County Heritage*, a publication of the Union County Historical Society. Mifflinburg, Pennsylvania: Mifflinburg Telegraph, 1976. (Miss Cook, although many years younger, was a personal friend of Jane Mathewson during the later years of Mrs. Mathewson's life.)

Cook, William A. *The 1919 World Series: What Really Happened.* Jefferson, North Carolina: McFarland, 2001.
Cottrell, Robert Charles. *The Best Pitcher in Baseball: The Life of Rube Foster, Negro League Giant.* New York: NYU Press, 2001.
Curran, William. *Strikeout: A Celebration of the Art of Pitching.* New York: Crown, 1995.
Danzig, Allison. *Oh, How They Played the Game.* New York: Macmillan, 1971. (For football in the 1890s.)
Dictionary of American Biography. The original volumes and the supplements.
Durso, Joseph. *The Days of Mr. McGraw.* Englewood Cliffs, New Jersey: Prentice-Hall, 1969.
Fleming, G.H. *The Unforgettable Season 1908: The Cubs, Giants, and Pirates in the Greatest Race of All Time.* New York: Holt, Rinehart, 1981.
Foster, John. "The Magnificent New Polo Grounds." *Baseball Magazine*, October 1911.
Fowler, Gene. *The Great Mouthpiece: A Life Story of William J. Fallon.* New York, 1931.
Fuchs, Robert S., and Wayne Soini. *Judge Fuchs and the Boston Braves.* Jefferson, North Carolina: McFarland, 1998.
Gallos, Phillip L. *Cure Cottages of Saranac Lake: Architecture and History of a Pioneer Health Resort.* Saranac Lake, New York: Historic Saranac Lake, 1985.
Giamatti, A. Bartlett. *Take Time for Paradise: Americans and Their Games.* New York: Summit, 1989.
Gonzalez, Raymond. "Hitting Homers Off Christy Mathewson." *The Baseball Research Journal*, No. 9, 1980.
Graham, Frank. *McGraw of the Giants.* New York: Putnam, 1944.
Green, Paul. *Forgotten Fields.* Waupaca, Wisconsin: Parker Publications, 1984.
Hannan, William M. "Christy Mathewson's First Baseball Contract." *Baseball Magazine*, December 1914.
Hardy, James D., Jr. *The New York Giants Base Ball Club: 1870 to 1900.* Jefferson, North Carolina: McFarland, 1996.
Hill, Carmen P., with Paul Green. *The Battles of Bunker Hill: The Life and Baseball Times of Carmen P. Hill.* Iola, Wisconsin: Krause, 1985.
History of Luzerne, Lackawanna, and Wyoming Counties. New York, 1880. A description of Factoryville is contained on pages 505–6.
Ivor-Campbell, Frederick, Robert L. Tiemann, Mark Rucker, editors. *Baseball's First Stars.* Cleveland: SABR, 1996.
James, Bill. *The Bill James Historical Baseball Abstract.* New York: Villard, 1988.
Jansen, Larry, and George Jansen. *The Craft of Pitching.* Indianapolis: Masters Press, 1997.
Jordan, Pat. *Pitching: The Keys to Excellence.* New York: Sports Illustrated, 1988.
Kaese, Harold. *The Boston Braves.* New York: Putnam's, 1948.
Katcher, Leo. *The Big Bankroll: The Life and Times of Arnold Rothstein.* New York: Harper, 1958.
Kavanagh, Jack, and Norman Macht. *Uncle Robbie.* Lincoln, Nebraska: SABR, 1999.
Kindall, Jerry. *Baseball: Play the Winning Way.* Lanham, Maryland: Sports Illustrated, 1993.
Kohout, Martin Donell. *Hal Chase: The Defiant Life and Turbulent Times of Baseball's Biggest Crook.* Jefferson, North Carolina: McFarland, 2001.
Lane, F.C. *Batting: One Thousand Expert Opinions on Every Conceivable Angle of Batting Science.* Reprint, Lincoln, Nebraska, SABR, 2001.

Liddell Hart, Basil Henry. *The Real War: 1914–1918.* Boston, 1930.
Lieb, Fred. *Baseball as I Have Known It.* New York: Coward, McCann, 1977.
Liggett, Hunter. *A.E.F.* New York: 1928.
Lowenfish, Lee, and Tony Lupien. *The Imperfect Diamond: The Story of Baseball's Reserve System and the Men Who Fought to Change It.* New York: Stein and Day, 1980.
Mann, Arthur. *Branch Rickey: American in Action.* Cambridge, Massachusetts: Riverside, 1957.
Mansch, Larry D. *Rube Marquard: The Life and Times of a Baseball Hall of Famer.* Jefferson, North Carolina: McFarland, 1998.
Mathewson, Christy. "How I Became a Big League Pitcher." *St. Nicholas Magazine*, May 1912. Found in the Mathewson file at the National Baseball Library.
_____. Mathewson collection, Miller Library, Keystone College.
_____. "My Life So Far." *Baseball Magazine*, December 1914.
_____. *Pitching in a Pinch.* 1912. Reprint, New York: Stein & Day, 1977.
_____. "Why We Lost Three World's Championships." *Everybody's Magazine*, October 1914.
Mathewson file, National Baseball Hall of Fame and Museum, Cooperstown, New York.
Mathewson file, Special Collections, Bertrand Library, Bucknell University.
"Mathewson's Folks." *Baseball Magazine*, December 1914.
Mayer, Ronald A. *Christy Mathewson: A Game-by-Game Profile of a Legendary Pitcher.* Jefferson, North Carolina: McFarland, 1993.
McCarver, Tim, and Danny Peary. *Tim McCarver's Baseball for Brain Surgeons and Other Fans: Understanding and Interpreting the Game So You Can Watch It Like a Pro.* New York: Villard, 1998.
McGraw, Blanche, with Arthur Mann. *The Real McGraw.* New York: David McKay, 1953.
McGraw collection, Friedsam Library, St. Bonaventure University.
McGraw, John J. *My Thirty Years in Baseball.* 1923. Reprint, Salem, New Hampshire: Arno, 1974.
Moreland, George L. *Balldom.* 1914. Reprint, St. Louis: Horton, 1989.
The New York Times, 1900–1925. Abbreviated *NYT* when cited in chapter notes.
Okkonen, Marc. *Baseball Memories: 1900–1909.* New York: Sterling, 1992.
_____. *Baseball Uniforms of the 20th Century.* New York: Sterling, 1991.
_____. "Team Nicknames 1900–1910." *The Baseball Research Journal*, No. 27, 1998.
Oliphant, J. Orin. *The Rise of Bucknell University.* New York: Appleton, 1965.
Pitt, Barrie. *1918: The Last Act.* New York: Norton, 1963.
Reichler, Joseph L. *Fabulous Baseball Facts, Feats and Figures.* New York: Collier, 1981.
_____, editor. *The Baseball Encyclopedia.* New York: Macmillan, 1976. Other editions were consulted from time to time, but this third edition was utilized in the main.
Rice, Grantland. *The Tumult and the Shouting.* New York: Barnes, 1954.
Ritter, Lawrence S. *The Glory of Their Times.* New York: Morrow, 1984.
Schacht, Al, with Murray Goodman. *Clowning Through Baseball.* New York: A.S. Barnes, 1941.
Schechter, Gabriel. *Victory Faust: The Rube Who Saved McGraw's Giants.* Los Gatos, California: Charles April Publications, 2000.

"Sentiment and 'Matty.'" *Literary Digest*, 12 August 1916.
Seymour, Harold. *Baseball: The Early Years*. New York: Oxford, 1960.
_____. *Baseball: The Golden Age*. New York: Oxford, 1971.
Sher, Jack. "Christy Mathewson—The Immortal Big Six." *Sport Magazine*, October 1949.
Shieber, Tom. "The Evolution of the Baseball Diamond." *The Baseball Research Journal*, No. 23, 1993.
Spalding, Albert G. *America's National Game*, 1911. Reprint, San Francisco: Halo, 1991.
The Sporting News. 1904–1910; 1916–1925. Abbreviated *TSN* when cited in chapter notes.
Stark, Benton. *The Year They Called Off the World Series*. Garden City Park, New York: Avery, 1991.
Sterling, E.A. "Christy Mathewson as Man and Boy." *The National Pastime*, No. 16, 1996. A reminiscence by CM's friend throughout life.
Sutton, Keith. *Wayne County Sports History: 1871–1972*. Honesdale, Pennsylvania: 1972.
Taylor, Robert. *Saranac: America's Magic Mountain*. Boston: Houghton, Mifflin, 1986.
Thorn, John, and John Holway. *The Pitcher*. New York: Prentice Hall, 1987.
_____, and Pete Palmer, with David Reuther, editors. *Total Baseball*, 2d edition. New York: Warner, 1991.
Thornley, Stew. *Land of the Giants: New York's Polo Grounds*. Philadelphia: Temple University Press, 2000.
Tiemann, Robert L., and Mark Rucker, editors. *Nineteenth Century Stars*. Kansas City: SABR, 1989.
Toland, John. *No Man's Land: 1918—The Last Year of the Great War*. New York: Doubleday, 1980.
Veeck, Bill, with Ed Linn. *The Hustler's Handbook*. Reprint, New York: Fireside, 1989.
Wheeler, John N. "'Matty' as the Champion of the Friendless." *Literary Digest*, 26 December 1925.
Wolff, Rick. *Playing Better Baseball: Inside Tips to Improve All Areas of Your Game*. Champaign, Illinois: Human Kinetics, 1997.

Index

A.J. Reach Co. 166
Alexander, Grover Cleveland 96, 97, 113, 128, 132, 167
American Association 62
Ames, Leon "Red" 36, 42, 87, 92, 101
Anderson, Fred 115
Anson, Cap 41
Attell, Abe 149, 152, 154
Aulick, W.W. 77
Austin, Jimmy 80

Babb, Charley 35
Baker, Frank "Home Run" 88–91, 104, 105
Baker, Newton 132
Bancroft, Dave 151, 161, 163–4, 166, 167, 168, 170
Bancroft, Frank 124
Barnes, Jesse 143, 160, 167
Barry, Jack 88, 92
Barrymore, Ethel 80
Baseball Writers Association 103
Bausewine, George 43
Bedient, Hugh 98, 99
Bender, Chief 47, 48, 91, 104, 108
Benton, Larry 167
Benton, Rube 115, 143, 144
Berra, Yogi 66
Bescher, Bob 107, 111
Boeckel, Tony 164
Bowerman, Frank 25, 44, 46, 51, 53, 54, 56, 59, 60, 61, 85, 117, 155
Braves Field 158, 163, 164, 166

Brennan, Ad 102
Bresnahan, Roger 29, 30, 34, 44, 46, 47, 48, 49, 51, 53, 74, 75, 95–6, 155, 168
Bressler, Rube 132, 164
Bridwell, Al 60, 65–6, 72, 81, 84–5, 93
Britton, Helene 123
Brouthers, Dan 40
Brown, Three Finger 37, 42, 58, 59, 62, 64, 70, 108, 112, 120–1
Browne, George, 34, 60
Brush, John: changes position on World Series 44; death 100; dislikes American League's Harry Pulliam 32, 34, 38, 50, 73, 76; Dr. Creamer 73; fires club secretary 93; investment in Marquard 62, 67; Mason 52; new Giants owner 30–1; Polo Grounds 42, 52, 82–3; refuses '04 World Series 38–40; reportedly dissatisfied with McGraw 60; rivalry with Highlanders (Yankees) 51, 54; sickbed 68, 177; successful franchise 37, 73, 77
Bucknell University 11–2, 14, 15–7, 21, 23, 27, 32, 168
Bulger, Bozeman 20, 77, 80
Burns, George 95, 101, 111, 142, 160–1
Burns, Sleepy Bill 95, 144–5, 149–50, 152, 181
Bush, Bullet Joe 105
Byron, Bill "Lord" 127

Cady, Forrest 98
Camp, Walter 21, 169
Camp Sheridan 131
Capwell (Doolittle), Christiana (CM's maternal grandmother) 3, 5, 6
Capwell, George (CM's maternal grandfather) 3, 5
Carey, Max 103
Chance, Frank 53, 64, 66–7, 69–70, 72, 86, 160
Chase, Hal 50, 73, 78, 80, 108, 120, 123, 124, 126, 128, 130, 131, 132, 133–4, 141–2, 143–4, 146, 152
chemical warfare 114
Chemical Warfare Service 135, 137, 139–41
Chesbro, Happy Jack 21, 40
Chutes Park 56
Cicotte, Eddie 129, 145, 146–8, 149, 150
Clarke, Fred 21, 64, 76, 91
Clarke, Tom 127
Clive, Henry 81
Coakley, Andy 43, 47, 59
Cobb, Ty 63, 95, 100, 116, 125, 135, 139–40, 166, 171
Cohan, George M. 40, 88
Cole, Leonard "Old King" 87
Collins, Eddie 88–9, 94, 105, 116, 132, 145, 146–7, 148
Collins, Shano 146, 147
Columbia Park 45, 87
Comiskey, Charles 106, 129, 145
Conlon, Arthur 158, 163
Coolidge, Calvin 164
Coombs, Jack 88, 89, 91–2, 105, 114
Corbett, James J. 45, 48, 171
Corcoran, Tommy 54, 59
Costello, James 133, 152
Coveleski, Harry 67–8, 73
Cox, Channing 159
Cox, George 31, 32
Crandall, Otis 61, 87, 91
Cravath, Gavvy 102
Creamer, Dr. Joseph 62, 69, 73–4
Cronin, Jack 29, 35
Cross, Lave 46, 48, 49, 176
Cross, Monte 46
Crowder, Gen. Enoch 132
Cueto, Manuel 127, 134

Cunningham Bill, 161
Curley, James 111, 159

Dahlen, Bill 35, 56, 60
Davis, George 19–20, 23, 27, 33
Davis, Harry 48, 88, 93
Dean, Dizzy 37
Delahanty, Ed 33
Demaree, Al 101, 103, 105
Devery, William "Big Bill" 54, 102
Devlin, Art 35, 43, 53, 56, 60, 65, 68, 80, 85, 95, 155, 163
Devore, Josh 78, 81, 84, 88, 91–2, 94, 98, 101
Doheny, Ed 20
Donlin, Mike 38, 40, 46, 50, 51, 52, 54–8, 59, 60, 61, 63, 68, 73, 75, 83–4, 106, 111, 117, 175, 179
Dooin, Red 102
Doolan, Mickey 106
Doolittle, Albert (CM's half-uncle) 6, 106
Doolittle, Benjamin (CM's half-uncle) 6
Doolittle, Christiana *see* Capwell, Christiana
Doolittle, Nelson (CM's step-grandfather) 5, 6
Douglas, Phil 143
Dovey, George 60
Doyle, Jack 50
Doyle, Larry 59, 60, 63, 65, 70, 72, 80, 82, 84, 92, 104, 105, 106, 114, 117, 120, 126, 142, 151, 152, 182
Dreyfuss, Barney 34, 76, 83
dropkicking 12
Drucke, Louis 79, 95
Drysdale, Don 104
Dubuc, Jean 144
Dunn, Jack 62

Eastern League 54, 74, 166
Ebbets, Charles 35–6, 51, 76, 115
Ebbets Field 102, 108, 114, 134
Elberfeld, Kid 33, 101
Eller, Hod 124, 133, 143, 150
Elliott, Claude 36
Emerson, Ralph Waldo 153
Emslie, Robert 43, 53, 66
Engle, Clyde 99–100

Evers, John 39, 64, 65, 69–70, 94, 109–10, 132, 151, 177
Exposition Park 43

Factoryville, Pa. 3, 5, 6–7, 74
Fallon, William 145, 152
Farrell, Frank 54, 80, 82, 102, 106
Faust, Charley 86–7, 97
Federal League 107–8, 112, 113, 115
Felix, Gus 167
Feller, Bob 96
Felsch, Happy 145, 147, 150
Fenway, Park 97, 98, 111
Ferguson, George 60
Fitzgerald, John "Honey" 97
Fleischmann, Julius 31
Fleischmann, Max 31, 130
Fletcher, Art 79, 84, 90, 91, 92, 104–5, 117, 125, 142, 151
Foch, Ferdinand 138
Fogel, Horace 27, 28, 95, 102
Forbes Field 76, 83, 86, 168
Foss, Eugene 97
Foster, John 129, 160–1
Fournier, Jack 163
Frazee, Harry 157
Freedman, Andrew 21, 23, 27, 28, 29, 30–1
Frisch, Frank 142, 162
Fromme, Art 101
Fuchs, Emil 157–8, 160, 161, 162, 164, 165, 166–8, 170
Fullerton, Hugh 91, 107, 146–7, 151, 155
Fultz, David 100–1, 103, 115, 123

Gaffney, James 158
Gandil, Chick 145, 147, 149–50
Garfield, James 3
Gautreau, Walter "Doc" 167
Gaynor, William 38, 97
Genewich, Joe 160, 161, 162
Gilbert, Bill 34, 42, 54, 155
Gill, Warren 64
Gleason, Kid 146–7, 149, 154
Goslin, Leon "Goose" 164
Gowdy, Hank 84, 110, 128, 158, 160, 165
Graham, George "Peaches" 95
Grant, Eddie 103, 104, 128, 139
Grant, George Washington 157, 158

Gray, William 93
Griffith, Tom 123, 126, 127
Groh, Heinie 120, 123, 128, 135

Hancock, Winfield 3
Hanlon, Ned 35, 52
Hanna, Mark 26
Harley, Dick 28
Harris, Bucky 164
Harris, John Howard 11, 17
Hart, James 37, 38, 76
Hartley, Grover 102, 104, 107
Hartsel, Topsy 46, 47, 48
Haughton, Percy 135
Held, Anna 10
Hempstead, Harry 100, 102, 107
Hendricks, Jack 28
Henriksen, Olaf 99, 100
Herrmann, August "Garry" 32, 52, 101, 117–8, 120, 123, 131, 134, 140–1
Herzog, Buck 61, 62, 63, 69, 73, 85, 87, 89–90, 107, 109, 117–8, 125, 132, 144, 180
Heydler, John 74, 76, 107, 141–2, 151
High, Andy 167, 183
Hilltop Park 82–3, 102
Hite, Mabel 54, 61, 75, 84
Hoblitzell, Dick 144
Hofman, Solly 66–7, 70
Holke, Walter 142, 164
Honesdale, Pa. 11, 14, 15
Hooper, Harry 97, 99
Hoppe, Willie 50
Hornsby, Rogers 123, 162, 170
Howard, Del 70
Hubbell, Carl 20
Hudson, Frank 12
Huggins, Miller 123
Hughes, Charles Evans 121
Hull, Harry 161, 168, 171
Humphreys, Joe 40, 53, 75
Huntington Park 38
Huston, Tillinghast 102, 112, 124, 129

International League 143
Iron and Oil League 146
Isaminger, Jimmy 103, 152

Jackson, Joe 132, 145, 149, 150
Jackson, Travis 161, 165

Jeffries, Jim 41
Jennings, Hugh 74, 75, 77, 117, 125, 131, 160, 168
Johnson, Ban 25, 28–9, 32, 34, 38, 93, 95, 99, 103, 124
Johnson, Walter 106, 164–5, 171
Johnston, Jimmy 167
Johnstone, James 43, 53, 62, 69, 70, 73
Jones, Davy 95
Jones, Fielder 33
Joseph, Enos 42

Kauff, Benny 108, 113–4, 115–6, 142
Keeler, Willie 117
Kelleher, John 163
Kelley, Joe 29, 36, 38
Kellogg, Ray 16, 174
Kelly, George 143
Kerr, Dickie 149, 150
Keystone Academy 5, 6, 8–9, 10–11, 27
Keystone Division (28th Pennsylvania National Guard) 140–1
Killefer, Wade 118
Kinsella, Dick 59
Klem, Bill 60, 69–70, 73, 77, 92, 111, 167
Kling, Johnny 53, 69–70, 177
Knetzer, Elmer 127
Knowles, Fred 54, 76
Kopf, Larry 126, 147

Lamb, Charles 154
Landis, Kenesaw Mountain 112, 148–9, 158–60, 167
Lapp, Jack 90, 92
Lardner, Ring 155, 168
Latham, Arlie 75, 86
Lavender, Jimmy 117
Leach, Tommy 39, 77
Lewis, Duffy 97
Lieb, Fred 26, 82, 155, 157, 165
Liggett, Hunter 138
Lloyd George, David 116
Lobert, Hans 63, 73, 106
Lundgren, Carl 44
Luque, Adolfo 143

Magee, Lee 106, 130–1, 132, 133–4, 151–2

Magee, Sherry 102, 122–3, 129, 131, 133, 135
Maharg, Billy 95, 144, 152
Manhattan Field 23
Mann, Louis 45
Maranville, Rabbit 109–10, 132, 133, 157, 161, 167
Marlin, Texas 60–1, 82, 142
Marquard, Rube 62, 67, 75, 79, 81, 83, 86, 87, 88–90, 92, 96, 98, 101–2, 103, 105, 114–5, 158, 160
Marshall, Doc 52
Masterson, Bat 83
Mathewson, Christopher (uncle) 3
Mathewson, Christopher: affidavit against Hal Chase 141–2; approves trade for Andy High 167; army service 136–41; arrested for Sunday baseball game 129; asked to serve overseas with YMCA 132; at 1924 World Series, enjoys occasional drink 165; attends 1922 World Series 156–7; attends 1924 spring training 163; belief in Jimmy Ring 134; "Big Six" 26, 43, 174; "Big Six" board game 156; birth 3; birth of son 54; Bonesetter Reese 116; boys' books 77; Braves player salaries 162; as Braves president 157–67; card playing 27, 35, 78, 84, 161; checkers 27, 35, 76, 155, 156, 165–6; chooses Dave Bancroft as manager 161; on college men in baseball 163; college years 11–14, 16–17, 21, 23, 27; commercial endorsements 77–8; concern for brother's health 119; consecutive walkless innings 102–3; consecutive wins over Cardinals, Reds 63, 75–6; consecutive World Series shutouts 49; considers trade for Irish Meusel 165; contract negotiating policy 163; contracts 21, 23, 32, 75, 77, 108; diphtheria 51; disliked 28; eighth season with Giants 54–60; election to Hall of Fame 171; eleventh season with Giants 78–80; entrance into games 37; Ernest Sterling 9, 11, 14, 26, 54, 168; extends welcome to Ty Cobb

125; "fadeaway" 14–15, 19–20; Federal League 108; fifteenth season with Giants 108–11; fifth season with Giants 35–40; final illness 168; first return to Polo Grounds as Reds manager 120; first season with Giants 19–22; fourteenth season with Giants 101–3; fourth season with Giants 32–5; friendship with Frank Bowerman 44, 54; funeral 168; Giant coach 142–3, 151–2; golf 84; Grantland Rice 84, 90, 128; growing up 7–11; Harry Coveleski 68; home built in Saranac Lake 161; insurance business 74–5, 101; Jack Wheeler 89, 94, 128, 146, 162, 165; Jane Stoughton Mathewson 21, 27, 32, 136, 161, 168; joins Chemical Warfare Service 135; Larry McLean 131; last matchup with Three Finger Brown 120–1; last pitching appearance with Giants 117; learns from Joe McGinnity 30; Lee Magee trial 151–2; McGraw relies on CM winning 25 games a season 102; managerial method of conducting spring training 124; Marquard and Home Run Baker controversy 89–90; "Merkle" game 65–6; minor league career 11, 14–18; more wins than walks in 1914 113; movie role 111–12; Nicholas Mathewson's suicide 74; 1905 World Series 45–9; 1912 World Series 97–100; 1913 World Series 103–5; 1923 Opening Day 158–60; ninth season with Giants 60–72; no-hitters 25–6, 42; one game playoff with Cubs 68–72; participation in Giants' world tour 106; *Pitching in a Pinch* 94–5, 162; pitching strategies 15, 20, 47, 62, 76; plan to develop young, fast team 163; Players' Fraternity 100–1, 112; Polo Grounds benefit 155; reclusiveness 76; Reds manager 118, 119–35, 141; relations with fans 121; religious beliefs 24, 36; rematch with Jack Coombs 114; reports 1919 World Series 146–48, 150; returns to Saranac Lake after 1925 spring training 166; salary strategy proposed at 1925 league meeting 162; second season with Giants 23–6; sells Liberty Bonds 130; seventeenth season with Giants 116–17; seventh season with Giants 51–4; sixteenth season with Giants 113–15; sixth season with Giants 41–5; spring training regimen 82; strict accounting of money 162; stylish clothes 42, 121; suspends Hal Chase and Lee Magee 134; teammate support 80; tenth season with Giants 75–7; third season with Giants 27–31; thirteenth season with Giants 95–8; Three Finger Brown 42, 37, 64, 120–1; three hundred wins 96; traded from Giants to Reds 118; trades with McGraw 160, 161; tuberculosis and Saranac Lake 152–58, 162, 163, 167–8; twelfth season with Giants 81–7; as uncle 128, 156; vaudeville 80–1; visits Cuba 94, 112; visits John Brush's sickbed 68; visits racetrack 130; watches Dazzy Vance pitch 164; wildflower log 156; World Series 87–92; writes controversial magazine article 110–11

Mathewson, Christy, Jr. 54, 126, 161, 168, 170–1
Mathewson, Cyril (brother) 6
Mathewson, Edith Christine (sister) 6, 128, 179
Mathewson, Frances (step-grandmother) 5
Mathewson, Gilbert (father) 3, 5–6, 74, 156, 170
Mathewson, Grace (Van Lengen) 128, 177
Mathewson, Helen (niece) 128
Mathewson, Henry (brother) 6, 50, 51, 54, 58, 74, 106, 119, 126, 128
Mathewson, Henry (grandfather) 5, 173
Mathewson, Jane (sister) 6, 179
Mathewson, Janette (grandmother) 5, 6

Mathewson, Jeanette Stoughton "Jane" 21, 23, 27, 31, 32–3, 50, 54, 78, 94, 96, 106, 112, 119, 130, 136, 153–5, 156, 158, 162–3, 168, 170–1
Mathewson, Jessie (aunt) 5, 7
Mathewson, Marie (sister-in-law) 119, 128
Mathewson, Minerva (mother) 3, 5–7, 8, 9, 11, 24, 74, 128, 170
Mathewson, Minerva (niece) 119, 128
Mathewson, Nicholas (brother) 6, 74
Mathewson, Regina (niece) 128, 156
Mathewson, Wellington (uncle) 5
McAdoo, William 36, 38
McAleer, James 98
McCarty, Lew 108–9
McCarver, Tim 103
McClellan, George B., Jr. 41
McCormick, Harry "Moose" 38, 63, 65–6, 104, 128, 135, 155, 179
McDonough, James 157
McGann, Dan 29, 30, 34, 45, 56, 59, 60
McGinnity, Joe 29, 30, 34, 36–7, 38, 39, 40, 41, 43, 44, 47, 48, 51, 52, 58, 61, 63, 66, 69, 74, 117, 155, 163, 174, 175
McGraw, Blanche 33–4, 80, 94, 106, 112, 161, 170
McGraw, John: ability to incite crowds 43; absent from Pulliam funeral 76; agrees to 1905 World Series 44; Andrew Freedman and John Brush 29–31; apartment with Mathewsons 33; apathy 59–60, 115; arrested for Sunday baseball game 129; attacked in Philadelphia 102–3; attitude toward 1904 World Series 34, 38; baseball unions 112; basestealing strategy 84, 177; becomes Giants manager 29; Benny Kauff 113, 115–6; Braves Field as place for Giant cast-offs 160, 165; breaking negative tension on club 85, 86; Bugs Raymond 75, 83; calls CM at Saranac Lake 154; concern for CM's health 51; continued enmity for Ban Johnson 34, 38; Cuba tours 94, 112; Dave Bancroft 161; death 170; Edd Roush 115, 116, 118; fines CM 35; first decisions concerning Giants team 29–30; first seen by CM 20–1; Fred Snodgrass after "muff" 100; Fred Tenney 60, 67; greets CM at Polo Grounds 1923 opening game 160; Hal Chase 50, 133, 142–4; Hugh Jennings 74, 117; Iron and Oil League 146; Lambs' Club 152; Larry McLean 104, 131; "Little Napoleon" 38–9, 105; method of conducting spring training 124; Mike Donlin 38, 40, 50, 54–8, 59, 60, 63, 75, 83–4, 117; mourns CM 168; 1905 World Series 45–8; 1911 World Series 88–92; 1913 World Series 103–5; 1919 Giants team 142–4; 1922 World Series 157; Orioles manager and enmity with Ban Johnson 24–5, 28–9; part-owner of Giants 141, 145; pitches Tesreau in game one of 1912 World Series 97; players' regard for 81; pool hall on Herald Square 50, 145; reaction to "Merkle" game 67, 73; releases Marquard and Snodgrass 114–5; relies on 25 wins from CM each season 102; replaces Bowerman with Bresnahan as CM's regular catcher 44; runs team with tight reins 81–2, 110; salary 50, 100, 175; seeks to raid American League for players 33;; sends Doyle to pinch-hit for CM in playoff with Cubs 70, 72; sign language 39; signs Larry Doyle 59; speaks at John Brush's funeral 100; synonymous with Giants 125; threatened by Earl Smith 160; trades 35, 38, 41, 52, 60, 74, 84–5, 107, 113, 117–18, 126, 142, 143, 151, 160, 161; trades CM to Reds 117–8; umpire confrontations 28, 43, 53, 60, 67, 115, 127, 151; upbraids CM for playing golf 84; Wilbert Robinson 75, 81, 86, 105; world tour 106
McInnis, Stuffy 88, 158, 160, 165
McKechnie, Bill 115, 118, 126, 130, 170

Index

McKinley, William 26
McLean, Larry 104–5, 131
McMullin, Fred 145, 149–50
McNeely, Earl 165
McQuade, Francis X. 129, 141, 180, 182Mack, Connie 18, 21, 23, 44, 45, 46, 47, 80, 88, 90, 92, 105, 111, 145
Merkle, Fred 59, 61, 65–9, 73, 74, 76–7, 84, 87, 92, 95, 98, 99, 100, 103, 104, 106, 116, 117, 126, 165
Mertes, Sam 34, 41, 46, 52
Meyers, John "Chief" 62, 75, 77, 78, 80, 84, 88–9, 90, 91, 93, 99, 100, 104, 115, 155, 178
Miller, John "Dots" 77
Minoso, Minnie 39
Mississippi Valley League 163
Mitchell, Clarence 127
Mitchell, Fred 126, 127, 158, 160, 161, 166
Mollwitz, Fritz 121
Montgomery, Dave 40
Montgomery, Alabama 131
Moran, Pat 142, 148, 150
Murphy, Charles 66–7, 95
Murphy, Danny 89, 92
Murphy, Tom 51, 62, 82, 176
Murray, Billy 76, 129
Murray, Red 74, 77, 82, 84, 91, 92, 98, 99, 110, 113

National Agreement 32
National Commission 32, 74, 93. 112, 151, 156
Neale, Earle "Greasy" 119–20, 126, 132, 134, 142, 147, 150
Needham, Tom 60, 61
Nehf, Art 143, 157
Neis 165, 166
Nichols, Kid 15,
Nicklin, Sammy Strang *see* Strang, Sammy

O'Brien, Thomas "Buck" 98
O'Day, Hank 28, 64, 66
Oeschger, Joe 161
O'Loughlin, Frank "Silk" 98
O'Neil, Mickey 167
O'Rourke, Orator Jim 39

Packard, Dr. Edward 153–55, 158, 168
Padden, Tom 25, 174
Padgett, Ernie 164
Peitz, Heinie 43
Perritt, Bill "Poll" 113, 117, 133, 142, 143
Pershing, John J. 115, 136–39, 157
Pfeister, Jack 65, 69
Phelon, William 91, 121, 123–5, 127–8, 130–3, 143–4, 146
Phillippe, Deacon 43
Pinchot, Gifford 14
Plank, Eddie 45–6, 88, 104
Players' Fraternity 100, 112, 123
Players' League 54
Poe, Edgar Allan 10
Polo Grounds 20, 25, 30, 41, 54, 58, 62, 63, 75, 77, 80, 86, 87, 95, 108, 109, 114, 115, 117, 120, 132, 134, 151, 170; "Burkeville" 52; capacity 37; clubhouse 42; fire 82; game time 175; Highlanders/Yankees become tenants 102; Mathewson benefit game 155; McGraw's hiding place when ejected 43; "Merkle" game 65, 67; 1905 World Series 46, 48; 1908 play-off game 69, 70; 1911 rebuilding 83, 85; 1911 World Series 88, 89, 91, 92, 93; 1912 World Series 98; opening days 23–4, 27–8, 51, 61, 82, 159; proximity to Mathewson apartment 33, 50; Sunday ball 36
Powell, Albert 157, 168
Powers, Mike 48
Price, Jim 50
Pulliam, Harry 32, 33, 34, 41, 50, 53, 64, 66–8, 73–4, 76

Radbourn, Charles "Old Hoss" 20
Rariden, Bill 115, 127, 142
Rawlings, Johnny 133, 152
Raymond, Arthur "Bugs" 63, 74, 75, 78–9, 83, 95, 97
Redland Field 125, 132, 135, 146, 148
Reese, John "Bonesetter" 116
Regan, Mike 128, 132, 142
Reulbach, Ed 67
Rice, Grantland 84, 90, 121, 138

Rickey, Branch 36, 129, 135, 136, 137–8, 140, 153, 162, 166
Rigler, Charles 134
Riley, Edwin 168
Ring, Jimmy 127, 134, 142
Risberg, Swede 145, 147–50
Ritter, Lawrence 81
Robertson, Dave 113
Robinson, Wilbert 75, 81, 86, 105, 108, 114, 115, 134, 167–8
Rogers, Will 116
Roosevelt, Theodore 11, 13, 26, 43, 173
Rothstein, Arnold 50, 145, 149–50, 152, 157
Rotterdam (troopship) 141
Roush, Edd 108, 115–6, 118, 124, 126, 128, 130, 133, 145, 147, 148, 150
Rowland, Pants 142
Royal Rooters 40, 97–9
Rucker, Nap 102
Rudolph, Dick 158, 164
Ruel, Muddy 165
Ruether, Dutch 146, 147
Ruppert, Jacob 102, 129, 159
Rusie, Amos 21, 25, 174
Ruth, Babe 84, 132, 152, 157, 159, 166, 171

Sallee, Slim 94–5, 143, 148
Saranac Lake, N.Y. 153–4, 156, 158, 161, 162, 166, 167
Schacht, Alexander 43
Schaefer, Herman "Germany" 106, 116
Schalk, Ray 148, 150
Schlei, Admiral 74, 75
Schneider, Pete 120, 125, 127, 132, 133
Schreckengost, Ossee 46, 48
Schulte, Wildfire 65, 70
Schupp, Ferdinand 143
Schwab, Marty 127
Seaton, Tom 102
Seeley, Blossom 101–2
Selbach, Kip 26
Selee, Frank 37
Seybold, Socks 47
Seymour, Cy 52, 53, 62, 65, 68, 70, 78

Shafer, Art 79, 104
Shannon, Spike 52, 61, 63
Sharman, Ralph 131
Shay, Dan 52, 59
Shean, Dave 123–4, 127, 131
Sheckard, Jimmy 58, 70, 87
Shibe, Thomas 166
Shibe Park 87–8, 91, 92
Shotton, Burt 129
Shreveport, Louisiana 123, 125
Sinclair, Harry 108, 113, 115
Sisk, Harry (CM's cousin) 32
Sisler, George 135, 140
Slattery, Jack 170
Sloan, Tod 40, 50
Smith, Al 156
Smith, Earl "Oil" 160
Smith, George 28
Smith, Harry 62
Smith, Phenomenal John 15–18
Snodgrass, Fred 61, 75, 76, 78, 81, 84, 86, 90–1, 92, 99–100, 104, 111, 113, 114, 165, 178
Snyder, Frank "Pancho" 143, 166
Sousa, John Philip 146
Southworth, Billy 158, 160, 161
Spahn, Warren 65
Sparks, Tully 28
Speaker, Tris 97, 100, 106, 147
Stahl, Jake 98–9
Stallings, George 80, 109–10, 113, 123, 128–9
Stanton, Frank 11, 17, 173
Steinfeldt, Harry 53, 66, 70
Stengel, Casey 161, 166–7
Sterling, Ernest 9, 10, 11, 13, 14, 26, 32, 54, 77, 168
Stevens, Harry 40
Stevenson, Robert Louis 153
Stock, Milton 107
Stone, Fred 40
Stoneham, Charles 141, 159, 160
Stoughton, Margaret (CM's sister-in-law) 32
Strang, Sammy 43, 47, 53, 56, 61, 62
Strange, Gladys 132
Street, Gabby 78
Strunk, Amos 92
Sullivan, Sport 145, 150
Sunday baseball 24, 35–6, 129, 165

Sutton, Larry 122
Sweeney, Col. Walter 141

Taylor, Jack 37
Taylor, Luther "Dummy" 23, 37, 38, 39, 42, 61, 62, 74, 96
Taylor, Zack 167
Tener, John K. 107, 113, 127, 141
Tenney, Fred 36, 41, 60, 61, 63, 66, 67, 68, 69–70, 78, 155
Tesreau, Jeff 95, 96, 97, 98, 99, 105, 117
Thomas, Ira 90
Thomas, the Rev. Welling 32
Thorpe, Jim 101, 106, 110, 126, 129
Tierney, James "Cotton" 163, 164, 165
Tinker, Joe 62–3, 64, 66, 70, 87, 108, 121
Toney, Fred 120, 124, 126, 127, 129, 130, 131–2, 143, 144
Torporcer, George 72, 164
Trudeau, Dr. Edward Livingston 154
Tully, May 80
Tuthill, Harry 42, 51, 53, 59
Tyler, George "Lefty" 110, 111

Vance, Dazzy 164
Vaughn, James "Hippo" 126
Veeck, Bill 39
Veeck, William (father of Bill Veeck) 151
Vila, Joe 31, 52, 59
Villa, Pancho 115
Virginia League 16, 18, 19

Waddell, Rube 43, 45, 88
Wagner, Honus 21, 34, 35, 44, 63, 77, 86, 94, 116, 129, 171

Walton, George 128
Warner, Jack 21, 25–6, 36, 41
Washington Park 35
Watson, Johnny 160
Weaver, Buck 145, 149
Welch, Mickey 20
Welsh, Jimmy 166
Wheat, Zack 108
Wheeler, Jack 89, 94–5, 115, 128, 146, 162, 165
Whitman, Burt 163
Whittlesey, Charles 138–9
Wicker, Bob 37
Williams, Claude "Lefty" 132, 145, 148, 149, 150
Williams, Dave 14
Williams, Ted 8, 163
Williamson, Ned 152
Wilson, Art 78–9, 102–3, 104, 126–7
Wilson, Owen 64, 65
Wilson, Woodrow 121, 125, 132
Wiltse, George "Hooks" 52, 68, 72, 92, 104, 111, 155
Wingo, Ivy 106, 117, 120, 130, 147
Woman's Christian Temperance Union 5
Wood, Gen. Leonard 112
Woodruff, George 16
world tour 106

Yerkes, Steve 97, 98, 100
Young, Cy 15
Youngs, Ross 143, 170

Zimmerman, Heinie 125, 126, 142, 144

www.ingramcontent.com/pod-product-compliance
Lightning Source LLC
Chambersburg PA
CBHW020923230426
43666CB00008B/1551